Modern Indian Drama: Issues and Interventions

Modern Indian Drama: Issues and Interventions

Edited by

LAKSHMI SUBRAMANYAM

Srishti
PUBLISHERS & DISTRIBUTORS

SRISHTI PUBLISHERS & DISTRIBUTORS
N-16 C. R. Park
New Delhi 110 019
srishtipublishers@yahoo.com

First published by Srishti Publishers & Distributors in 2008

Photo Courtesy:
A Scene from Muthusami's *Padukàlam* Photo: Courtesy Koothu-p-Pattarai.
Sabitri as Marilyn Monroe in *Ezzat* (2000), directed by Kanhailal. Photo: Courtesy KKM Archive.
Safdar Hashmi as the Sack of Grains (Ration ka Bora) in *Samrath Ko Nahi Dosh Gosain*. Photo: Courtesy Jana Natya Manch.

ISBN 81-88575-64-X

Typeset in AGaramond 11pt. by Suresh Kumar Sharma at Srishti

Printed and bound in India

Contents

Acknowledgements

My warm thanks to all my contributors who made this collection possible.

Kanhailal, Tripurari Sharma and Alarippu, Koothu- p-Pattarai, Sudhanva Deshpande and Jana Natya Manch need special mention for their generosity in lending photographs for this anthology.

I deeply appreciate the meticulous and comprehensive editing of the manuscript by Promodini Varma.

I must thank Tripurari Sharma and G J V Prasad for their useful suggestions and Taisha Abraham for her critical insights.

The encouragement and support received from my daughter Chitra and my husband Subramanyam went a long way in completing this book.

Introduction

Lakshmi Subramanyam

Robert Leach in his book *Makers of Modern Theatre* provides a crucial and useful definition of the term "modern" in the context of Western drama:

> The modern theatre is the theatre of today. 'Modernist' theatre refers to the theatre of the first fifty years or so, years of the last century when Stanislavski, Meyerhold, Brecht and Artaud flourished. Their Modernism however infiltrates and influences all aspects of modern theatre. They bestride the gap between Modernism and modern.[1]

The word "Modern" in the title of this volume has been used in a similar sense to examine the concept of modernity in post-Independence Indian theatre and drama. Sixty years of Independence provide a crucial marker to renegotiate and reinterpret the past decades. The terms "drama" and "theatre" are often defined as written and performance texts respectively. Ric Knowles, however, interprets drama as a more "serious literary mode" and defines theatre as the "translation of the text into different (and usually unstable) codes of semiosis of enunciation, gesture, embodiment, design and so on".[2] For the purposes of this book, the two terms have been used in a more flexible manner as the intertexuality between drama and theatre is a fluid and dynamic one. Though the title limits itself to "drama" for the sake of convenience and brevity, performance texts are also the focus of several essays featured in this volume.

In post-Independence India, modernist trends began to emerge in the works of playwrights like Vijay Tendulkar, Badal Sircar, Mohan Rakesh and Girish Karnad. Naturalism, realism and existentialism dominated the drama of this period. Samik Bandhyopadhyay contends that "Every single director who dominated the 50s and 60s starts with Ibsen."[3] In Bengal, Utpal Dutt's first production in the 1950s was Ibsen's *Ghosts* followed by *A Doll's House* (1957). Modernism in Indian drama was also deeply influenced by European drama in its questioning of traditional values in religion and culture, a self-conscious reflection on the fragmented nature of the urban experience, avant-garde movements and an emphasis on experimentation in form and theme. Family, with its frictions and fissures, was an important subject in this period. There was a "stress on the exploration of the individual in society and the society's responsibility to the individual".[4] While proscenium theatre dominated mainstream drama, a counter discourse was visible in experiments that were deeply influenced by Bertolt Brecht's epic theatre and alienation techniques. Further, street theatre proved to be a useful forum for theatre practitioners deeply involved in political and social issues. In recent years the aesthetics of performance and its processes have engaged several theatre directors. Focusing on multiple devising techniques, non-linear composition, multi-media and emphasizing the material presence of the body are but a few of the techniques used to destabilize the concepts of realism and naturalism that marked the early phase of modern drama and theatre.

However, it would be simplistic to see a neat parallel between developments in the early phase of modern Indian drama and the modernist discourse of Western drama. Amkpa Awam, writing on the African post colonial experience, emphasizes that drama and its various modes of production have political and economic implications in the development of cultural and social discourses. He argues that in "most of the colonized world, to be formally educated means a simultaneous subordinate existence in two overlapping worlds – one a global space and system of knowledge derived entirely from Europe, and the other a local space fragmented by internal re-arrangement brought about by external encounters. Such cultural topographies typify colonized spaces and they discursively perform themselves as 'modern' and 'traditional', 'indigenous' and 'foreign', 'Eurocentric' and its 'other'." In this context, Amkpa stresses the sense of alienation and ambivalence that "inscribes" the postcolonial condition. He argues that the African dramatist seeks "in-betweenness" in order to "develop metaphors of subjectivity", and subverts colonizing discourses by "fragmenting, compacting and inscribing them with decolonizing energies". The post colonial society challenges complexity by "questioning the terms of relationship to European cultures and practices as well as through negotiations and internal disparateness of diverse people brought together by colonial premises". Theatre, Awam contends, is also a "forum of engagement within which external and internal dimensions of society are articulated".[5]

Indian dramatists faced a similar dilemma in the years immediately after Independence. On the one hand, they were negotiating with a Eurocentric view of modernism and on the other hand, they were actively engaged in a dialogue with the diverse folk and traditional forms of theatre, still alive and active in many parts of the country. This constitutes the "in-betweenness" of Indian dramatists. Aparna Dharwadkar rightly points out that modern and traditional theatres in India are not necessarily in direct competition with each other because they appear in "different locations and fulfill different needs in their audience".[6] Foregrounding of "indigenous cultures", "revisioning" or reproducing of "classical texts" which deconstruct the "hegemonic authority embedded in the original text", the "syncretic combination of indigenous and colonial forms in the post-colonial world", all contribute to the "decentring of the European norm". Theatre, thus, becomes a "site for resistance strategies" such as viewing the present through the lens of the past, interrogating our classical epics or focusing on questions of identity, language and nationalism.[7] The work of women dramatists and practitioners has also been the site for experimentation. Moving away from the conventional play, women dramatists and directors have created their own texts through a collective process or in close collaboration with other writers; reinterpreted and reconstructed source material whether it be from canonical texts or folklore and have evolved strategies of interpretation, as well as continued with experimentation and evolved new styles.[8]

Central to this volume is the group of essays dealing with mainstream dramatists: Vijay Tendulkar, Girish Karnad and Mahesh Dattani. In "Interrogating the 'Post colonial': A Reading of Plays by Girish Karnad, Vijay Tendulkar and Mahesh Dattani", (No.7 in this collection), Angelie Multani emphasizes the need to place post-colonial texts in the different spatio-temporal contexts that they were written/staged in. However, the line between the urban dramatist and the playwright using traditional/indigenous forms is blurred. Tendulkar largely writes in the naturalistic/urbanized mode but, as Multani points out, he uses the traditional form of Tamasha in *Ghashiram Kotwal.* She examines the role of the white man in the play as he is placed in the position of an onlooker, on the fringes of the action, unlike the white man in Dattani's play *Clearing the Rubble.* In Dattani's play Jeffrey, the white man, plays a crucial role and can be identified with the urban audience/reader in India who cannot understand the happenings in a Gujarat village. Multani describes Dattani's play as a "perfect post colonial text" both in terms of language and setting and because it brings to "light some of the problems of contemporary India". She questions the view that the playwright is less Indian because he writes in English. The divide between a regional language and English is also highlighted in another play that Multani discusses, Karnad's *Heap of Broken Images.*

Karnad's *Tughlaq,* feels Multani, lends itself to a postcolonial interpretation as the past is interrogated but the understanding of the play "has evolved and changed over the decades depending on the socio-political contexts prevailing at the time". Multani concludes her argument by emphasizing that the time has come to see colonialism as one more event in history and to engage with texts as simply texts by Indians.

GJV Prasad sees Karnad's *Tughlaq* (No.8 in this collection) in the context of contemporary Indian dramatists who interpret a literary and cultural past to "enact, construct and represent the modern". It is a play that remains contemporary even today because of the issues that it raises. *Tughlaq* is not only a "historical play about history making" but an existential-historical play in the emphasis it places on the inevitability and meaninglessness of death and the sense of no-exit that Tughlaq experiences at the end. The ambivalences and contradictions in Tughlaq's character range from his visionary nature to his being a master of intrigues. Tughlaq's negotiations with his policies of secularism are seen by Prasad as reflecting the crucial questions that post Independence India is facing, while the fictional characters show the "theatrical nature of his statecraft" as they play the roles assigned to them by the tyrant king.

In "Modernity and Hindi/Indian Theatre" (No. 9 in this collection) Jaidev Taneja sees modernity as related not to content but to a point of view. He sees the main issues of modernity reflected in mainstream Hindi theatre as well as in translations from other languages. Taneja highlights the effects of modern life on the family and on individual relationships, as well as on institutions like marriage, in a wide spectrum of plays. Western ideologies and philosophies have also played a crucial part in the evolution of Hindi/Indian theatre as is reflected in innumerable plays. He emphasizes the crucial role that theatre groups and government and semi-government institutions have played in the development of modern Hindi drama.

Sonali Jain interprets Tendulkar's *Baby* (No. 10 in this collection) from a psychoanalytic point of view. She argues that Tendulkar seems to portray the characters in *Baby* through their "psychic reality" as it helps to clarify their hidden, disguised motives and opens up the realm of relationships and gives meaning to identity. She analyses Tendulkar's use of madness and violence and the role they play in everyday life. Placing the play in the contexts of Heinz Kohut's work on narcissism, Elaine Klein's interpretation of the infant's destructive tendencies towards the mother and Freudian theories of the child and his phantasies of violence, she likens Tendulkar to a psychoanalyst who "helps his patients to go as far as possible in their representation of their internal worlds and of their relationship to the external". She sees the significance of the title of the play in the depiction of various forms of violence in the play and an "attempt to create a mental space in relation to confusing internal primary objects, locked in a violent primal scene, particularly in relation to the mother". It is interesting that one of Tendulkar's most controversial plays is here opened up to a psychoanalytic approach, underlining the fact that Western theories can assist the critic and reader in understanding plays that would otherwise be reduced to stereotypical interpretations.

Today, Indian drama explores issues which had remained largely marginalized earlier. As Daryl Chin has stated, pluralism and marginalism are important markers of post-modernism. He defines pluralism as an "acknowledgement of alternatives so that additional perspectives have the possibility of being understood. Marginalism is an accreditation of these additional perspectives by defining a dominant and ceding territory to the sidelines."[9] These issues are closely interconnected to the revival of traditional theatrical forms and the problems arising out of interculturalism and will be discussed further in this introduction. As Taisha Abraham has also pointed out, "More recent post colonial writings focus on groups such as the Dalits and their cultural exclusions and continued marginalization even in the independent nation-state of India."[10]

Maya Pandit in "Revisoning the Family and Nation: A Critical Look at Dalit Theatre" (No. 11 in this collection) looks at some of the crucial issues addressed by Dalit theatre with a detailed analysis of *Routes and Escape Routes* and *Kon Mhanto Takka Dila* by Datta Bhagat and Sanjay Pawar respectively. She sees Dalit theatre as a significant part of the political theatre of Maharashtra and the Dalit playwright as having a different, more compassionate and humane approach to issues of family, caste and patriarchy. The private space of "home" is interpreted very differently by them as compared to mainstream playwrights. Pandit interprets the word "Dalit" as connoting "revolt, pride, militancy and sophisticated creativity". She argues that Bhagat and Pawar present a re-visioning of the "home" and the family where a more humane relationship is worked out and the intricate patterns of caste and gendered relationships are sorted out. But Maya Pandit also accepts the fact that no easy solutions are to be found in a nation state which is still "occupied by feudal and capitalist powers and casteist ideologies".

An important issue among practitioners of the craft in modern Indian drama has been the debate that focuses on the revival of indigenous traditional forms. Government organizations like the Sangeet Natak Akademi promoted and officially patronized these forms. In a set of formal recommendations made by the Akademi in 1956, it linked the regeneration of Indian theatre to the revitalization of traditional folk forms. In 1984 Suresh Awasthi stated, at a national seminar on contemporary Indian theatre organized by the Sangeet Natak Akademi that "the return to and discovery of tradition was inspired by a search for roots and a quest for identity".[11] Vasudha Dalmia differentiates between experiments with folk forms in the 1960s and 1970s and the use of these forms in the 1980s. While the earlier experiments were "rooted in the concerns of the urban middle class and thus in a modern sensibility" they later became "export items", divorced from their content.[12] Dalmia is obviously referring to the highly popular "Festivals of India" when folk art and folk performances were showcased abroad as part of Indian culture.

The term "folk" itself has been open to much discussion. Kathryn Hansen has defined and modified the term in the context of forms like the Nautanki, Jatra, Tamasha and Bhavai. She argues that these forms do not entirely fit into the category of folk theatre if the word "folk" is defined as Roger Abraham does: "Folk drama exists on a village or a group level. The performers are members of the community and therefore known to most of the audience. The dramas are given on special occasions only, most commonly a seasonal festival."[13] Noting the changes that have occurred in forms like the Nautanki, Kathyrn Hansen finds it difficult to categorise them as a city or village form. She defines these forms as regional or traditional theatre occupying an "intermediate position between the simplest folk forms of drama and the highly elaborate Sanskrit theatre".[14] She categorises them as "intermediary theatre" that occupy a space between simple village forms and elaborate classical or urban theatre. These, she says, act as a "mediating agency between different populations, regions, classes and ways of life".[15]

The debate between dramatists who use traditional forms and others, who insist that this is a retrograde step, is a continuous one. Mahesh Elkunchwar was to condemn the appropriation of folk theatre by urban dramatist in 1991 while delivering a talk on "The Nature of Innovation and Experimentation in Marathi Theatre". He argued that folk forms are closely related to a "collective impulse", while "the urban theatre worker is an individuated one who does not represent an entire community".

Another critical area of debate in contemporary Indian drama has centred around the theories of interculturalism. Rustom Bharucha sees intercultural theatre as a "search for a universal theatre language across cultures". [16] He is critical of Schechner's celebration of cultures of the world as it shows "insufficient regard for their social, economic and political contexts".[17] Like Daryl Chin, Bharucha also argues that interculturalism can lead to cultural imperialism. Chin states that in the process of admitting other cultures, care should be taken that they are not made to speak in the language of the dominant culture. He urges diplomacy in intercultural affairs as it can lead to cultural imperialism as the "idea of interculturalism as simply a way of joining disparate cultural artifacts together has a hidden agenda of imperialism".[18] Bharucha also argues that one cannot entirely abandon the "legitimacy and potentially liberating force of the 'national', particularly in relation to those people's movements against globalization in Third World Countries which could be the only hope for challenging and redemocratizing the state".[19] Bharucha, therefore, posits the term "intracultural", a term "that I was compelled to invent for myself as a critical shorthand to differentiate intercultural relations across national boundaries and the intracultural dynamics between and across specific communities and regions *within* the boundaries of the nation state".[20] Intracultural, he states, explores the possibility of relationships between "different cultures at the regional level". At the same time, however, he warns of the dangers of the appropriation of forms that can create their own hegemony. Moreover, intraculturalism does not necessarily express the organic unity of Indian culture. Rather, the attention or importance given to some regional cultures over others highlights the "deeply fragmented and divided society of India". Intraculturalism is, therefore, concerned with "mobilizing a consciousness of differences among its participants".[21]

H S Shiva Prakash's "Theatre between Cultures" (No. 6 in this collection) focuses on the problems arising from interculturalism vs. intraculturalism. Shiva Prakash examines the unequal "exchange of theatres between different regions within India and also between India and other countries". Defining translation as not only linguistic translation but an exchange of religions, philosophies and ideologies he looks at the crucial role it plays in the histories of our theatre. Transplanting a Shakespearian play into Indian soil brings it closer to the audience than literal translation. He sees the performances of Gaddar as a form of translation as Gaddar uses folk theatre for revolutionary ideology. Shiva Prakash highlights the plight of states like Manipur and the "unequal exchange of theatre" between that state and the rest of India.

The reinvention of traditional theatres and intraculturalism find a common meeting ground in the group of essays that I am going to discuss now. The dramatists and practitioners discussed here explore an active collaboration between the two forms – modern and traditional – and consciously avoid the domination of any one of them. Kathryn Hansen's definition of intermediary theatre is particularly relevant in this context. These essays look at folk and traditional forms in the context of the experiments that contemporary dramatists have undertaken in their plays. The essays make some crucial points. The playwrights and directors are not consciously searching for roots or appropriating traditional forms to create an ambience of ethnicity. The attempt is to understand the essence of forms, which are changing rapidly and are often in decline. In interpreting the forms of Nautanki, Koothu, Tamasha, Nacha, Manipuri folk theatre and Meithei culture through the contemporary lens, these dramatists and directors provide an interesting perspective on modernity in contemporary drama.

Tripurari Sharma's "Nautanki, Gulab Bai and the Making of *Teen Betiyan*" (No. 3 in this collection) is a close study of the evolution of the Nautanki form and its decline. Her portrayal of the great Nautanki woman artiste, Gulab Bai, shows how the form changed in its nature when women artists took to practicing Nautanki. Partition, and the consequent migration of patrons, the growing commercialization of the form as popular entertainment and the impact of the film industry, all played a part in the decline of the form. Tripurari Sharma records in detail the complexities of using this form to tell an urban tale, woven around the famous incident of the three sisters of Kanpur who ended their lives rather than become a burden on their family. The script evolved through workshops and collaborative work with the Nautanki actors. The essay records meticulously the methodologies used, like discussions, alternate endings, the feasibility of introducing Nautanki artists on an urban stage, the use of dance and music, and the difficult and delicate task of inscribing a pre modern form with urban insights without appropriating it.

V. Padma's "Construction of Modernity in Tamil Drama and Theatre: Na Muthusami's Plays and Performances" (No. 4 in this collection) examines Muthusami's plays in the context of his response to caste, gender and the traditional form of Koothu. Coming down heavily on caste discriminations, he elevates the music of the Pariars to the "realm of art". As far as gender goes, Muthusami sees male and female characters on the level of abstractions. But the most fascinating aspect of Muthusami's plays is his experiment with the Koothu form and in fusing this "precolonial traditional form with a contemporary sensibility", V. Padma argues that the Koothu does not merely appear "in the external parameters of dance, music and drama but also in an abstract philosophic form" in his plays.

Lata Singh's article, "Tamasha Theatre and Sushma Deshpande's *Teechya Aeechi Goshta*" (No. 5 in this collection), looks at the role of the female performer in middle class discourse during the colonial period. The female performer was the "other", a disruptive force in contrast to the ideal woman. Lata Singh correlates the changes in the tamasha form to the rise of the middle class and the influence of the cinema. The middle class condemned Tamasha as a vulgar and low form of entertainment. Lata Singh examines Sushma Deshpande's play *Teechya Aeechi Goshta*, (*Her Mother's Story*), which centres on Hira, the Tamasha artist, and her daughter Ratna. Hirabai sees Tamasha as an art form and Deshpande foregrounds the Lavani performer as a professional who, however, has very limited choices in her life. Like the Nautanki form, the Tamasha lost much of its vibrant nature under state patronage. Lata Singh criticizes the system of awards whereby an artist given state patronage is made to fit into the "official definition of an appropriate cultural ambassador". In the process long term issues like financial support to help the form survive are ignored.

Another perspective on experimentation with traditional forms is to be seen in the theatre of Kanhailal and Habib Tanvir. My interview with H. Kanhailal and Sabitri (No. 1 in this collection) reasserts the continuing interest of contemporary dramatists in indigenous forms. Their rejection of Western theatrical conventions is indicative of the resistance strategies consciously adopted by several Indian dramatists. Influenced by the age-old Meithei culture and the rich tradition of Manipuri folk theatre, shamanism and ancestral worship, Kanhailal's theatre is also deeply political in its expression of resistance to political and state repression. In training his actors, Kanhailal not only focuses on the use of the body as a source of energy but also as an expression of flow and subtlety. Music and dance are seen as an expression of inner space and translating these outer and inner spaces into action and visual shape is the essence of Kanhailal's theatre. In his work meditative practices from different philosophies, and verbal and non verbal dynamics are paradoxically blended with a deep political commitment.

Sudhanva Deshpande in "Habib Tanvir and the Prism of Chattisgarh" (No. 2 in this collection) sees Habib Tanvir as one of the "seminal theatre directors of independent India". Influenced both by Sanskrit drama and Brecht, Tanvir evolved a "distinctive idiom of modern theatre". Besides experimenting extensively with theatrical forms like the Nacha of Chattisgarh he has also, according to Deshpande, borrowed "elements from rural dramatic tradition that has been more often than not utopic rather than revolutionary". Deshpande argues that Tanvir's theatre is "the theatre of modern sensibilities and modern concerns" as also a celebration of the plebian and draws its energy from the life of the Chattisgarhi peasants and tribals. Tanvir has always been a fierce critic of fundamentalism of any kind.

As Rustom Bharucha states, the task of any intracultural initiative in India is not to reconstruct "dying tradition but to create new possibilities of interaction and exchange within and across a wealth of 'living' traditions from vastly different time frames and cultural contexts".[22] One could argue that in viewing traditional forms in a contemporary context, the playwrights and practitioners discussed above are exploring the dynamics of intraculturalism in a different paradigm. The aim is not to dominate or search for homogeneity but to engage in a dialogue with forms and artistes in an attempt to understand the complexities of a culture and tradition that is no longer easily accessible. Bharucha further points out that the diversity of existing cultures in India ranges from the tribal to the rural to folk traditions and from mofussil, to urban to metropolitan contexts in "different states of vibrancy".[23] The shaping of an intracultural narrative, therefore, entails the "negotiation of more than one self, more than one history, and more than one language".[24] Therefore, the negotiation occurs in the "space between diversities and differences".[25]

Intraculturalism is further complicated by the diversity and plurality of Indian languages. All languages are not available to all Indians and, inevitably, a hierarchy emerges in these languages as some of them gain greater attention due to political or official patronage. Thus, while linguistic diversity can be seen as a manifestation of India's plurality, languages that are obliterated or marginalised can be a "manifestation of inequality and underdevelopment".[26] The efforts of directors like Kanhailal to recover little known dialects of Manipur and use them in theatre are a conscious effort to give space to marginalized cultures and languages. Similarly, the Jirsong Theatre in Assam has been involved in working with ethnic minority groups, especially the Karbis of Assam.

While the focus of this introduction has been on work for the proscenium theatre, it is important to consider the role of theatre that has moved out to other spaces. In Vidharbha a play, *Atma Hatya*, based on farmers' suicides, draws a crowd of 6000. P Sainath says that it is part of the Jhadi Patti theatre of the jungle belt, a tradition which he differentiates from the mainline theatres of Mumbai and Pune as well as the folk theatre of Maharashtra. With no sponsors, the Jhadi Patti has evolved from mythological themes to scripts written in Mumbai and Pune to plays now written in Vidharba itself. Jhaddi Patti is a "people's movement rooted in their lives…this is their theatre".[27]

In this context it would be relevant to consider Swati Pal's "Boundaries of Performance: Ritual and Street Theatre: A Case Study of Safdar Hashmi's *Samrath Ko Nahi Dosh Gosain*" (No. 12 in this collection). She sees a "desacrilisation of the performance space and a demystification of the actor-spectator relationship". In a close analysis of the text, she argues that the performance space becomes a site for confrontation between the performers and the spectators but the performance is ultimately seen to be fruitful as the spectators are shown as being open to ideas. She concludes that it is through the strategies of demystification and desacrilisation that *Samrath* seeks to transmit certain messages regarding political choices.

Even as I was writing this introduction, I was privileged to see a performance by H Sabitri at the Yoga Hall of the National School of Drama on 30th January 2008. Sabitri was demonstrating to a large group of students the outer and inner process of acting, based on the concept of theatre that she and Kanhailal have evolved over the past decades. Attired in her simple Manipuri outfit and with no make-up, she transformed the space into a living presence. She carried the audience with her as she played a variety of roles – of peasant, wife and mother – and in the process, revealed a gamut of emotions and gestures. She progressed from simple physical movements to vigorous steps, from facial distortions to subtle changes in mood and emotion, with expressions of joy, weariness and grief. Sabitri unfolded a variety of layers that constituted the acting process. Acting, for her, was an integration of body and mind, largely non-verbal except when interspersed with a few sounds (which almost seemed meaningless), gestural interpretations or folk songs. With no support from stage props, Sabitri's use of space reinforced the role that the actor plays, demonstrating that the politics of performance space is "germane to any theorizing about the post colonial condition".[28] Even though Sabitri's roots are deep within the Manipuri theatrical tradition, she uses the modernist non-verbal discourse to express the complex dimensions of the politics and philosophy of the Manipuri people.

The variety of approaches used in presenting this group of essays underlines the difficulty of defining modernity in Indian drama in a singular or homogeneous way. The several discourses problematize the issues and this is perhaps the only way that modernism can be understood in Indian drama.

Notes

1 Robert Leach, *Makers of Modern Theatre: An Introduction*, London and New York: Routledge, 2004, p. 1.

2 Ric Knowles, "Modern Drama: Defining the Field", *Modern Drama*, Vol. XIII, Number 4, Winter 2000, p. 526.

3 Samik Bandyopadhyay mentioned these crucial points in a conversation with me in September 2007.

4 Robert Leach, op. cit., p. 3.

5 Awam Amkpa, "Colonial Anxieties and Post-Colonial Desires: Theatre as a Space of Translations" in *The Routledge Reader in Politics and Performance,* ed. Lizbeth Goodman and Jane de Gay, London and New York: Routledge, 2000, pp. 117-18. Amkpa writes in the context of dramatists like Wole Soyinka, Ngugi wa Thiong'o, Ama Ata Aidoo, Micere Mugo and Rose Mbowa, among others. In referring to "in-betweenness", he is recalling "what Homi Bhabha (1994) calls a 'projective disincorporation' as they seek an in-betweenness between colonially determined axes of 'native' and 'foreign', barbaric and civilized, in order to develop metaphors of subjectivity".

6 Aparna Bhargava Dharwadker, *Theatres of Independence: Drama, Theory and Urban Performance in India since 1947*, New Delhi: Oxford University Press, 2005, p. 158.

7 Helen Gilbert and Joanne Tompkins, "Post-Colonial Drama: Theory, Practice, Politics" in *The Routledge Reader in Politics and Performance*, pp. 232-3.

8 For more details see Lakshmi Subramanyam, ed., *Muffled Voices: Women in Modern Indian Theatre,* New Delhi: Har-Anand Publications, 2002.

9 Daryl Chin, "Interculturalism, Post Modernism, Pluralism" in *Performance: Critical Concepts in Literary and Cultural Studies,* Vol.II, ed., Philip Auslander, London and New York: Routledge, 2003, p. 396.

10 Taisha Abraham, *Introducing Postcolonial Theories: Issues and Debates,* New Delhi: Macmillan India, 2007, p. 7.

11 Quoted in Vasudha Dalmia, *Poetics, Plays, and Performances: The Politics of Modern Indian Theatre,* New Delhi: Oxford University Press, 2006, p. 205.

12 Ibid., p. 200.

13 Quoted in Kathryn Hansen, *Grounds for Play: The Nautanki Theatre of North India,* Berkeley, Los Angeles: University of California Press, 1992, p. 41.

14 Ibid., p. 37.

15 Ibid., p. 43.

16 Rustom Bharucha, *The Politics of Cultural Practice: Thinking Through Theatre in an Age of Globalization*, New Delhi: Oxford University Press, 2001, p. 34.

17 Ibid., p. 5.

18 Daryl Chin, op. cit., p. 399.

19 Bharucha, op. cit., p. 6.

20 Bharucha, ibid., p. 8.

21 Ibid, pp. 11-12.

22 Ibid., p. 79. Bharucha examines the many problems faced by using intraculturalism in theatre. He gives the example of working on an original multilingual piece called "Prakriya", based on excerpts from Chekhov's *The Seagull.* While some access to the source language –Russian – and the target language – Hindi – was available, the Manipuri actor Heisnam Tomba faced problems as there were no resources for providing a Manipuri text. Bharucha's own experiment with intercultural theatre was the adaptation of Ibsen's *Peer Gynt.* Gynt is metamorphosed into Gundegowda in the Kannada version *Gundegowdana charitre.*

23 Ibid., p. 79.

24 Ibid., p. 78.

25 Ibid., p. 84.

26 Quoted in ibid., p. 85.

27 P. Sainath, "And All the World's a Stage", *The Hindu*, 25 January 2007.

28 Thiong'o, Ngugi, "Enactments of Power: The Politics of Performance Space" *The Drama Review*, Vol 41, No. 3., 1997.

1

H. Kanhailal and Sabitri

in conversation with Lakshmi Subramanyam[1]

LS: What made you turn to theatre as a profession?

Kanhailal: It was an instinctive choice. I was exposed to proscenium and folk theatre from childhood. My first choice was acting, but gradually I realised I was not suited to acting.

In 1958, while in college, I came in contact with G.C. Tongbra, who was known as the Bernard Shaw of Manipur. I joined his group and stayed with him for two years. After acting in a few plays, I decided that acting was not for me. I also felt dissatisfied with the methods of acting then prevalent and felt that I should start to learn from experience.

In the 1960's I started working with a few students in Imphal. This is also the time that I met Sabitri, when I selected her for one of my productions. In February 1962 we got married in true Meitei tradition by eloping. Sabitri was already an accomplished actor but gave up acting for a few years. Till 1969 she remained a housewife as we were part of a joint family.

In 1968 I got admission as a student at the National School of Drama, New Delhi. I was an introvert by nature and felt a misfit in the school. Being far away from Manipur and not knowing Hindi added to my sense of being an outsider. After three months I was asked to leave the School and came back to Imphal feeling very frustrated and disappointed. But it also motivated me to establish the Kalakshetra in Manipur in July 1969 with the help of Sabitri and other friends. Even then it took me nearly two years to discover my true direction.

By 1971 it had dawned on me that I should move away from the conventions and trappings of the proscenium theatre. I felt an urge to experiment with a new kind of theatre and performative techniques and this made me look into our traditions. I felt that one could read contemporary meanings in Manipuri folk tales. This was the genesis of the play *Tamnalai* (*Haunting Spirit*) produced in 1972.

LS: **In what way was *Tamnalai* important for your development as a director?**

Kanhailal: *Tamnalai* was the direct result of the social conditions prevalent in Manipur in the late 60's and early 70's. *Goondas* or anti-social elements flourished all over the place, in the *mohallas*, open roads and in street corners. Most of the anti- social elements were unemployed, uneducated and given to drink and would harass and threaten the people. There was an interesting case of a boy from a respectable family, whose parents had great hopes of him, but, unfortunately, he turned out to be a murderer. This story interested me.

LS: **So is your theatre rooted in political and social reality?**

Kanhailal: I can hardly ignore the reality or the state of society as it exists.

I wished to probe the local sensibility, how ordinary people reacted to *goondaism*, the roots of their fear and fury and their anger towards what was happening around them. I have always been fascinated by the emotions of fear and fury and the role of catharsis in Greek tragedy. I wanted to use these elements to express the sensibility of the Meitei people.

My theory of catharsis did not involve the idea of the purgation and purification of emotions. I define catharsis as the representation of an emotion, a kind of psychological representation that draws the spectator to the character. It involves the refinement of a subtle kind of emotion. So I might have assimilated ideas from Greek tragedy but transformed them by using them in a different context. In *Tamnalai*, I tried to develop a new kind of aesthetics where I wanted the spectator to become alert on the sensory level and thereby create a new kind of perception. This is conveyed in the acting methodology adopted by Sabitri.

Sabitri's process of acting is a way towards self-discovery, privileging her self over the character – the otherness. She cannot convince herself of the psychological motivation of pretending to live in the other self. She thus posits herself beyond the representational domain. She suggests the otherness through her self from the perspective of her social standpoint. Her way of controlling emotion and self-discovery is worked out by the inner action – a single vital force impregnated with a type of cathartic and psychic process. It works as the spiritual act of cleansing the body and distilling the emotions for its gentleness. The process of catharsis, as we understand it, is the transformation from coarse to subtle forms by concentrating on peeling layer after layer of psyche so as to reveal, say, a Sabitri underneath – her true self.

LS: **What impact do you expect your plays to have on the audience?**

Kanhailal: In Western theatre sympathy is evoked in the audience for the protagonist. But in my theatre, though I evoke sympathy for the protagonist, I also want to haunt the psyche of the audience, their mind and their inner being through images, even evoking a dream-like atmosphere. I want to awaken the imagination of the audience.

LS: **I sense a contradiction here. On the one hand your theatre is largely rooted in political and social reality, but you also talk of evoking a dream-like atmosphere on the stage.**

Kanhailal: Well, the primary aim of ideological or political theatre is to teach the audience, but I consider my theatre political in a different sense. I don't assert a particular ideology as you see in the theatre of Piscator, Brecht and Badal Sircar. I admire Badal Sircar and learnt a lot from him. But Badal Sircar conceived of theatre as social action. My theatre does not express a constructed structure of political thought. I believe that theatre cannot change the whole of society. One can only hope to create awareness. I often create a performance by putting myself in the place of the audience. The idea of resistance in my theatre is incarnated by the body of the actor and represents a collective and communal vision.

For the last two decades, I was suffering from the pain and anguish of suicide and silence of women-victims of rape by the army in our local context. I was just wondering if those women-victims could open their mouths in public casting away their shyness at the loss of izzat (woman's chastity), simply because rape is an accident, not the loss of izzat . So, women need to be spirited enough to make it public and protest themselves. This is the reasoning behind me to do a play that can disturb the audience and not simply educate them intellectually. Surprisingly, I found the material in the story of Draupadi written by Mahasweta Devi that worked instinctively in me to create the play *Draupadi*.

In 2004, the Manipuri women who protested against army atrocities were all ordinary women who felt oppressed. They could not articulate their ideas verbally but when they were physically confronted with a situation they reacted and it was their survival instinct that made them react in this manner. As a theatre director, in my local context, it is more practical to invoke this spirit of resistance which comes instinctively. It was not only the educated Manipuri woman but women from all walks of life who confronted the army and it is this spirit that I want to acknowledge and honour.

My plays are about common people, and their instinct to fight and through my theatre I want to awaken their spirit, their senses and their survival instinct.

In my play *Draupadi*, I celebrate this spirit. Though it was performed in 2000, it was almost prophetic of the events that occurred in 2004.

LS: **How far was your dramaturgy influenced by the Meitei culture?**

Kanhailal: Historically speaking, the Meiteis are considered to be almost a 2000 year old civilization. The Meiteis are actually a conglomeration of small communities who migrated from the southern part of China and from Tibet and Burma. The language of the Meitei belongs to the Tibetan-Burmese group. Culturally, we have a great affinity with South-East Asia, especially Indonesia. The Meiteis have a pronounced martial tradition. Within the Meitei group many clans and communities have fought with each other, some clans dominating at one particular period and others at other times. The men folk were primarily warriors while the women looked after domestic affairs.

Today, the insurgency in Manipur is led mainly by Meiteis. Though, again, there is little unity amongst them and they are divided into seven or eight groups. The Meiteis have taken to insurgency because they feel that they have been forcibly merged into India and been Hinduised. However, our ancestors permitted us to maintain an equal balance between ancestral beliefs and Hindu traditions.

The Meiteis have a rich repertoire of folk culture, ancestor worship and animistic religion. The *maibi* or shaman tradition is also widely prevalent. All these factors influenced the Meitei's perception of the universe and their use of the body expressed these elements. In fact, our ancestors assimilated the Hindu tradition also. I have used many of these elements like nature-lore and body-techniques in my theatre.

LS: **Is there a performance tradition amongst the Meiteis?**

Kanhailal: The *Laiharaoba* ceremony is the root of theatre in Manipur. It can last from seven days to one month and has a beginning, middle and end. The ritual begins at a river or pond where the deity, which represents both the male and the female, is evoked. This is linked to the cycle of fertility. On an auspicious date a temple is built in a selected place. The Maibi goes to the river or pond and evokes the spirit of the deity. It is believed that through this ritual, life is invoked into the Deity, which is then worshipped through dance, music (*pena*) and rituals. At the end of the *Laiharaoba*, there is a performance where the *Maibi* takes on the role of a woman, the *Nurabi*, and a male dancer who is very skilful in his movements takes on the role of the *Nongpok*. An enactment of the sexual union of the two is performed in very subtle terms and there is a powerful element of theatre in it. Transforming material in a refined way is inherent to the Meitei psyche.

LS: **How did you develop the nature lore element in your dramaturgy?**

Kanhailal: The Meitei tribe developed their animistic beliefs through their perception of nature-clouds, wind etc. We, Meiteis, conceive of the universe as circular and our movements also convey this idea. We identify the human body with a snake and represent it with the figure "8" which is symbolic of a coiled serpent.

The phrase "spineless spine" which I use in my dramaturgy is indicative of this idea. The spine is the origin of energy, an idea that has been transmitted by our ancestors from generation to generation. We train the actors to use the spine not only for vigorous movement but also for very subtle, soft and delicate gestures. This, verily, also imitates the movement of the snake. When angered, it hisses with a vigorous movement. Otherwise it moves with a flow. The style of our performers also has a flow; it is circular as it has no beginning or end but it can also be quite vigorous.

LS: **How do you translate these theories in terms of training the actor?**

Kanhailal: Let me make it clear that while my ideas were shaped to a large extent by Meitei culture, I don't believe in imposing it on my actors. I try to define my theatre language in a practical, objective manner which can be universally accepted. The approach should be similar even if the actors are different culturally. The difference is only on the physical level; the manner in which the psyche is provoked is quite similar. I select that which is universal, not the specific.

(*Sabitri demonstrates this idea through the emotion of grief, starting with short quivering breathing and ending by weeping.*)

Kanhailal: You can see that the eyes might look different but the act of crying is the same.

LS: **You mention that instinct and intuition are important. How do you define these words?**

Kanhailal: The instinct is linked to how we develop and observe through sensations. The mind registers these sensations and creates a sensorial memory.

When we open the senses we also open the repertoire of sensorial memory. For example, if an actor has to weep or express fear, he draws on his sensorial memory. He must have cried or felt fear at some time and he draws upon this memory bank to express these feelings. These moments occur instinctively and cannot be logically explained.

Besides memory, we also evoke emotion through music and dance. We have taught our actors songs not only from the Meitei tradition but also from Tripuri and other tribal regions, like Reang (Tripura), Rabha (Assam), MaoNaga (Manipur). We have taught our actors not only to sing from their larynx but from their inner being, to capture the rhythm of the music so that they can move from their consciousness to open the doors of their hearts.

Dance opens infinite space and makes them encounter many images and teaches them to use their body without any social inhibitions.

Let me explain this further by showing how we worked out this process in our play *Pebet* (1975)[2]. The idea came to us from a Meitei lullaby. At first, Sabitri and I kept singing this lullaby silently to ourselves. This opened the door to many images as we continued to focus on the song. The process then moved on from point to point, first concentrating on the theme of guarding the children, then the ordeal of the children, the capture of the child by the cat and the cat slapping the child.

These images—sometimes dreamlike—present themselves to an actor. The difficulty lies in transmuting these impressions into action and giving them a visual shape.

At this stage, Sabitri explains her approach to acting. She speaks in Manipuri and Kanhailal translates into English.

Sabitri: In my acting, the outside—the physical world—moves inwards and the inner world moves outwards. At the physical level, there is an immediate reaction to anything that impacts it from outside. Then the memory flows and the action starts from inner to outer.

Sabitri enacts the crucial scene from Kanhailal's play Draupadi (2000) *where Draupadi registers her reactions after the "rape" scene.*[3] *She begins with expressive, non verbal gestures and then moves on to verbal articulations of helplessness and fear.*

Kanhailal: For the actor, rape is an imaginary state. She imagines the physical effect of rape but psychically has to express the inner fire.

Sabitri: In the enactment of Draupadi's reaction, I register the physical impact on my skin and muscles, but when I deliver the lines I manifest the inner emotions, what I call the psychical. The breathing pattern reflects this. *(She demonstrates this)*.

First I breathe out deep from the navel, where the energy is stored in the solar plexus. Then I slowly move upward as I start taking deep breaths from the chest and finally move further upwards, to the focal point, which is the *bindu* on the forehead. It is there that the root of emotion lies. I feel this breathing exercise is essential for the actor to learn how to express his emotions.

LS: **Your breathing pattern suggests you have been influenced by the process of meditation!**

Sabitri : No, it does not follow the exact pattern of meditation. In my breathing technique there is a circular movement, which involves deep rhythmic breathing and focusing on vital points of the body from top to bottom. The inner focus moves from the top to the central part of the soles of the feet and then from the soles to the spinal cord to the navel. The flow of energy has to be understood by the actor. When the actor really concentrates on his lips on the stage he can feel the vibration from the *bindu*, the dot on the forehead.

Kanhailal: Yes. Some of the principles of meditation have been adapted here. Some elements of Vipasana, too, have been incorporated as also elements from *Hirikomba*—a Manipuri form of meditation. *Hirikomba* concentrates on vital parts of the body and was taught to the male warriors. Through this technique, one could sense the presence of any one about to attack from behind and be trained to defend oneself against such an attack.

We investigated into the nature and practice of meditation. All these materials have been transformed in our laboratory into a process, which becomes our own.

LS: **Sabitri, were you influenced by the Maibi tradition?**

Sabitri: In the Maibi tradition the physical manifests the psychical.

I might use some of the techniques of the Maibi but I am neither religious nor mystical in my approach to acting. In fact I wish to demystify the Maibi. The first stage is to throw out all one's preconceptions. Then I feel a vibration through the whole body as in a Maibi trance. The inner eye sees images which are not preplanned. I respond physically, with the eyes half closed, feeling emotions of happiness. Then, as the energy moves upwards, I look as if I am peering far away into the distance. The hands move gently sideways just as the body moves gently in a slow rhythmic movement, as if I am in ecstasy. There are expressions of fear, wonder and surprise. It is as if I am in communication with myself, in an inner dialogue, where I take the images I see close to my heart in a process of self revelation.

(Sabitri demonstrates this process.)

Sabitri: Let me share an experience with you. Once, when I played the role of Thambal in *Migi Sarang* (*Human Cage*) in August 1991, I was immobile on the stage but I saw my own image in the space in the rear of the auditorium. The experience was transcendental, but it also disturbed me! In this play, I had to enact silence on the stage. This is a painful process for the actor. Though he is externally immobile, there is a lot of movement in the blood and muscles. But this is different from the silence of meditation. The actor has to be alive to the working of his body as well as to his inner world.

Kanhailal: I call this "practical objective impact". The central focus of my plays is the actor. Besides training his body I also work with the heart and brain continuum- celebration and cerebration —the brain says "yes", the heart says "no". I want the actor to be human with the human and natural with nature.

LS: **But your use of space is also meaningful.**

Kanhailal: I see the stage from two perspectives. The stage is transformed by the actor into a space where he acts.

(Sabitri demonstrates how any room, any space is transformed when it is taken over by the actor. She creates a sense of distance by gazing past the viewer as if looking at a far-off object.)

Kanhailal: When the door of the heart opens, the stage becomes a space which opens up to hills and mountains. This is the power of the actor who can transform space through his/her inner-outer being.

The actor-character-text replaces the western concept of actor-text-character.

LS: **Tell us the process by which you transform a written text to a performance text.**

Kanhailal: The text, whether it is a folk lullaby as in *Pebet* or a play by Tagore as in *Dakghar* (2006), is first discussed amongst the actors. It is a collaborative effort through which the performance text seems to move away from the written text.

LS: **How was this process used in your production of *Dakghar*?**

Kanhailal: I did not follow Tagore's text verbatim. I selected specific lines and captured the essence of the text. I made the actor's body respond to the verbal poetry of Tagore's text. I deconstructed and reconstructed it. Sabitri played the role of Amol the young boy. The gender factor was not important here. I interpreted the role of Amol from a psychological point of view. He is symbolic of the desire of the human spirit to live in a free world. Amol's desire to be a postman suggests that a postman recognizes no barriers. The physician, who wants to close all the windows, symbolizes the excluding of nature and the dogmatic, reductive view of the human soul.

LS: **What are the recent experiments you have been working on?**

Kanhailal: I am now moving to other parts of the North-east and working in different tribal areas. In November 2005 I worked on Shiva Prakash' s play, *Sati,* in three different rural areas of Assam. The workshop was conducted by me and the play was directed by H. Thomba. I worked with the Bodo and the Rabha tribal communities. Their response to this play was instantaneous as they found the story not alien to them, like a Picasso painting. It was a part of their life. The experience of working with the Rabha community in Rampur was not only rewarding but also an eye opener. Our rehearsals took place in a hut which had no walls. Many elders and children came and watched the rehearsals. Their laughter was spontaneous and there were no inhibitions in their reactions. This innocence and instinctive and spontaneous reaction is what we have to learn from them.

I also saw how they live, in complete harmony with nature. When we were there a herd of elephants intruded, trampling down their paddy fields. The elephants were in direct confrontation with the villagers. There was a general uproar. The women lit fires to protect the fields. The men took long bamboo sticks with a pointed spear at one end, which had been turned red hot in a smouldering fire, and then poked them at the elephants, accompanied by the beating of drums and the bursting of crackers. But the interesting part was that none of the intruding elephants got seriously hurt. Though they were slightly scalded, they were only nudged to move in a direction which would take them back to the forest — an escape route without loss of face, as it were. It is this close understanding of nature and the ability to live in harmony with one's surroundings that we should imbibe from the tribals.

Notes

1 The interview with Kanhailal and Sabitri took place in two sessions on 6 October, 2006 and 7 October, 2006 in New Delhi. Kanhailal remains in the foreground of modern Indian Theatre in his quest for experimentation even as he draws his inspiration from the long theatrical traditions of Manipur. The semiotics of Kanhailal's theatre ranges from non verbal to verbal techniques as he emphasises both, the physical and psychological development in his actors at Kalakshetra Manipur. The success of these experimentations lies in Sabitri's superb ability to translate them on stage. In these

interviews I have focused on Kanhailal's and Sabitri's dramaturgy and performative techniques rather than on individual plays and performances.

2 *Pebet* (1975) was noted for its political theme, centering around the Meitie's struggle for cultural survival. For more details see Rustom Bharucha 's *The Theatre of Kanhailal: Pebet and Memoirs of Africa* , Calcutta: Seagull Books, 1992.

3 *Draupadi* was based on Mahashweta Devi's short story of the same name. Sabitri's interpretation of Draupadi was largely seen as an expression of female resistance to political repression.

2

Habib Tanvir and the Prism of Chhattisgarh*

Sudhanva Deshpande

Born in the 1920s, they are the seminal theatre directors of independent India: Habib Tanvir (b. 1923), Ibrahim Alkazi (b. 1923), B.V. Karanth (b. 1928), Utpal Dutt (b. 1929). To this list of directors who shaped the "theatres of independence", one must add the name of Satyadev Dubey, even though he was born in the next decade (1936).[1] Their contrasting careers make for a fascinating study.

Alkazi — patrician, disciplinarian, master of the monumental. He did his early theatre work in Bombay with Dubey, went to England to train at the Royal Academy of Dramatic Arts, eventually became Director of the National School of Drama, where he imparted to students what he had learnt at RADA. He quit the NSD in the early 1980s and, apart from a brief return in the late 1980s, he has stayed away from theatre ever since. Karanth — peripatetic minstrel, visionary, musical genius. He began with the Gubbi Veeranna theatre company, trained in Hindustani music in Benaras under Pt. Omkarnath Thakur,

---

*An earlier version of this article under the title "Upside Down Midas" has been published in *The Drama Review*, Volume 48, No.4 (T184), Winter 2004. Moloyashree Hashmi, Javed Malick and Sameera Iyengar had given useful comments on that earlier version.

joined the NSD as a student in 1962, eventually succeeded Alkazi as its Director, and went on to become the first director of two repertories: the Bharat Bhavan Rangmandal in Bhopal and the Rangayana in Mysore. He dabbled in cinema as well, directing some Kannada films and giving music for many others. Utpal Dutt — feisty Marxist, acid-tongued, master of heroic melodrama. Beginning with English theatre and Shakespeare in Calcutta, he flirted all too briefly with the Indian People's Theatre Association, formed the People's Little Theatre, wrote scores of plays, acted in Jatra as well as in cinema—in Bengali films by Satyajit Ray and Mrinal Sen, but also in trashier Hindi films, through which he subsidized his theatre work. Satyadev Dubey — urchin, teacher, master of speech. Originally from Madhya Pradesh, he is a naturalized Maharashtrian; has directed dozens of plays, mostly in Bombay but also many for the NSD. He has mentored playwrights and introduced generations of actors, including some very famous ones, to the difficult pleasures of the spoken word. Unique among the five, he has not headed a theatre institution, nor has he run a theatre company for any substantial length of time. He, too, has dabbled extensively in cinema, especially as script and dialogue writer to his friend Govind Nihalani.

And then there is Habib Tanvir. Like Alkazi, he went to RADA but unlike him, shed his learning like a snake's skin. Like Karanth, he experimented extensively with Indian theatrical forms, especially the Nacha of Chhattisgarh but unlike him, he always stayed close to the modern European theatre as well. Like Utpal Dutt, he is an actor-director-playwright-manager but unlike him, did not subsidize his theatre work by earnings from cinema. Like Dubey, he too is from central India but unlike him, he sought his theatrical identity in the region. And unlike the other four, Habib Tanvir's identity is inextricably tied up with that of his theatre company, the Naya Theatre. Many of its best-known members are dead but till recently, the Habib circus was quite a sight.

There was his wife Monika who, planted in a chair, made sure the costumes were ironed, the props in place, the toilets clean, the actors fed. Her knees ached, but she had perfected the art of dozing while sitting. There is Nageen, their daughter, deceptively fragile looking but with a clear, resonant singing voice that never slips a note. Then there are the actors: Bhulwaram, now dead, who joined Habib Tanvir in 1958, a year before Naya Theatre itself was formed, with majestic white hair like a halo around his dark, gentle face—probably Chhattisgarh's last great singer; Govindram, now retired, an actor of immense skill, dignity, and simplicity; Devilal Nag, composer of countless songs; the gentlemanly Udayram, actor and organizer; Ramcharan, past 80 and retired, the funniest stage actor I have ever seen; Ramchandar, younger and handsome in a rugged sort of way, educated and, along with Dhannu, the organizational backbone of Naya Theatre; Chaitram, Bhulwa's son, mulish and impulsive in equal measure, the exterior only partly concealing a baby's heart; Agesh, Devilal's daughter, still learning the actor's craft; Shankar, clarinet player, whose ex-wife, an ex-Naya Theatre actress, is married with child to another ex-Naya Theatre actor; Amardas the tabla player, who uses his mouth for tobacco rather than talk; and finally, Shyama, who has spent many years playing those unheralded bit parts without which any play is incomplete. Shivdayal, one of the original 1958 group, who spent years in jail on a false criminal charge, died in August 2003. Brijlal, another of the senior actors, died before Shivdayal. Some of Naya Theatre's finest performers died even earlier: Madanlal, Thakurram and Laluram, the great Nacha performers; Fidabai, an actress of incomparable power, grace, and subtlety; Malabai, a singer with an astonishing range.

Most importantly, there is the Pied Piper himself. His father was a Pathan from Peshawar, and Habib Tanvir retains the arrogance and quiet determination of those sturdy tribesmen[2]. Urbane and sophisticated, pipe in hand, he is a man of sartorial panache, charming and wickedly funny, delighted with the ordinariness of the world. Sage-like and forever immersed in work, he sizes up people instantly. Grand patriarch, benevolent dictator, he can surprise you with a completely open and accommodating mind. With his own writing he can be brutal, deleting fabulous passages because in performance they hinder the flow. To actors of intelligence, he can give unlimited space—well, almost. For the rest, he is a tyrant. As someone once said of Marx, freedom of man does not include for him the freedom to be stupid.

This circus has been on the road since 1959 and nearly fifty years later, after some have died, some retired and some gone away, finally looks like it is going to wind up sooner rather than later.

The Early Years

Christened Habib Ahmed Khan by his *hafiz*[3] father, the young Habib, a budding poet, took the *takhalluz*[4] "Tanvir". The *takhalluz* stuck and he, too, has composed poetry through his life, apart from the hundreds of songs he has written for his plays. He matriculated from Raipur in 1942, graduated from Morris College, Nagpur in 1945 and went to Bombay to pursue an acting career in cinema. It was an exciting time to be in Bombay. The film industry was expanding, new talent was emerging and he soon had a circle of friends among film personalities, writers, actors and poets. The War was winding down, the Quit India movement had already poured volatile youth on the streets, and he recalls the heady days of the RIN Mutiny. The Indian People's Theatre Association was formed in Bombay in 1942 and he soon found himself a part of it, drawn to the personality of Balraj Sahni. He did a variety of things to support himself, including working for the radio, but this was the time when he made, partly consciously and partly fortuitously, the decision to devote his energies not to cinema, nor to poetry, but to the theatre.[5]

Habib Tanvir shifted to Delhi in 1954 and worked for Qudsia Zaidi's Hindustani Theatre. He also worked in children's theatre and some of his playscripts from that time are still delightful. He met the young actress/director Monika Misra here and although they did not take to each other initially, in time they were married. His first significant play, *Agra Bazaar*, dates from this time. It is a celebration of the life and work of the plebian poet Nazir Akbarabadi, an older contemporary of Ghalib's. Hardly any biographical information is available about Nazir, so Habib Tanvir was forced to do a play in which the protagonist never appears. The play, as the title suggests, is set in a bazaar, the locale that has kept Nazir's poetry alive. With virtually no plot, the play was a stylistic novelty in its time. Habib Tanvir drew into the play the residents of Okhla village in Delhi in an experiment that was to be repeated on a more sustained basis with Chhattisgarhi rural actors some years later.

Qudsia Zaidi died prematurely and Habib Tanvir set off to train at the Royal Academy of Dramatic Arts (RADA), London. He was already in his early thirties then, not a novice learning the rudiments of his trade but an experienced craftsman of some standing. At RADA he learned many things, including British discipline, the principles of blocking[6] and some tricks of a director's craft,[7] but mostly he learned what he did not want to do. It seemed to him that Western theatre, particularly English theatre, was too rigid to allow the free movement that Indian theatre demanded. Western theatre, following Aristotle, demanded the unities of time, space and action, while Indian theatre, both the ancient Sanskrit and the rural, broke these unities constantly, admitting only one unity, that of *rasa*. For example, "In act II of

Mrichchhkatika, the Samvahak is being pursued by a couple of fellow gamblers. It is a street scene. He first enters a temple and then Vasantasena's house in the course of the chase. In both instances the scene is enacted—replete with dialogue and visuals—simultaneously inside as well as out in the street. Some translators have divided this act into Part I Scene i, Scene ii, Scene iia, Scene iii, etc., refusing to face up to the fact that Sudraka, the playwright, had no use for such unity of space. Unity of time is likewise broken. . . . The judge orders an officer to go on horseback to the Pushpakarandak garden to see if a female dead body is lying there. In the very next line, the officer confirms the existence of the dead body in the garden. The point here is that the officer has not gone off the stage."[8]

He roamed around in Europe for a while after that, watching plays, learning gypsy songs, sometimes earning money for passage by singing at bars songs from his native Chhattisgarh. He eventually arrived in Berlin determined to meet Bertolt Brecht, whose Berliner Ensemble was giving practical shape to the master's plays and dramatic theory. The year was 1956 and by the time he made his way to the Berliner Ensemble he discovered that Brecht had died a couple of months earlier. But Brecht's productions were alive and Habib Tanvir got to see those. He also got to see the legendary actor Helene Weigel, whom Brecht had married, and was struck by the simplicity of her expression. Indeed, simplicity and directness were the hallmarks of Berliner Ensemble productions under Brecht and Habib Tanvir must have been reminded of Sanskrit drama, with its "absolute simplicity of technique and presentation". Simplicity, he felt, was "intrinsic to Sanskrit drama"; "it had to be so in order that its complicated plot is put across in a comprehensible manner".[9]

By the time he got back to India he was determined to unlearn much of what he had learnt at RADA. It wasn't easy.

The Prism of Chhattisgarh

Theatre became serious business in India only in the 1970s. The number of those who remember plays from the 1960s and earlier is dwindling. I myself started doing, and watching, theatre seriously enough only in the mid 1980s. We encountered Habib Tanvir fully-formed. *Gaon ka Naam Sasural, Mor Naam Damaad*, his first significant Chhattisgarhi production, was done in 1972. *Charandas Chor* was crafted in 1973–74 and won the Edinburgh Fringe First Prize some years later, catapulting its creator and his band of rural actors to stardom. It even did a run on the London stage, playing to packed audiences. *Mitti ki Gaadi*, his Chhattisgarhi adaptation of Sudrak's Sanskrit classic, was done in 1977;[10] *Bahadur Kalarin*, an oral rural Oedipal tale, followed soon after. *Shajapur ki Shantibai* (Brecht's *Good Person of Schetzuan*), with the incomparable Fidabai in the lead, was done in 1978 and *Lala Shohratrai* (Molière's *Bourgeois Gentleman*) in 1981. In other words, by about the mid 1970s, Habib Tanvir had already evolved his distinctive idiom of modern theatre and subsequent years have basically seen him elaborating this idiom, refining it, polishing it, rather than evolving a new form. Those of us who came to watch and love his theatre tend to take this idiom, his style, for granted. It can, therefore, be quite easily forgotten that it took *him* fourteen long years, from 1958 to 1972, to come to it.

On Habib Tanvir's theatre, it is quite common to hear two views. One sees him as developing the legacy of IPTA, the other sees him as a practitioner of "folk" theatre. Both are incorrect. IPTA sought to build an all-India network of revolutionary cultural groups in close association with the Communist movement. Habib Tanvir, after his early years with IPTA, has never again done that kind of work. Certainly, in his theatre *practice* there isn't even a whiff of IPTA: while IPTA used "folk" forms essentially as carriers of revolutionary ideology to "the masses",

Habib Tanvir has fashioned a popular modern theatre, borrowing elements from rural dramatic traditions, that has been, more often than not, utopic rather than revolutionary.[11]

Habib Tanvir put together his first set of six rural actors in 1958. He did several plays between then and 1972 but most were, to a greater or lesser extent, failures. These failures led him to wonder: rural actors, when they do Nacha in their own setting, are fabulous. What made them stilted and trite when they acted in *his* plays? He identified two main reasons: "mother tongue and freedom of movement". "[I realized], after many years, that I was trying to apply my English training to the village actors—move diagonally, stand, speak, take this position, take that position. I had to unlearn it all. I saw that they couldn't even tell right from left on the stage and had no line sense. And I'd go on shouting: Don't you know the difference between the hand you eat with and the one you wash with? . . . I realized that those who were for years responding to an audience like this [without bothering about whether the audience was on one side, or three, or four, or whether some of them were sitting on the stage] could never try to unlearn all this and rigidly follow the rules of movement and that was one reason why Thakur Ram, a great actor [one of the 1958 six] wasn't able to be natural. Another reason was the *matrubhasha*—he wasn't speaking in his mother tongue, so it jarred on my ears, because he was speaking bad Hindi and not Chhattisgarhi, in which he was fluent, which was so sweet. This realization took me years—naïve of me, but still it took me years. Once I realized it I used Chhattisgarhi and I improvised, allowed them the freedom and then came pouncing down upon them to crystallize the movement—there you stay. And they began to learn. That quite simply was the method I learnt."[12]

That was the method all right, but it was used to channelize the rural actor's energy to tell modern stories. Habib Tanvir's dramaturgy and stagecraft is also modern. His *Kamdev ka Apna, Basant Ritu ka Sapna* (Shakespeare's *A Midsummer Night's Dream*) is played on a bare stage, the only element of set being a hand-held, beautifully embroidered half-curtain which sometimes reveals, sometimes hides and sometimes becomes a backdrop to the action. With its simplicity, its directness and minimalism, Habib Tanvir's theatre would have been considered avant-garde had it not been so popular and so funny. If you talk to his actors they all, without exception, make the distinction between Nacha, where they originally trained, and "theatre", that is, Habib Tanvir's theatre. His is a theatre of modern sensibilities, of modern concerns. Besides his own plays, look at the range of dramatists he has tackled: the ancient Sanskrit writers Sudrak, Bhasa, Visakhadatta and Bhavabhuti; European classics by Shakespeare, Molière and Goldoni; modern masters Brecht, Garcia Lorca, Gogol, Gorky and even Wilde; and Indian writers Rabindranath Tagore, Sisir Das, Asghar Wajahat, Shankar Shesh, Safdar Hashmi and Rahul Varma. He has adapted stories by Premchand, Stefan Zweig and Vijaydan Detha for the stage, besides adapting oral tales from Chhattisgarh. The stories he tells are the stories of our times, told with the simplicity and directness and energy of the rural performing traditions.[13]

His writing methods are eclectic. In plays that are original pieces authored by him, like *Agra Bazaar* or *Ek Aurat Hypatia Bhi Thee*, he is prone to write and re-write and edit and amend and cut and expand, till the text acquires the desired level of perfection. All this is based both on the voracious reading he does as research for the play, as well as on the basis of what he sees on the rehearsal floor as working or not working. When he uses traditional material, in *Gaon ka Naam Sasural* or *Charandas Chor* for instance, he encourages his actors to improvise and enrich the play – but he also reins in the over-exuberant actor. On the other hand, in pieces like *Ponga Pandit*, he presents the traditional Nacha performance with no authorial intervention, because he considers it a masterpiece, a gem. When he translates from Shakespeare or Brecht, he feels free to substitute Indian references for the western rather than translate quite strictly, word for word. When he picks up a play by a contemporary playwright, he makes it his own, improving the dramaturgy, adding music and songs, writing link scenes, enhancing the humour, and so on. When the playwright in question is generous, like Safdar Hashmi, Habib Tanvir is acknowledged as co-author, when not, not – but this scarcely deters him. The critical issue, always, is the *performance*. The best writing in the world is no good if it doesn't work in performance, as a *play*. As a director, he has a story to tell – whatever helps him take the story forward, he keeps (or inserts, when it is not in the original text); whatever hinders the flow of the story, is ruthlessly cut, no matter how beautiful it may be as a literary text.

Habib Tanvir, then, is a citizen of the world, borrowing, reading, soaking up influences indiscriminately, but he has become, through a long, hard, creative struggle, a resident of Chhattisgarh. Chhattisgarh is the prism that refracts his creative expression. He is writing his autobiography, *Ek Matmaili Chadariya*—a life woven with multiple threads, a life the dusty colour of earth. He is a Midas turned upside-down: whatever he touches loses its sheen, it becomes rough and turns to Chhattisgarhi. As Brecht once put it: "True art becomes poor with the masses and grows rich with the masses."[14]

Celebration of the Plebian

This is the man the Hindu Right has hounded since the early 1990s.[15] To argue, as the Hindu Right does, that Habib Tanvir is anti-Hindu and, by extension, anti-Indian, is of course a reflection not on the man and his work but of the depraved, pea-sized worldview of his attackers. To spit at the moon is to spit on your own face.

Yet Habib Tanvir is no revolutionary. Indeed he, along with a large number of intellectuals and artists close to the CPI, flirted for a while with the Congress (I) in the 1970s. He campaigned for the party in the 1971 elections with a play called *Indira Loksabha.* In what some saw as a return of the favour, he was nominated to the Rajya Sabha and, to the dismay of those to the left of the CPI, he did not resign his seat when the Emergency was declared in 1975. It is only later, in the 1980s, that he became, in private conversations at least, more critical of the Congress (I). He directed a play for Jana Natya Manch in 1988 and was in the forefront of the protests that followed Safdar Hashmi's murder at the hands of Congress goons in 1989. Over the years he and the left have both moved closer to each other, and in the context of the attacks on him by the Sangh Parivar over the last decade and his refusal to bow to their dictates, he has become something of a hero for left cultural activists.

The politics of his plays is somewhat harder to categorize. If there is one theme that runs consistently through all his creative output, from *Agra Bazaar* and even earlier to the present, it is the celebration of the plebian. The culture, beliefs, practices and rituals of the Chhattisgarhi peasants and tribals, their humour, their songs and their stories have given his theatre its incredible vitality. His characters do not lack religiosity but have a down to earth, commonsensical relationship with god. Charandas prostates himself in front of god in all sincerity before purloining the idol. A peasant or a tribal can turn a rock, a tree, an animal, anything, into god. Habib Tanvir is fascinated by this openness and eclecticism. He opposes Hindutva because, among other things, it seeks to destroy this freedom and regiment the belief structures and practices of peasants and tribals.

Habib Tanvir has been the enemy of parochialism, of bigotry, of fundamentalism and of the kind of development that crushes the poor. If *Jamadarin/Ponga Pandit* critiques, in the lively, robust manner that he has perfected, the caste system, superstition and priestcraft, his other play, Asghar Wajahat's *Jis Lahore Nai Dekhya Voh Janmya hi Nai*, the story of a Hindu woman left behind in Lahore after Partition, attacks Muslim fundamentalism. His latest production, *Raj Rakt*, based on Tagore's *Visarjan*, is also a critique of superstition. An earlier play, *Moteram ka Satyagraha*, based on a story by Premchand and written in collaboration with Safdar Hashmi, is a humorous look at what happens when religion starts meddling with politics. In the aftermath of the demolition of the Babri Masjid in December 1992, he produced, for a Delhi group, Sisir Kumar Das's *Baagh*, an allegory on the communal tiger on the prowl. In 1999, he wrote and directed for Jana Natya Manch *Ek Aurat Hypatia Bhi Thee*, on the 4th century. woman mathematician from Alexandria, lynched on the streets by Christian bigots.[16] *Sadak*, a short play, is a comic critique of "development" that ravages villagers, tribals, their land and their culture. *Hirma ki Amar Kahani* is a more profound look at what development has meant for tribals. An early short children's play, *Gadhe*, is a rip-roaring take-off on the education system that produces asses. His latest production, Rahul Verma's *Zahareeli Hawa*, is a fictional recreation of the Bhopal gas tragedy.[17] Then there is *Dekh Rahe Hain Nain*, perhaps his most refined play philosophically, the story of a king's futile quest for a calling that will harm no other being.

This, then, is Habib Tanvir, a man who represents two great traditions of Indian theatre—the tradition of the actor-director-playwright-manager, as well as the tradition of an active involvement, through the theatre, in larger social and political causes. The first tradition is now near-extinct and Habib Tanvir is probably our last link to it. The second tradition, happily, survives and some of the credit for this must go to Habib Tanvir himself, for showing us the way.

Notes

1 See Aparna Dharwadker's superb study, *Theatres of Independence: Drama, Theory and Urban Performance in India since 1947*, New Delhi: Oxford University Press, 2006, for a detailed and well-researched look at how the field of post-independence Indian theatre was shaped. The other names that one could possibly add to the list of the first generation of post-independence seminal theatre directors are Shombhu Mitra, Badal Sircar, K.V. Subbanna and Shreeram Lagoo. However, of these, Shombhu Mitra and Lagoo were basically actors who took to direction so they could do the roles they wanted to. Badal Sircar's main contribution, before he cut himself off from urban theatre, was as a playwright, and even though later, as a practitioner of what he called the "third theatre" in those days, he had a huge impact on street theatre, others learnt little from him. Subbanna is in a category all his own, his main contribution being the setting up of the theatre institute Ninasam, in rural Karnataka. For more on the careers of Alkazi and Habib Tanvir see Vasudha Dalmia, *Poetics, Plays and Performances: The Politics of Modern Indian Theatre*, New Delhi: Oxford University Press, 2006 and the special issue of Jana Natya Manch's magazine on Naya Theatre, *Nukkad Janam Samvaad*, 7:23-26, April 2004-March 2005, as well as Prithvi Theatre's sumptuous Yearbook, *On the Road with Naya Theatre*, Mumbai 2006. For more on the careers of Utpal Dutt and Badal Sircar see Rustom Bharucha, *Rehearsals of Revolution: The Political Theatre of Bengal*, Calcutta: Seagull, 1983, and Shayoni Mitra, "Badal Sircar: Scripting a Movement", *The Drama Review*, 48:3 (Fall 2004). For more on Subbanna see Rustom Bharucha, *Theatre and the World*, New Delhi: Manohar, 1990, and Sudhanva Deshpande, "The World was his Village", *Frontline*, 22:17, August 13-26, 2005. For more on Lagoo see his autobiography in Marathi, *Lamaan*, Popular Prakashan, Mumbai, 2004, and its review in English, Sudhanva Deshpande, "King of Actors", *Theatre India*, 11, 2005.

2 On productions of Sanskrit plays, he says: "I've always found others' productions ... wanting. I've liked mine better. I've enjoyed my *Mitti ki Gaadi* better than all other productions all over the world." Interview with Reeta Sondhi, *Contemporary Indian Theatre: Interviews with Playwrights and Directors*, New Delhi: Sangeet Natak Akademi 1989, p. 187

3 One who memorizes the entire text of the Holy Quran. His father's name was Mohammad Hayat Khan. His mother was Nazirunnisa from Raipur, where he was born.

4 Literary name, normally used along with the real name as in Faiz Ahmed "Faiz", Ramdhari Singh "Dinkar" and unlike *the nom de plume* which replaces the real name altogether as with George Orwell and Mark Twain.

5 Though he has dabbled in cinema as well as poetry through his life. In cinema, in the early days, he acted in several films, including some he does not remember the names of. By his own account though, it did not seem like he would be the kind of success Ashok Kumar already was and Dilip Kumar, who is about Habib Tanvir's age, was on the way to becoming. (Habib Tanvir, an entertaining raconteur, tells a lovely story of how invisible sparks flew between himself and Dilip Kumar when the two met on the sets of *Footpath*. Dilip Kumar is the hero of the film and Habib Tanvir does a bit role of an unemployed youth who unsuccessfully tries to kill him.) Later in life Habib Tanvir collaborated with Shyam Benegal when *Charandas Chor* was turned into a children's film. As an actor in cinema viewers will recall Habib Tanvir in films like Sudhir Mishra's *Yeh Voh Manzil to Nahi* and Nana Patekar's *Prahar*. Habib Tanvir's poetry has not yet been collected in a published volume, and when it is, Urdu-Hindi readers will surely admire his formally accomplished and stylistically elegant verses, powerful when political and tender when not. Perhaps Habib Tanvir rues not being recognized as a poet in his own right, perhaps not. His theatre work dwarfs everything else.

6 "Blocking" refers to the moves that a director assigns to each character in a play and, therefore, also the position of a character in relation to other characters and the locale in a scene. While there are overall principles of blocking, there are no rules, and directors play with blocking to create—or demolish—meaning. A director once got Hamlet to say his "To be or not to be" speech in a corner of the stage with his back to the audience, hunched over, trying to tie his shoelaces and making a mess of it

7 More than thirty years later, in 1988, I worked with Habib Tanvir for the first time. We were racing against what seemed to me an impossible deadline. When I asked him how on earth he thought he was going to get our play ready for its first performance, he told me a trick he had learnt from one of his teachers at RADA: "When you have no time, work on the beginning and the end. The middle takes care of itself." It did.

8 Habib Tanvir in an interview with Reet Sondhi, *Contemporary Indian Theatre : Interviews with Playwrights and Directors*, New Delhi : Sangeet Natak Akademi , 1989, p.187.

9 Ibid.

10 He had done this play earlier in Qudsia Zaidi's Hindi translation in 1958. The Chhattisgarhi version was, however, not a simple re-creation of this earlier production.

11 For a good discussion of the "utopian horizon" of Habib Tanvir's plays, especially

Charandas Chor, see Javed Malick's "Introduction" to Habib Tanvir, *Charan the Thief*, translated by Anjum Katyal, Calcutta: Seagull Books, 1995. Malick also discusses this point in "Habib Tanvir: The Making of a Legend", *Theatre India*, No 2, November 2000.

12 Habib Tanvir, "It Must Flow—A Life in Theatre", *Seagull Theatre Quarterly*, No 10, June 1996, pp. 21-22.

13 Habib Tanvir has argued that we cannot access the ancient Sanskrit theatre through the texts, only through the so-called "folk" theatre. In other words, the "classical" and the "folk" are not as clearly distinct as we sometimes imagine

14 Bertolt Brecht, "Two Essays on Unprofessional Acting", *Brecht on Theatre*, ed: by John Willet, London: Methuen, 1978.

15 For details of a relatively recent spate of attacks, see Sudhanva Deshpande, "Habib Tanvir Under Attack", *EPW*, August 30–September 5, 2003.

16 Ever since the Gujarat carnage, he has been on the lookout for a play that can address that horror.

17 And is, incidentally, very different in style and form to what one has come to expect from Habib Tanvir. For a review of this production see Sudhanva Deshpande, "Performing Bhopal", available online at www.znet.or

3
Nautanki, Gulab Bai and the Making of *Teen Betiyan*

Tripurari Sharma

A rose would probably smell as sweet even by another name, but that would not be true for a voice and persona that mesmerised audiences for long from the Nautanki stage. The name of Gulab Bai, affectionately called Gulab, Gulabo, Gulabjaan, evokes the magic and memory of a phenomena that was treasured by a whole generation of audience for its beauty and power.[1] " If she sang at Phool Bagh, the voice would float on the banks of the Ganga," Professor Satyamurthy would recount with great fondness. "Her voice had both melody and strength. Even if you resisted, it would pull you towards itself." [2] Professor Satyamurthy prided himself on his association with the modern, urban intellectual theatre scene but his eyes would light up at the very mention of Nautanki, which I did while directing Indira Parthasarathy's *Nandan Katha* for the Darpan group of Kanpur.[3] He was very keen that I meet Gulab Bai, who then lived in Rail Bazar, surrounded by relatives and well protected by the summer heat and light. She was unwell and seemed a pale shadow of the person described by another admirer as a "young girl in full bloom, with pink silken cheeks and feet as white as lotus petals". Her simplicity was distracting. Clad in a crumpled saree she was devoid of any adornment and frills.

Polite and attentive, she was happy and interested in my production of *Nandan Katha* but refrained from commenting on it. Soft spoken , with delicate and small gestures, she seemed to be of gentle demeanour, withdrawn from the world and at ease in the cool, unlit corner of what seemed to me a long corridor. This was the woman who had dared to desire a space for herself on the Nautanki stage–a place hitherto coveted and dominated by the male actor.[4] She made history by being the first woman performer of this popular form and she did it in such a way as to become one of its most famous icons. That was no easy achievement, for Nautanki was then a form that dominated the entire northern belt. The full throated singing, supported by the drumming on the nagara, filled the monotone of life with vibrancy and colour. [5] Its sharp rhythmic beat would echo over the placid flat fields and mango orchards, the sound waves electrifying the air and generating a flutter of activity. Crowds would begin to converge in the direction of the sound, prepared for a performance that would rob them of a whole night's sleep and yet leave them happy and cheerful at daybreak. Women would cook early, then head for a space from where a glimpse of the show or a whiff of the music could reach them. "Sometimes the parties would use our house as a base", Jayanti Devi, my mother-in-law, would reminiscence, "then it was all the more exciting. We could see them digging holes for the bamboos, putting up tents, arranging curtains. They would take out glittering clothes from their trunks, put on the paste while their ghungroos jingled all over the place." Her favourite was *Sultana Daku.*[6] The twinkle in her eyes reflected the delight created by the wonder world of the unreal and the exaggerated and the untiring projection of emotion and energy. It was an event that lingered on in memory even after it was over. With time, not only did the music and the narrative become part of life but the costumes adorned by the actors also influenced the way people dressed. Krishna Chandra Pahlwan had a tailoring outlet that would design and sell outfits fashioned in accordance with popular productions.[7]

The Nautanki, at its core, is centred on a dramatic narrative, emotion heightened through the singing of the actors, the impact accentuated by the nagara. Its origins lie in the simple and modest tradition of the musical which could be performed on a bare platform, the *chabutra*, or a hastily assembled stage made of *takhats* (wooden cots of a standard size and no decoration). It is generally acknowledged that the form acquired strong roots in Uttar Pradesh in the late nineteenth and early twentieth century with Mathura emerging as an important centre of performance and reference. Narratives like *Roop Basant* and *Sathya Harischandra* were developed into performances.[8] Natharam Gaur, one of its main proponents and directors, travelled with his troupe throughout Uttar Pradesh and each tour added to his laurels.[9] *Doha, Behar, Tabeel, Lavani, Khamsa* and various other metres were evolved so that layers of drama could unfold according to the subject, situation and intensity of the moment. The actors were also singers with histrionic abilities. Dance and dialogue, acrobatics and folk songs were also part of Nautanki. The actors would change position or create movement when the nagara played. Comic interludes were often interwoven into the main text. The available published scripts show a strong element of conflict and connected emotion but comedy does not seem to be central to the story telling. (The most popular text even to day is *Sathya Harischandra*, according to book sellers in Kanpur). While the Mathura School draws its power from music, the singing being melodious and intricate, the Kanpur vein has more of drama, dialogue and conflict. The singing, too, is often straight and direct–more like speech in metre set to notes and phrased so as to evoke emotion with varying pitch and intonation. The Mathura-Hathras tradition is older and is considered by many to be the primary and pure rendition of the form. Kanpur had witnessed *Inder Sabha*, *Shirin Farhad* and other productions of the Parsi Theatre companies before it developed its own version of Nautanki.[10]

There is a story that Natharam Gaur challenged Kanpur to produce something that would equal his work in merit. The artists of the city, led by Bandi Khalifa, accepted the challenge and created a performance using more than nine nagaras for drumming. According to some people this was the first time that the word Nautanki was used. Others believe that it is called "Nautanki" as it draws on the nine Rasas. The performance was a great success and even though the pioneers moved away, Kanpur Nautanki had come to stay. Krishna Chandra Pehalwan was quick to see the enormous scope for profit in this form, certainly more than in garments. He floated his own company which in no time multiplied into four, with performances lined up as far as Karachi. So popular was the form that he set up his own publishing house. Another company was set up by Trimohan Lal who is remembered as a great exponent of this style.[11] The Kanpur Nautanki assimilated the rural traditions and combined them with the dazzling grammar of the professional stage so as to create something with which the people could identify and yet have enough novelty so as to be commercially viable. Trimohan Lal ultimately had to sell his company's assets, including scripts, to the rival group of Krishna Chandra. To Lal goes the credit of introducing, to the Nautanki audiences, Gulab Bai who, later on became a challenge for him to reckon with. The Nautanki stage was thus a highly competitive space when young Gulabi first stepped on it. It contrasted with the rustic, less extravagant and less sophisticated, partly improvised performances put up by the local villagers. Nautanki was an organized venture in which big money could guarantee the success of a performance. While artistic merit was an important, and perhaps the most essential component, success could not be measured by appreciation alone. It had to translate into returns brought to the company, which could not sustain itself without the monetary benefit and the highly decorative structure needed to support it.

Born into a poor family, as the eldest of ten children Gulab Bai, however, had access to the rich treasure of song , music and dance which eventually proved to be invaluable assets. While watching Trimohan Lal's company perform *Bahadur Ladki* (a Nautanki in which she was later to play the lead role and which, years later, she directed with her daughter Asha playing the lead role) she persuaded her father to take her to meet the director. Trimohan Lal was impressed by the girl's talent, but the company was a place for men and boys. The girl was adamant, not dissuaded by the prospect of being stationed at Kanpur, the large indifferent city where she could receive training but no remuneration. Ultimately, Trimohan Lal relented and at her father's insistence also agreed to an allowance of fifty rupees for personal expenses like soap, oil etc. Thus, Gulab Bai joined his company in 1929.

Soon, her salary rose to two thousand rupees a month, excluding gifts of cash and kind that came her way. She delighted her teacher and employer with the Dadra "Nadi Nare Na Jao" ("Don't go across the river") which was an instant hit on the Nautanki stage as well. News spread like wild fire that the latest sensation in Trimohan Lal's company was a woman. Her performances drew crowds and she was the star of the show in their eyes. Her success attracted other woman performers. Other companies were quick to follow suit and new faces and boys entered the profession. Many of them, like Gulab Bai, are no more. However, some like Krishna Bai, Radha Rani and Kamlesh Lata, who carved a niche for themselves, continue to be involved with this form in different ways.[12]

"The work in Nautanki was very demanding and rigorous," says

Krishna Bai. "We would begin early with the practice of music, dance and speech. Perfection was demanded and diction had to be absolutely correct." This need for clarity and correctness arose from the very nature of the Nautanki writing which included words from Braj, Avadhi, Bhojpuri alongwith chaste Urdu and urban Hindustani. Literary metaphors were placed alongside popular idioms and common phrases, creating a mixed and interesting flavour, representing the cultural linguistic plurality of the region.

The opening invocation is often not addressed to Ganapati but refers to symbols of various religions, (Ram, Rahim) as the music too is drawn from a variety of sources. The diversity of the milieu, along with the nature of the performance, posed a challenge to the actor and she had to struggle with herself to sharpen or develop the skills necessary for the stage. There was also drama, the depiction of conflict and the need to emote with heightened energy and conviction, which needed to be communicated convincingly to the audience, so that they could move along with the performer. While it is true that many of the women came from families and caste groups that by birth and tradition defined them as performers, it is also evident that they were not content with the level of the skills they possessed. Technically, it may have meant extending a singer/dancer into an actor. Control of breath, pitch, gesture had to be enhanced. But the difference was deeper. Traditionally, the women would be called to sing and perform on occasions like marriages and births and for community celebrations of popular festivals like Holi. Landlords would also organize *mehfils* in their houses where women performers would engage the attention of the gathering for the entire night. Most of them were well versed in classical singing, dance and the art of pleasing the viewer who, in most cases, was the male patron. A carpet would be spread on the floor and the audience sat all around with the performer in the centre. The performer would face the host and patron while the others sat around. Encircled by them, performing in their midst, she could develop an intimate rapport with them – and yet this intimacy also made her vulnerable. Incidents of high caste men taking advantage of this arrangement were not unheard of. It also meant that the male gaze she addressed could often be domineering and encroach into her space and such proximity may not have always added to the comfort of the performer. Stepping on the stage was, thus, a cultural leap, significant in more ways then one.

The Nautanki stage may have been a temporary structure but it was higher than the audience. This height dramatically altered the position and stature of the performer – making her a larger than life image. The stage and audience faced each other but the two were separate areas – one belonged to the performer and the other to the viewer. Distance had been created. The circle of the *mehfil* or the *mujra* was broken.[13] By the time the women came to occupy it, the Nautanki stage had incorporated curtains in its décor and created a proscenium like façade that further heightened this separateness. For the woman who was vulnerable in the circle, this was a space that not only liberated her from various insecurities but it enhanced her dignity and status as a performer. She was also no longer performing for a special patron at any given time but for the hundreds who bought tickets to see her – the numbers gave support to her presence. The Nautanki plays with an awareness of the audience and, in the case of a woman performer, it meant performing largely to the opposite sex. Yet , in this context, it meant the widening of the male gaze thus making it seem more general and anonymous. Compared to the woman who could be rendered helpless in the circle of intimacy, she had more power and a more pronounced identity. During mujra both she and the viewers were aware of the social system and the hierarchy to which they belonged – and as by caste she belonged to what the patron considered inferior to his standing, she was compelled to play within the parameters of social expectation. The Nautanki stage temporarily created a world where she could assume a persona and hence address and be addressed through that image, thus transcending her social status. True, the system of the "once more" and the offering of cash persisted but in most cases it was routed through the manager and was not confined to the woman performer alone.

The transition also changed some aspects of life outside the performance. As a performer defined by caste, the woman had to engage in social interaction for her livelihood and there she almost always found herself at the receiving end. In Trimohan Lal's company she received a salary as an artist. True, there were grades and categories but these were according to skill and not determined by caste. The company owners were also aware that the presence of a large number of women professionals was in sharp contrast to the acceptable norms of a conservative society that demanded that women remain faceless. This dichotomy created a delicate situation. It brought audiences to the performances and yet a framework of respectability was necessary. The company gave the artist freedom and there was little interference in their personal lives but a form of discipline was maintained. The living quarters of men and women were segregated. "One of the special features of company life was the purdah," says Radha Rani, a prominent actor of her time. "By purdah, I don't mean the customary purdah of covering the face – but of decency and distance. It is true we travelled a lot, but always in covered vehicles. And wherever we went, it wasn't as if we were going sightseeing or on a shopping spree. We couldn't just go to people's homes or talk to anybody on the street. Too much familiarity was not considered good. If we wanted anything it was brought to us. If we wanted jewellry, the leading jewellers would be called. If it was sarees, the whole market would be laid before us. Whether it was perfume or flowers – we had to name it – and it was there at our doorstep."

At one level it protected the artists and ensured a certain privacy and generated respect making it evident that access to them was not easy and that they were beyond the reach of all and sundry. This seclusion created a distance that further mystified the show world. Pictures and posters, whispers and rumours made the artist an enigma that could only be revealed in the lustre of light, heralded by music. Needless to add, the actors used heavy make up and very little of the real self would be revealed. However, the curiosity aroused could take on bizarre forms as Vidya Bai recounted, when some students from Aligarh kidnapped her "out of sheer admiration." On the other, hand Trimohan Lal's Company was issued orders by the Police Commissioner to leave Kanpur within twenty-four hours as their performances were creating a law and order problem. "Gulab Bai was a crowd puller," says Awasthi ji, "so it was not possible to keep track of the people coming and going." Another version is that during a performance some rowdy elements created an ugly scene, challenging each other with knives, thus disrupting the show, ironically, of *Bahādur Ladki*. According to Asha, Gulab Bai's daughter, the play was popular for a scene in which a British officer tries to molest an Indian girl and she in retaliation slaps and humiliates him. As the play was anti-British and drawing huge crowds, the administration had to ban it in 1942. But of course they did not want to state the political reason and used a vague pretext to have Trimohan Lal's company removed from Kanpur. The Company moved to Kannauj and continued its performances. Gulab Bai remained the central star till she was denied an advance to meet the expenses of her sister's medical treatment who had fallen from a terrace.

A woman of quick and quiet resolution, Gulab Bai left the company and returned to Kanpur determined to float her own banner – a logical outcome of an ambitious career in the performing arts. There was the risk of losing money as well as earning the ire of other company owners. But she was steadfast and slowly built her group by contacting people who had worked earlier with her or taught her music.[14] Curtains were stitched and tent canopies were made, housing more than a thousand people. She accepted small and big assignments – marriages, fairs, public functions and ticketed shows. "My mother had a huge company," recollects Asha, her eyes beaming with pride and brimming with nostalgia, "its hugeness is even beyond the imagination of the men in business today. You won't believe it, but there were over a hundred people – actors, dancers, singers, acrobats – and that many musicians, technicians, cooks, guards and attendants. Then there were the sets, tents, all sorts of curtains, trunk loads of costumes, properties and all the rest that goes with it. When we went from one place to another it was like a long convoy on the move. We would be in caravans, while trunks and cartloads of luggage followed. Some would be dragging machines used for special effects while others would carry posters and banners, with the children running behind them and the people in the fields staring at us, filled with awe." Her voice quivered with the excitement of someone who had lived in the centre of performance and known the flutter in the wings and the glory of being on the stage.

Building largely on the goodwill Gulab Bai had accumulated, the company's profits soared and its assets increased. Gulab Bai was now also director and proprietor and in a position to demonstrate and dictate. Was she then able to bring about any changes in the Nautanki presentation? Could she bring in women oriented subjects or evolve a new and distinct way of dealing with the female persona? Radha Rani, who also handled a company for a while, smiles at my query. "Running a company was not an easy task," she tells me, "because stiff competition was the order of the day. You could feel it intensely – especially at fairs.

Competitive groups had tents facing each other and it was a real tussle to have the largest ticket sale. Men would go around the fair publicizing their Nautanki – just as drapers sent their men to the bazaars to advertise their wares. There was always tension before a show. Companies would send their agents secretly to the shows of others to find out what was attracting the audience. Dialogues would be copied, action would be imitated and sometimes, as a last resort, actors would be bought over. Generally song and dance numbers were the biggest crowd pullers – so if another company had seven songs we would have to have at least eight. As film music became the craze, Nautanki too latched on to it. Companies vied with each other in this aspect. It was cut throat competition and if you lost at the box office – you lost it all."

Krishna Chandra Pahlwan had seen Nautanki as a lucrative commercial venture before investing in it. As the popularity of the form soared more money poured in, more companies sprouted and competition intensified. To keep the box office ticking the audience had to be kept entertained and happy. This gave them the right and power to demand and reject. The "once more" syndrome was very much a part of commercial Nautanki and an artist who was repeatedly called for was certainly the envied one. "There was a new girl who had joined the company," narrates Asha. "She was so beautiful and delicate that we all kept staring at her. When she danced, it seemed that she had springs in her feet. The audience loved her and wouldn't let her go. The girl started acting pricy. The audience was clamouring for her and she refused to leave the wings. My mother scolded me for leaving the stage empty. But I was in tears. Why perform when you are not wanted? But my name was announced and it was not booed, so I went. This must have been around midnight. It had also rained and there were puddles even on the stage. But the audience wouldn't let me stop and so I went on in ankle deep water till it was morning. I was so dizzy I didn't know where my feet were. When the music stopped, I just collapsed."

"So many were talented," says Vidya Bai, ruefully. "But talent needs someone to appreciate it." She had worked in companies run by both men and women, including Gulab Bai. "We were pressurized to attract more people. The young girls were the worst hit. Talented ones, from nearby villages, were made to go on stage clad scantily, in circus type of clothes, which were so tight that the girls could hardly move. The going got really bad. There was no joy in performing and no proper money either so I returned home."

"But couldn't a company owner make a difference?" I asked.

"No, not really," she answered pensively. "Because Nautanki was the same. The audience was the same. And the company's need to make money was the same – else it had to shut down."

The women owners were more hard pressed, more insecure, because the men had been in the game much longer and were well versed in the art of manipulation as well as tact. "My mother was a hard task master," says Asha. "She would make you work, often to the point of a break down. The company flourished, but she was burdened by the task of management and accounts. In addition, there were challans by petty officials who threatened to disrupt performances. After Independence she was instrumental in getting a number of taxes abolished but even so it was difficult to keep the show going. The managers handled the finance and kept a record of the purchases, sales of tickets and distribution of salaries besides getting various clearances, permission of travel, performance space etc. She trusted them but it was they who cheated her."

Despite investing her personal resources she became vulnerable to the manoeuvrings of the managers she had hired. The inability to read and write had not mattered as long as she was just a performer but the culture of written records and accounting baffled those who were the stalwarts of the oral tradition. Radha Rani moved out of the fray. So did Gulab Bai. After a performance near Meerut, she returned home empty handed. Friends and sisters asked her to retrieve her assets so as to recover some money from their sale. She declined, saying that it was better not to touch the remnants of her passion lest it again overtake her. Shuffling the embers could set the fire aglow again, so she moved away. With ruthless detachment she pulled herself away from the world she had energized and whose spirit she had come to personify. Silent and still, she grew pale and weak – that is how she was when I met her in the early summer of 1981.

By then the Nautanki scenario had changed. Many companies had shut down even as new ones continued to sprout. The nagara was heard but in the midst of many other sounds. The urban stage had created and celebrated the Nautanki in *Ala Afsar* (a musical adaptation of *The Inspector General*) and opened a new area of discourse. On the rural stage the narrative, in many cases, moved away from centre stage making room for performance – a phenomena that can be analysed in more than one way. "Nautanki" still implies popular entertainment and there are banners that do brisk business. "Who would not want to do real Nautanki even today?" says Murli, who has a small company in Lucknow. "What I do is to keep my body and soul together so that the few artists who remain with me can earn something. They all need to live. They are good dancers and singers. But Nautanki is much more and that is gone. The arena is soiled and the audience spoiled. And that is because the women who were allowed on this stage played with the form and made it vulgar."

"What is vulgar?" counters Awasthiji. "It is just a notion. When women were kept in purdah, even the toe of an uncovered foot was considered immoral. When women were kept cloistered in the house, for someone to stand amongst men and sing could be termed as vulgar. Today these notions have changed. What is called vulgar today is very much acceptable tomorrow. Whatever was shown on the Nautanki stage good, bad, commercial – is definitely not more than what is seen in films today. But families watch them together; educated girls and boys act in them. So there is no right or wrong. If you like it, you go – if you don't, you stay away." But the argument does not seem to end here. Like a refrain it comes up in many conversations and discussions.

Jhabu Mastan, a well-known comedian of his times says, "Nautanki was doomed from the day woman set foot in it. You people talk of glory, art and contribution. Ask me. I know what it meant." The anger and hostility does not subside even as he elaborates, "they ruined the actor – destroyed his very art." He was not only referring to the actors who had played feminine parts and were now replaced by women – but to the overall displacement of actors and the very art and method of acting. "You have read Nautanki texts, haven't you?" he counters. "Do they deal only with songs and dances? No. But this is what remained when women stepped on the stage. What should have been in snatches became the main show. The story, the dialogue, the emotions are forgotten – and slowly, so is the actor. He is all dressed up – with make up on his face and his lines on his lips. He paces up and down in the green room repeating them to himself. The audience is too preoccupied with the dancing and the parade of flesh to be bothered about him and his role. Outside the tent, the board says *Sultana Daku* but the whole night passes and no-one sends for him. He waits till sunrise when the curtains are drawn then he and goes home. The ones with any self-respect left the stage. The needy stayed to puff and pant in the group dances - like extras in films."

The intensity of the resentment is heart-rending. It is a common saying: everywhere, a woman employed renders a man unemployed. But there should have been a place for the woman to begin with. The woman also needs to be there – not to oust a man but in her own right. She is claiming the space that she has been deprived of. They say women in the work force are willing to work for less money, are better workers and create less trouble. This is more so in the case of single women especially if she is a parent – for she needs the job more. And the Nautanki stage discovered that they were also more saleable. When men have no social access to open interaction with women, her very presence is a gift to the eye. Denial at one level led to a kind of presentation that would get audiences that were largely men. The female personae, when adorned by men in forms like khyal, also elicits a similar response. It is encouraged by the company owners for the returns that it brings in. The woman – or the notion of a woman and her body – becomes a commodity that is a financially feasible proposition for the investors. As commerce was inbuilt into this style of Nautanki, the owners took the road that served their interest, for they were clearly in it for the business of making money. The responsibility for this must rest with the owners. As Awasthiji says. "To assume that women performers were not talented would be wrong. Many of them stood tall on the stage in terms of talent and dramatic ability – often higher than their male co-actors."

Radha Rani and Krishna Bai, who perform even today with grace and strength, prove this point. Radha Rani, too, left a regular performing career because, as she says, "My children had grown up and felt it was causing me too much strain. Besides, Nautanki was getting a bad name because it imitated dances from Hindi films and displayed too much body. So where is the art? That is something deep within – almost like a prayer. I don't need to stoop to such compromises to keep it alive."

The loss of the actor cost the form heavily, for he/she was a carrier of its content and music. Thus, the narrative too became redundant. The displacement of the narrative also meant that new texts stopped emerging and the creative resourcefulness connected with the form was squeezed of its energy.

But there were other reasons as well. The Bombay film industry capitalized on the audiences of this belt. It appropriated many of the songs and tunes that had been popularized on the Nautanki stage – more or less in the same way as Nautanki had appropriated folk songs and the informal *swang* into its fold. True, it continued to perform in the same area and, for a fee, gave back to the audiences a scale so grandiose that it was far beyond the reach of the rural singer/actor.

It is significant to note that the women came on to this scene rather late – in 1930s. By this time the Hindi cinema had already gone beyond the silent era and was all set to expand further. This had already sent jitters in the Parsi theatre. Themes, stories, narrative structures, music and actors were moving to the new medium – which was the popular cultural form and had acquired a mass base.

It is quite possible that the entry of women on the Nautanki stage was facilitated by the dwindling feasibility of the form in the context of the changing scenario. The emergence of the woman on stage, as a charismatic entity, probably helped to extend the life of the form which may have collapsed earlier had this not happened, considering the onslaught of the cinema. The novelty and energy that women performers brought, changed the face and character of Nautanki, thereby giving it a fresh lease of life. Responsible women performers like Krishna Bai (like many male actors) have tried to keep the core and narrative alive, not only as performers but also as organizers of groups. However, the kind of support that was needed to nurture these efforts was missing. In the pre-independent phase, Nautanki artists were gripped with the fervour of nationalism and there are instances of many of them performing in villages on the sly (without the huge company trudging along). However, post independence they did not get the care and attention from the state that they deserved and needed. Independence also brought the Partition. This region (the Ganga-Yamuna belt, falling in Uttar Pradesh) was not partitioned, but there was heavy migration which altered its cultural face. Many patrons, who had earlier sponsored performances and were well versed in the art of appreciation – whether it were emotion, music, verse or language, left. Many of the themes that emerged in Nautanki reflected the language with which this group could identify. The damage caused by the Partition to the social and cultural fabric of the region has never really been assessed. With some patrons gone, the state not sufficiently proactive and isolated factories creating pockets of single men, the popular stage took many turns, constantly adapting to the changing nature of the audiences. But the parameters of success, commerce and popularity had begun to change even when the companies were at the height of their glory.

Part II – The Making of *Teen Betiyan urf Dehleez Ke Par*

As one listens to the Nautanki singing, one can feel the compelling power of the performance. I had seen some performances and dabbled with it somewhat in 1981. The desire to learn and discover that which was outside the scope of my city-bred education and grooming remained. The resonance of the nagara drum enchanted me and the very thought of an actor amidst thousands of spectators dazzled and teased the mind. Many large companies still go by the name of Nautanki, though they have moved away from the narrative and have a loose amalgamation of songs, skits and dances that nevertheless create chemistry between the audience and performer, though in an altered context. The narrative performance was in existence prior to the companies and thus can be said to contain the seed of the form.

Fortunately, the prevalence of narrative Nautanki has not yet become a matter of the past. Though very few texts have been added in the past few years, there are still groups that continue to create performances on existing texts. Even today, traditional and familiar texts have an overpowering impact on audiences that delight in the known manoeuvrings of drama. Krishna Bai has built and kept up an active group in Mathura that sustains a regular stream of performances. For her traditional texts like *Puran Bhagat* are meaningful and relevant. She has not felt the need to add extra song and dance sequences to attract audiences. Her focus is on the inherent drama of values, the intricate singing, the play of contrasts and the rhythmic flow of action. An accomplished singer and a graceful performer herself, she has trained a group of men and women who blend joy with dedication while performing Nautanki.

In places less than fifty kilometres from Delhi, sale of tickets for a night performance easily fetches the group a revenue of about forty to fifty thousand rupees. Returns are substantial, though not regular. Yet, Krishna Bai smiles and says, "Often the proceeds are given away to charity. So many schools have been built in this area by money raised through performances."

Radha Rani, too, performs occasionally, her favourite role being that of Taramati in *Satya Harishchandra*. She does not interpret Taramati as a meek and docile wife but as a woman of substance who questions Harishchandra and demands to be an equal participant in his ordeal of truth. Her performance is enhanced by her stance and voice, seasoned by years and practice. She projects the Veerangana (warrior) image which makes a virtue of sacrifice. I give credit to Radha Bai for altering the image of Taramati that had been stored for so long in my mind. According to a Kanpur bookshop, *Satya Harishchandra* is the most widely sold Nautanki text – the clientele being largely from rural areas. It probably serves as a base for emerging young talent aspiring to be on stage.

"Shall we make a performance out of the life of a woman performer?" I asked Asha and Madhu. Their mother Gulab Bai had recently passed away and this could be a tribute to her memory. They looked at each other and shook their heads. "It won't work," they said in unison. "A performer's life is very different and may be interesting, but the audience wants something it can relate to - or something that moves it." The two were, however, not averse to the idea of creating a new text. They felt it was crucial for the form to keep pace with the times – not only in terms of content and story but also in terms of treatment – the use of sets, lights and the overall technical design. Both have been associated with theatrical activities in Kanpur and have thought critically about the various dimensions involved in mounting a production. They were quite clear and precise in their views. Rejecting the idea of a comedy, they emphasized that the core of Nautanki must be a serious subject and "a situation that has drama."

We then discussed the tragic story of three sisters from Kanpur who had ended their lives together, as a subject. The most commonly held reason for their death was lack of dowry but it could also be seen as a case of denial of opportunity, suffocation due to conservative norms, being undervalued as persons, treated as unwanted, merely because they were women. Asha and Madhu agreed that the subject had sufficient substance for a performance. But this was just the starting point. The purpose of the performance was not to document their lives but to generate dramatic moments based on the development of the plot. The darkness and gloom of such a story is pervasive and overpowering, but translating it for the stage demanded a certain objectivity. We had to look for threads that could be built into the story or bring in other factors that would contain the situation, thus enlarging the scope for fictionalization and subsequently weaving a new plot. Death had also to be seen in contrast to life. But how alive could life be, in the bleak environs of a lower middle class home in Kanpur? A father, worried and burdened with three daughters; a mother desperate without a son and the three daughters oppressed by the parents and seen as being oppressive by them – these were the shadows and shade that realism could capture. And yet, it could not all be static. There had to be movement and resistance. Partly in search of drama and hope, we looked at various possibilities that could have happened but did not.

This was the beginning of my long association with the daughters of Gulab Bai that was to grow and develop through an Alarippu initiative that was exploring ways to relate with popular forms outside the ambit of the urban scenario.[15] Gulab Bai had breathed her last while her daughter was talking to us on telephone. The poignancy of that moment created a bonding that was strange and inexplicable, for it cemented different spaces and connected strangers to a common memory. Soon Asha and Madhu were working with me on the draft of the narrative. Asha took the responsibility of composing the music while the younger Madhu was to mount the scenes, handle the actors and look after the overall production. My role was to help with the structuring of the narrative and the design and other related areas with Bhanwar Gopal, my colleague from Alarippu which was to support and strengthen the initiative. We requested Siddheshwar Awasthi, who was familiar with Nautanki and also known to the Gulab Bai family, to create the Nautanki text, which he readily accepted. The challenge was to convey a contemporary experience in a language that was simple yet poetic, explicit yet not banal, indicative but not abstract. Popular metaphors and images had to be incorporated into ideas that were not so traditional. The lifelessness of the house had to be conveyed without the support of any ambience. The use of silence, monosyllables, subtle gestures and disjointed actions, used in the realistic genre, manage to convey mood and relationship. But the Nautanki prides itself in the use of well orchestrated verse in specific metres and dialogues that are crafted for impact. This provided scope for articulation of thoughts or view points bringing dynamism to the narrative.

The storyline was simple and the characters were ordinary. Three sisters, a conventional mother and a conventional father. One sister wanted to read poetry but was not allowed to do so and, suffocated by her surroundings, ends her life. The other sister wanted to dance but knew that she would not find the space in the house and, after the sister's final act, just leaves the house. The third obeys the parents but is confronted with a number of questions.

We envisaged a series of situations that created tension and thus brought out a certain restlessness, levels of disagreements and understanding which in turn sharpened the characters. The keyword was "drama" and discovering this in everyday situations was not only interesting but, at times, very revealing. For example, when Nina dances, she touches the empty cradle waiting for a son. This brings in the mother who, on seeing this, laments her situation. The girls now react differently and chide their mother suggesting that there could be choices other than suffering. The mother's pathos is real but the daughter's argument questions its validity, creating drama and a counterpoint. The helpless mother is a reality in many homes. Audiences can identify and relate with this character but care had to be taken so that this helplessness was not seen to be a virtue.

The father, an authoritarian figure within the home, is not a successful person outside it. Constantly vexed by his inability, his aim is to play safe with tradition and convention. Both parents are so troubled with the burden of their daughters that they barely notice the spark of life in them. The three daughters also have predictable characteristics. The eldest keeps her peace with her parents but is protective of her sisters. The other sister, Bina, is defiant, outspoken and is unwilling to live without her passion for books. Nina, the third sister, gains impetus from Bina's act of final withdrawal and moves out of the sphere of the house. Frequent use of words like *bahen* (sister), *humshakal* (look alike) and *hamsheena* (bred on the milk of the same breast) creates an emotional intensity that is easily grasped. Other metaphors used, like *safina* (boat of life) and *chuniya* (drape) also denoted fluttering of the sail or the noose.

Initial discussions and drafts in the realistic genre evoked no more than a grunt from Awasthiji. His command over language and fluency with metres was impeccable. He wanted to use phrases in a more innovative way. The script took time to shape up. With just two days to begin rehearsal, we received four sheets of paper which, on editing, were reduced to two and a half! After a short prayer, we began with a language "steeped in bitterness" as the Ranga mentioned "a substantive conflict between father and daughter" and thus the tale was introduced to the audience:

> Three lanes and in the corner of the third is a house
> A courtyard with three doors and that's where we pause.
> (The three sisters describe the house in contrasting hues.)
>
> *Meena:* Standing on this threshold, ever since I opened my eyes.
> Since then I've seen these walls and this space.
> This is the floor on which these feet have moved.

This shelter alone provides me with shade.

Bina: Shelter? These tiny rooms filled with dampness and cold all around. No flowers to be seen. Neither do rays of the sun touch this doorstep.

(sings)
the face of sadness, steeped in darkness.
This life stifled by torment
So many new turns, new shores and ways
Here we greet a crumbling phase.

Nina (speaks): Each wall of this collapsing house stands defeated by its own inadequacy.

(sings)
the ageing truth like a gem without lustre
chiselled on the floor fills it with shame!

The opening sequence created a visual image that became the central idea for the set design. The bare stage was appropriate. It was a space which could be any place, anywhere. On the other hand, a meaningful set could indicate the nature of performance and set the tone for the audience's expectation. It could also establish the contemporary theme of the Nautanki and its treatment. In the opening scene we wanted a set consisting of three arches constructed separately but placed in such a way as to form lines of connection. The arches were to be the distinct spaces for the sisters and each door could also represent a path to be taken or a journey that may or may not happen. The threshold, *ḍahleez*, is popularly seen as the space for a pause – a moment of dilemma. Three arches and an empty cradle was the basic constituents of the design. Each unit was moveable. Whenever possible, we used lights to accentuate mood and moments. But by and large we used general lights, creating plasticity of composition.

It gradually became evident that the culture of rehearsals was not understood by the Nautanki actors. A long new play with distinct dialogue and a great deal of singing meant a lot of work and there were not many takers. Some seasoned actors were, however, enthusiastic and happy to be part of the process.-A huge hall had been hired for rehearsals and the preparations showed a great deal of professionalism. The musicians and the actors would arrive early. Asha would read the new lines, count the beats on her fingers and ask the musicians for a specific note and a specific beat. Then she would sing the verse. The musicians and the actors would give the feedback. After a few trials, the tune would be set and the actor would start practising, picking a note suited to her or his voice. The younger actors who had never really followed a collective process, were both amazed and a bit lost but gradually warmed up. Awasthiji came to the rehearsals regularly and enjoyed every moment that gave shape to the words. At night we would sit in the light of a kerosene lamp, (as, most often, the electricity would have gone), sipping tea and munching biscuits while words were written, scratched and replaced.

Once the actors had prepared their individual parts, work began on the "assembling" of the scenes. However, care was taken to see that the thread of the story and its realism was carried by the performers even though the gestures were fairly standardized. The actors were to convey the mood and the emotion through their singing. Some variation in notes was also made once the scenes began to acquire shape. Sometimes interesting questions arose. How would Nina dance? Would it be a dance picked from Hindi films or would it be in the Nautanki tradition? A small romantic song had been composed and the actor playing the role tried to improvise the steps, an assortment picked from Hindi films. These songs and dances delve into a choreography often unrelated to the story- a shy character may seem totally uninhibited during the dance and the audience, too, does not seem to be disturbed by the discrepancy. The problem lay not so much in the dance being too skillful, as in the sexual undertones in the manner of execution, which did not connect with the character. The problem we faced was regarding the kind of relationship we wished to make with the audience. Should the dance be an engrossing and happy piece without seeming to titillate–like a folk dance or was it all right for the actress to design her piece according to her own understanding and carry on with it? This question was hotly debated and Madhu felt that the dance should not in any way titillate the audience. "The audience," she said, "is used to reading into this kind of style. And they come with a set mentality. If we want them to look at us differently then we must give them something different. Once I asked an elderly person who was highly educated and cultured and for whom I have a lot of respect, what a man expected from watching a woman on stage? And he said that a man wants to see as much as-possible of the woman, extract as much as he could from the spectacle." Such an attitude sees the body as a commodity. The actor does not exist in isolation – the performance is received and perceived by the other and the range of sensibility is measured in that experience. Yet, the performance on the stage, the body in motion is there to be seen. Inhibiting it would shrink its aura and take away the flow from the form. However, in this case, the narrative is about the lives of women. Can a woman's concern be highlighted if her presence in stage is not? Can the performer make the audience swing in and out of the story if she is also to play the character she depicts? Would the seed of thought reach and stay with the audience irrespective of the overall ambience of performance? It is a question not just of ethics but also of aesthetics, central to the nature of performance.

Nautanki is a living connection. The body is not just an image – it is a person. The young actors are used to engaging with male attention.

A few days later, one of the actors came along with her mother who had been a dancer on the Nautanki stage. She showed us many pieces and listened carefully to all our comments. Then she tucked in her sari, veiled her face, and began to dance. The harmonium stopped playing and the nagara beat grew fast and loud. With vigorous steps she moved all over the stage, bouncing with energy and rhythm. There was no denial of her sexuality but the rhythmic energy that her body transmitted filled all of us with wonder and awe. This was joy–pure joy of being. She was able to shift our attention from the dancer to the dance. She had not used the lines of the song and there were no illustrative gestures. Many folk dances also do not have illustrative gestures. The repetitive pattern of steps and the rhythm give it tempo. Even while the meaning of the lines may change, the steps sustain the sequence. Classical dances are highly codified and measured. The grammar of mudras and the expression of bhavas exhibit precision and control. The illustrative gestures that accompany the singing are often apparent in the mudras, which are also addressed to the male gaze and flatter it. It can interfere with the free flow and energy that surfaces when the dancer responds to rhythm within her own sphere, not conscious of the viewer. By veiling her face, the mother had distanced herself from the gaze of spectators. Beyond recognition, she surrendered her identity to the dance. The veil allowed her to concentrate on her actions and be free. The actress playing the role was not familiar with the dance steps that her mother was so adept at. She gave up the illustrative mode and the song was also trimmed. She created her steps drawing on the vigour of what she visualized as the dance. It gave her power and a sense of abandonment. The actress was also directed not to address the audience and at times to allow the character to relate with her sisters. By just moving away and distancing herself from the gaze, she qualitatively altered the sequence which had initially seemed like an invitation to the spectator.

However, the presence of the audience was an important consideration in developing most of the sequences. What will be the impact of such an action on the audience? Will it lead to the desired result? For each of the senior actors, used to playing scenes with an awareness of mood, it was crucial that the point of view and feeling of their character should reach the audience. Munnibai got so involved with the mother's predicament that her co-actors found it quite difficult to refrain from sympathizing with her. Bit by bit, equations began to balance out and the sequences developed smoothly. Madhu displayed her craftsmanship while assembling a scene between the father and his youngest daughter. It was sparsely written. The logic of the plot needed to build up to the point where the daughter's decision to end her life would seem convincing. Madhu insisted that the actors play it with intensity. The book, as the central prop, was used with added significance. The father's modulation was enlarged so as to be a clear reason for provocation. Observing the sequence, as it evolved, was very interesting for me. A scene from contemporary daily life, when woven into a popular traditional genre, blends into it when treated according to the known grammar of the form. This was the scene where conflict had to be at its height – in a way the "climax" for what happens next, the ending of life is the consequence of this moment and is not shown on stage. The entry of the father, the quick turn, the stamping of feet, the arrogant gesture in tearing and throwing the book were built upon so that in this particular sequence the "ordinary" father revealed horrific qualities of negativity that could not be overlooked. It was a short sequence – almost a glimpse, but not without effect. Madhu also contemplated bringing in the corpse of the girl. This is not unusual in

Nautanki – *Satya Harishchandra* being an outstanding example. However, that would have meant focusing on the event itself rather than dwelling on the impact that it had on the other sister.

Much discussion centred on the concluding sequence. Nina leaves home. Meena obeys her parents and get married. But happiness eludes her as her husband is involved with another woman who, as in a perfect story, turns out to be her sister. We wondered how the story should end. After a great deal of discussion, the possibility of the two sisters coming together was suggested. It would not have been forever and the story remains inconclusive. Madhu worried that the audience would not be able to absorb it and instead see it as an attempt to misguide women or as an advocacy for breaking homes. For days we discussed and pondered. Madhu's worry was that because of this one factor, the Nautanki would lose its impact. The audience suddenly seemed a static mass that would not accept an unconventional idea even on a stage that was known to indulge in fantasy. I appealed to Madhu to let the original ending stand and if it did not work with the audience, then another could be worked out. Ultimately, Madhu agreed keeping in mind that the ending was only a tentative one.

As the rehearsals neared completion, the actors became keen to work out their attire and physical appearance. It also spoke of their sensibility and experience that they did not make any demands for glittering clothes or hair styles, so typical of Nautanki. They wanted costumes that would go with the story. Like any budget-conscious group, the cheapest markets were surveyed in great detail.

The initial performances were put up for women's groups. They not only identified with the characters but were also appreciative of the treatment, primarily because of the unconventional turns. They saw it both, in the context of the popular genre and the exposition of the plot. This gave us the confidence to put up the Nautanki without any alteration.

Performances were arranged through various cultural organizations and NGO's, mainly through Shramik Bharati and Mahila Manch, in the nearby towns and villages. In some places, local bodies took the initiative in providing us space and making arrangements like setting up the stage, getting electricity connection, water and accommodation etc. Most of the performances were at night but some, arranged by women's groups, were during the day, so that a large number of women could come to see the performances. At some places like Kanpur, large audiences turned up. In Maharajpur, the Nautanki was put up on special request. By and large, the audience seemed moved with the story, and their interest intensified towards the culminating scenes, in both the first and the second half. In Kakori, there was disappointment expressed that the Nautanki did not have enough song and dance sequences. It was while travelling with the performers, to hitherto unknown places, that one realised how courageous they were to move about in this fashion, accepting the hospitality of strangers and giving performances late into the night, miles away from home. However, they had an inherent vulnerability that made them cautious and alert even during a performance – but that did not deter their enthusiasm while on stage.

The print media responded warmly to the Nautanki. The local press gave a fair coverage to the shows. The Nautanki was also invited to participate in a festival of plays held at Rabindralaya, Lucknow. Writers' conferences at Kanpur and Unnao also organized shows of the Nautanki. On 8 March 1997, two shows were organised at different venues. In Lajpat Bhavan, where a morning show was held, there was a strange scene. When Madhu began her dance, as part of a wedding scene, the women from the audience climbed on to the stage and joined her, stepping down only when they were utterly exhausted. It was, indeed, an unplanned interlude that changed the very meaning of the dance itself, making it part of a celebration larger than the situation on stage.

However, for the actors, the performances given at colleges were the most important ones. Asha would later remark, "Taking Nautanki to a college – a place of learning – where educated people can see the performance – is the highest form of tribute that one can pay to any art form."

The women's colleges that were approached in Unnao and Kanpur warmly welcomed the idea. For most of the actors it was a novel experience to perform for an exclusively female audience. Over the years, Nautanki audiences has been mostly male though some actors had performed for mixed audiences. Performing for women, the actresses seemed more relaxed and danced with greater abandon. For Madhu, the entire experience assumed a special meaning, especially, when she performed in the college where she had once taken admission. "But then, my mother fell ill and I had to discontinue my studies and work on the stage. I hated Nautanki then. But I couldn't believe that I had come to the same college and performed before the students, who were watching me with such close attention. Later, during discussions, they asked me questions and wanted answers from me. For the first time, I felt, Nautanki had given me this power."[16]

Notes

1 Gulab Bai, the first woman to appear on the Nautanki stage was born around 1918 and died on 13 July, 1996.

2 Professor Satyamurthy was the founder director of Darpan, an important theatre group in Kanpur.

3 An adaptation of Indira Parthasarathy's Tamil play, *Nandan Katha* in 1980.

4 Gulab Bai often claimed that she joined Trimohan Lal's company in 1929 when she was 11 years old. Companies were large theatre groups. Refer to the interview given in *Navbharat Times* and quoted in Kathryn Hansen's *Grounds for Play: The Nautanki Theatre of North India*, Berkeley, LosAngeles, Oxford: University of California Press,1992.

5 There were two kinds of nagaras – the smaller one had a sharper tone and the bigger one had more base to it.

6 *Sultana Daku* belonged to a popular genre of drama of the 1920's which depicted dacoits as heroes who robbed the rich and helped the poor.

7 Shri Krishna Chandra Pehalwan was the main influence, in the 1920's, on the Kanpur style of Nautanki. Born on 12th December 1891, his first Nautanki , *Hakekat Rai,* was presented in 1913.

8 *Roop Basant* was a popular adventure story about two brothers and their conniving stepmother. *Satya Harischandra* dealt with the well known story of King Harishchandra, who renounced everything for truth and a life of asceticism. Both plays were very popular on the Nautanki stage.

9 Natharam Gaur also known as Natharam Sharma Gaur, (1875-1943) , was a poet and publisher who also played female roles on the Nautanki stage.

10 *Inder Sabha* or *The Court of Indra* was an important nineteenth century musical written during the reign of Wajid Ali Shah (1847-1856) by Agha Hasseb Amanat, an Urdu poet of Lucknow. It revolved around the events in the court of Indra, King of Gods. *Shirin Farhad* was a romantic love story between a queen and a stonecutter which ends in tragedy.

11 Trimohan Lal belonged to Kannauj but later established his company in Kanpur in 1903.He made a significant contribution to the Kanpur Nautanki and published all his plays first in Kanpur and then in Kannauj.

12 Radha Rani was born in Pilibhit district in a village called Nadipur Bhagariya. She devised a Nautanki where women played all the roles. Radha Rani used to play the role of Majnu in the play *Laila Majnu* and also the role of Sultana Daku. She established her own company in 1956. Kamlesh Lata is the younger sister of Radha Rani. Krishna Bai is from Shikohabad in U.P. Vidya Bai came from Mahoba district.

13 A *mehfil* is a private musical gathering and *mujra* is a dance performance by a *tawaif* (courtesan) for a private and intimate gathering.

14 Gulab Bai's theatre company was known as The Great Gulab Theatre Company.

15 *Alarippu* is an organization working in theatre, education and culture since 1984.

16 *Teen Betiyan* had nearly 25 shows in Kanpur, Lucknow and other areas like Unnao.

4

Construction of Modernity in Tamil Drama and Theatre – Na. Muthusami's Plays and Performances*

V. Padma ('Mangai')

Modernism is usually defined as a movement that sprang up in the twentieth century in the field of arts and literature in different parts of the world, in disparate contexts. At the same time, modernity is seen as not referring to any movement but as a moment of departure in time and history. As a sociological concept, modernity is primarily associated with industrialization, secularization, the bureaucracy and urbanization. In a colonised nation, however, modernity is closely associated with colonization vis-à-vis westernization. Most often identified with the technological innovations brought into a society, modernity ushers in change with a jolt. Railways, the educational system, legal measures and documentation are some of the most pronounced signs of modernity that India experienced as part of colonial rule. These changes changed our perspectives as well. In a newly independent country, these factors of modernity become symbols of "progress". The same tools of modernity become the instruments to seek our pre- colonial identity, thanks to the anthropological studies of

---

*This paper is a revised version of a paper presented in Tamil in a seminar organised by Kaavya Publishers at the National Folklore Support Centre, Chennai on July 15, 2006, on the occasion of Muthusami's 70th birthday.

the early colonizers! Or they are retained as legacy of the colonizer to help continue the neo-colonial remnants.

The construction of nationhood, once India became independent, faced the challenge of bringing together two disparate strands of our historical past: our pre-colonial (and therefore pre- modern) traditions and the new modernity (therefore progress) had to come together to form a new nation. Nationalism had, also, to accommodate various regional identities. In the field of theatre this call for a national theatre has seen at least three phases so far: the pan-Indian cultural movement that was part of the anti-colonial struggle, spearheaded by IPTA; the Nehruvian cultural policy to seek unity in diversity through centralised organizations like the Sahitya Akademi, the Sangeet Natak Akademi and the National School of Drama in the fifties; and the seventies' call for "back to the roots" to decolonize our theatres.[1]

Tamil Nadu, however, has its own disjuncture with these three phases. The proscenium stage, painted back curtains, stage props, scenic design, the use of the harmonium and the introduction of dialogues in prose were imbibed as a colonial legacy via the parsi theatre into Tamil theatre in the latter half of the nineteenth century[2]. Sankaradas Swamigal assimilated these changes in his Isai Natakam / Balar Sabhai (Boys' Companies). Pammal Sambhanda Mudaliyar introduced these changes in amateur groups functioning from cities and small towns[3]. Tamil cinema evolved from these two major trends. From the early years of the twentieth century, the Self- Respect Movement consistently raised the issue of the casteist, religious and gender hierarchies operating in both these traditions. Led by E.V.R.Periyar, the Movement also questioned the concept of Indian nationalism. Tamil nationalism became the major impulse born out of this ideology. The Annamalai University, which was the result of the move to establish regional universities, focused on indigenous traditions of language and music.[4] Inheriting the rationalist traditions of western epistemology and education, artists belonging to the Dravidian movement attempted to disentangle the puranic aspects from drama. C.N. Annadurai, M. Karunanidhi, Tiruvarur Thangaraju, M.R. Radha, N.S. Krishnan, M.G. Ramachandran and Shivaji Ganesan were some of the artists who pioneered this trend. Muthusami grew up as a youth inspired by the Dravidian movement in its heyday, thanks to his student days at Annamalai University, and began to enter the field of Tamil literature (fiction, poetry and drama) at a period when the Dravidian movement had lost its radical edge. A brief sketch of Muthusami's life will help us to understand his place in the construction of modernity in Tamil drama and theatre.

Muthusami was born on 25 May, 1936 in Punjai village of Nagapattinam District in Thanjavur. His parents were Natesa Aiyer and Pattammal. In his twenties he moved to Chennai, then Madras. He began his literary career as a short story writer and a poet. Tamil had a strong literary culture, as did many other Indian languages, right from the thirties. In poetry a new wave of modern *Pudu Kavidhai* (New Poetry) began to raise disturbing questions about traditional prosody and contemporary sensibility. The *Pudu Kavidhai* movement, in turn, had two major schools of thought. One group advocated a forceful Marxist outlook and the other decried it as empty rhetoric. The latter concentrated on the aesthetics of multi-disciplinary arts. They wanted to enrich Tamil literature by absorbing the avant-garde trends from all over the world[5] . Ka. Na. Subramaniam and Si. Su. Chellappa were the major exponents of this trend in Tamil literature. *Ilakkiya Vattam* (1963-1965, 38 issues in all) and *Ezhuthu* (1959-1972) were the two magazines edited by them respectively. They focused on translations and newer forms of literature. Muthusami's first short story was published in *Ezhuthu*. Chellappa, was keen on drama as well and announced membership for drama performances on the pattern of the sabhas[6]. That may have been the major inspiration for Muthusami to enter drama. The younger generation of writers in *Ezhuthu* went on to start *Nadai* (1968-1970, 8 issues), *Akq* (1972-1980, 22 issues), *Kasadathapara* (1972-??) and *Pregnai* (1972/3-1980). Muthusami's plays were published in *Nadai*. All these little magazines were active in the seventies. Muthusami entered the field of theatre in full earnest in 1977 with the founding of the theatre group Koothu-p-Pattarai. He won the Sangeet Natak Akademi award for playwright in 2000. One must remember his early inspiration and consequent disappointment with the Dravidian movement, his participation in parallel literary activities and active involvement in little magazine circles, and his avant-garde initiation while evaluating his place in the construction of modernity in Tamil drama and theatre.

One cannot separate any discussion on Muthusami from that of Koothu-p-Pattarai. He was the founder of the group along with Veerasami. In due course only Muthusami remained. Most of Muthusami's plays are performed by this group. He also attempted directing a few plays, seeking to evolve a new language of theatre. He has written extensively on training for actors. Koothu-p-Pattarai is recognised by the UNESCO as a training institution. It was funded by the Ford Foundation for a specific period but unlike Subbanna's Ninasam or the Thrissur School of Drama, which became part of Calicut University, Koothu-p-Pattarai did not consolidate its institutional base with the Ford grant. However, it has been a strong presence for the past thirty years in contemporary Tamil drama and theatre, in spite of ups and downs because it did not have a solid support system.

Modernity brought in changes in various spheres of life. In terms of culture, modernity unsettled the power dynamics of earlier systems.

Chief among the systems operant in India were caste and gender. In theatre, the unquestioned accolade given to classical arts and theories came under severe scrutiny. That led to a reappraisal of the traditional forms of the various regions, classified as "folk". This paper attempts to read the construction of modernity in Muthusami's plays and performances as well as analyse his responses to caste, gender and the traditional form of Koothu. These three aspects are read as discursive spaces. In discussing these aspects I will also take a look at his writings on theatre and drama. They become the positions from which to examine his practice of theatre.

Caste has been the focus of public discourse in Tamil Nadu from very early times. In fact, it is the only state where caste surnames have almost completely gone out of usage. Periyar, and before him Iyotheethass, had attacked Brahminism and its hegemony[7]. The eighties saw the growth and consolidation of dalit movements. In such a context, it is surprising that Muthusami did not directly address the issue of caste in his plays. In *Engilandhu*, the temple chariot is pushed by the members of the paraiar community of that village. They beat the tappu and Mallari raga is played by the musicians accompanying the procession. Tappu and Thudumpu are the major percussion instruments used in Koothu-p-Pattarai's productions. Very early in his career, Muthusami wrote about why he grew a moustache (Yatra). It is significant that he used it to be a marker of his anti- brahminic beliefs.

In his introduction to *Oodadi*, a play written by Elangovan, a Singapore based playwright who writes in Tamil and English, Muthusami speaks overtly about his experience of growing up in a village which practiced untouchability.[8] He refers to how Elangovan's play documents the history of dalits in Singapore. Writing his preface in Mumbai, he weaves the memory of his childhood friend Vaidhyanathan alias Kuppu. Kuppu had just passed away and that triggers off his memory. Muthusami and Kuppu had entered the *cheri* (Dalit quarters) for the first time during the first general elections in Independent India. He records how they had often passed that way but never entered the *cheri*. Later, when he went in, he found the cross worn by some of the children in the *cheri.* He refers to it in one of his poems that is included in his play *Engilandhu.* He says, "It seems impossible to write the history of dalits without writing the history of conversion."[9] He talks about the two tea-shops in the village, one belonging to a Congress supporter and another to a DMK supporter. As they congregated there to listen to musical records, the youth of the village would stand in the separate space assigned to them while having tea.

"I have no memory of moving away from them due to issues of untouchability....In school, there was a bench allotted for Scheduled Caste students. There was no rule against the students of other castes sitting on that bench. It still revealed the separation that robbed them of the liberty of being seated wherever they pleased, unlike the other students. Girls too had a separate bench. All these strike my consciousness now; but then, they were accepted as given."[10] He adds, "While saying all this, I cannot escape the sense of shame in having behaved with an upper caste pride. I feel it even while reading Bharathi, who has transcended caste."[11] He also records how the shepherd boys sang, "Will not the Agraharam Brahmins die;/ will not their bodies be burnt on the riverbed", especially within the earshot of his *Periappa* (father's elder brother).

His views on Parai and Paraiars of Punjai village are documented in his article on his play *Engilandhu.* It is important to quote him at length in order to understand his logic in elevating the music of the Paraiars to the realm of art. One must bear in mind that in Tamil Nadu, like in many other parts of India, the traditional forms were revived, nurtured and studied by various theatre groups.

> The Paraiars of Punjai have torn the parai hung on the walls of the Mariamman temple. They refused to carry dead carcasses and refused to beat the parai in funeral houses. Instead of tearing the parai, they should have made more of them. Men and women should have played the beats, even the forgotten ones. They should have played the parais in the festival of Mariamman and while lifting the carcasses. They should have played with clarity, every rhythm with a sure beat. The carcass should have been taken for burial with more respect than the dead man. A new ritual should have been invented. They should have played in front of a Perumal temple and a Pillaiyar temple. They should have played on days not marked for their playing. They must have played from a distance especially, when the Brahmins of Punjai were leaving the village. Then parai would have lost its caste dimension. It would be just a musical instrument. It would become a weapon.[12]

A heated debate over whether the parai could be treated as a part of the identity of the dalits if it signified their lowly status has raged in Tamil Nadu among dalit organizations. Even if it could represent dalit identity, the traditional contexts of playing tappu/ parai were never considered liberative by the dalits. Muthusami's sensitivity to the art form is beyond doubt. But he does not seem to have considered the attitude of the community towards it. Emphasis on the artistic status itself then becomes a modern version of feudal hierarchy. One cannot deny that caste is a relatively silenced discourse in Muthusami's plays. In the performances of Koothu-p-Pattarai, however, parai is a significant presence. In his admission of a critical attitude towards Brahminism, Muthusami is far ahead of his contemporaries.

Gender was another major variable that was redefined drastically with the advent of colonial modernity. Tamil Nadu had the added influence of the Self- Respect Movement that drew many women into the public sphere. These women did not merely add to the quantitative strength of the movement. Periyar did not indulge in mass mobilization of that nature. These women were co-opted on the premise of their intellectual ability articulated in all spheres of life. Their arguments, like those of all Self- Respectors, were premised on knowledge, analysis and logic.[13]

The earliest "modern" plays in India, like *Andha Yug*, *Adhe Adhure*, *Hayavadana* and *Silence! The Court is in Session* had female protagonists. A changing perspective on gender was obvious in these plays. In Tamil Nadu, S. Ramanujam adapted the Greek play *Trojan Women* as *Veriattam* (1990). In its powerful use of keening as the major form holding the play together, it remains till date a strong statement of women as victims and survivors of war. Most of Ramanujam's major plays have women as protagonists. His critical writings, however, are silent on his views on gender. But by far he has been the most sensitive, in Tamil theatre, to the discourse of gender in his performances. Mu. Ramasami's adaptation of Sophocles *Antigone* was set against the background of police violence on Naxalites and was called *Durkira Avalam* (Creon's Tragedy). The play was also adapted by Shenbagam Ramasami and Ramasami (1986). Indira Parthasarathi, another major contemporary playwright in Tamil, focuses on female characters in plays like *Mazhai, Porvai Pothiya Udalgal* and *Kongai Thee.* I have written elsewhere about how his women are psychological victims and have no say in their own lives, leave alone the world they occupy.[14]

Muthusami has not made clear his views on gender. His plays do not operate on the plane of male or female characters. They work at the level of abstractions. His *Narkkalikkarar*, (The Person in the Chair) directed by Ramanujam, has the powerful presence of female actors as the narrators of the play. It adds an interesting dimension to the play which is a commentary on the middle class, non-committal attitude to life. In a recent production of the same play, Ramanujam made *Narkkalikkarar* take on the gestures of a transgendered person which I felt was a cliched way of looking at the play. Anyone unable to take a firm decision is compared to a *nabumsak*, neither male nor female. Ramanujam seemed to have extended that metaphor onto the character of *Narkkalikkar*, which is ultimately attacked by both parties.

The two plays written by Muthusami that deal directly with gender as an articulate category are *Undhi Chuzhi*(Navel) (1981) and *Kattiankaran* (Narrator) (1981). *Undhi Chuzhi* imagines a new method of reproduction. A woman can lay an egg each month and a child would be born from it. The *Muttaikkaran* (Eggman) explains the reason for this shift thus: "Our male pride will not be hurt any longer. Aren't you treating women as the lesser species because they have to carry the child in the womb for ten months? You keep yapping about chastity and faithfulness! Scientists have changed the story now. It shall be thus from now on. Human beings will be born from eggs. You should also take part in the incubation of the egg. Or else, both should have a common incubator. Now, sexual pleasure has increased among human beings. There need be no fear any longer. Things have become common for both." Once the child is born, however, the men fight over whose child it is. The play moves into the complications caused by lack of kinship markers. A young girl comes in. Men are torn between desire and their relationship with her. The man who has sexual union with her dies and the ensuing discussion proves it to be a suicide for the man realized that she was actually his daughter, whom he had abandoned since he was not sure if she was born of his egg. When she invites another young man for sexual intercourse, the other men dissuade her, saying that he is actually a brother to her. A frightening moment follows when she threatens to undress in front of them. The play is a terrible indictment of male authority that is taken for granted in pregnancy and child-bearing. The insecurity of human existence seems to be tied to the umbilical cord. The title signifies so.

Muthusami's *Kattiakaran* deals with the utter commercialism that has crept into our lives. Muthusami dedicates this play to the protagonist of Sundara Ramasami's novel *J.J. Sila Kurippugal*. Situated within an existential framework, the motif of the play is the commercialization of sexuality which is seen as the springboard of creativity. It is the libidinal economy that motivates the *Makkal Vangi* (People's Bank) to market the masks of the titillating heroines of the Tamil film world. The logic is to help men derive greater pleasure by imagining their partners as one of these heroines on screen and also to help them have variety. When the women wear the masks in order to be more attractive, the male imagines the number of women who might be in the mask. When average faces are also produced as masks in order to win them the status of heroes, the question of identity begins to loom large. It is the woman who voices an alternate view. She refuses to accept her husband fearing that someone else has come wearing his mask. He tries to prove to her that he is "real". The play employs two narrators. The hilariously comic situation places the human predicament in its most complex form. Fear of unsettling the hetero-normative monogamy prevalent in our system actually becomes a warning signal against mindless commercialism. The woman's voice becomes a strong advocate of retaining some sanity in this confusion. The structure of the play complicates the issue of sexuality and the prevalent homophobia is exposed to the maximum. The play makes a powerful plea for anti-establishment value systems. The performative aspects inherent in the text and executed in the production assimilated the koothu tradition with a contemporary consciousness and both are made self-conscious in the process. I consider this play to be a major modern Indian play, dealing with the nexus of sexuality, creativity and commercialism.

A more recent play, *Padukalam* (2002), (Battle Field), dealing with the performance and ritual of Duryodhana's death woven into the everyday lives of the performers, has a scene where the artists are getting made up. On stage we find a temporary greenroom erected with dried coconut leaves. Through the gaps, the villagers watch the performers getting ready. That scene transgresses the mythological framework and questions how the actor playing Bhishma is present in the same room used by Draupadi and Gandhari. The commentary informs us that Bhishma was the mute, voyeuristic witness of Draupadi's disrobing in the court. The female actors go about their business completely indifferent to these comments. When a few villagers enter the room and try to approach the female actors with sexual overtones, the women actually handle them with ease and wield their power, however temporary it is.

Draupadi- Actor: Shall I place my leg comfortably on your head? (To the man kissing her feet.)

Person 1: Of course, of course, by all means. Please do. (She places her feet on his head and he pines over them.)

Person 3: (To the Bhanumathi-Actor)Let me hold your hips. Exactly as Karnan did…just a little…Oh! Heavenly.

Person 5: (To her) Shall I collect or string the beads? (Mimes collecting the beads dropping from her necklace). Stop dropping them…stop…look they keep rolling down.

Draupadi: (To the man holding her feet) Don't stare like that, as Duryodhana did.

Bhanumathi: As they did while disrobing. (Looks at the villagers) Shoo…go away. Is anyone dancing in the nude here? Go, go. (They give a giggle). Do not tear the coconut leaves, making large holes. Your looks have already made holes in the old sarees. Get lost.

Draupadi: Those were the days when there were no latrines. Women used to wake up at dawn…or wait for dusk…till it was dark everywhere. So what? The treetops of the grove that women used for shitting would be crowded. That is how it is in the imagination of women…dark. They cover their faces with the pleats of the saree hanging down. Still in the Narrunaiyappan grove, when she squats, she hears…what those five saw, let me also see…a voice she knows not if true, false, imagined or real. It feels like being watched from the treetops in the grove…It feels the same, the way these people ogle.[15]

This scene operates as a terrible indictment of the male gaze. The way puranic references are woven into the everyday act of shitting at once becomes an ironic double and traces the long tradition of the patriarchal mode of constructing the female body as an object. The voices of women re-present not their own victimization but the stale, unimaginative and crass interference of the male gaze. This section becomes a major exposure of masculinity as it projects itself and the violent intrusion it makes into female space and existence.

The major aspect of modernity in Indian theatre was articulated by fusing the pre- colonial traditional forms of each region with contemporary sensibilities. However, most of the directors who have worked with the various indigenous forms (with the exception of Habib Tanvir), hardly mention the traditional artists who have provided them the impetus. Habib Tanvir is the only director who has incorporated the Chhattisgarh artists into his repertoire. His Naya Theatre remains the meeting ground of traditional and modern actors. There may be criticism about how successful the interaction has been, but at least the traditional artists have a name, face and space. Most directors however refer to the forms as an abstraction without reference to the actual performing artists. This mode of interaction seems to be the method followed by international directors like Schechner and Peter Brook, who conduct their field studies in which information becomes crucial, while the informant is almost an anonymous being.[16]

The interaction of Muthusami and Koothu cannot be studied without referring to the Purisai Koothu Company. This group was initially led by Veerasami Thambiran. After his demise the group was led by Ragava Thambiran. E. Krishna Iyer refers to how Ragava Thambiran concentrated on acting and perfection of the form.[17] Muthusami makes his intentions of interacting with Koothu quite clear: "I have no scholarship to identify the classical rhythms found in Koothu. Nor is it my job to seek prestige, quoting Koothu's classical traits. We are proud enough to claim the due respect to a form based on its own inherent characteristics."[18] He refers to an incident where he was mocked at for raising a question on the similarities and differences between Kathakali and Koothu.[19] It is important to bear in mind that Koothu did not have any reformer to sanitise it and give it a classical garb. In Karnataka, Shivram Karanth helped Yakshagana attain a classical status; Vallathol and Kerala State made efforts to project Kathakali as a classical form; in Tamil Nadu all effort was concentrated on upgrading Sadhir into Bharatanatyam. Krishna Iyer, a pioneer who helped establish Bharatanatyam as a respectable form, was aware of Koothu. He, however, did not focus on it. Except for Padma Subramanyam and Shyamala Balakrishnan, the other Bharatanatyam dancers did not find any inspiration in Koothu. When Muthusami made it a source of inspiration, he was not in any way considering reforming the form. In this sense, his interaction with Koothu cannot be read as part of the "Back to the Roots" mission or the nation-forming agenda mentioned earlier. Perhaps that is why his contribution and life-time interaction with Koothu have not been considered important by the State cultural offices or academia. He was interacting with Koothu as a form and with Koothu artists as theatre performers. He had no archival intentions or desire for documentation.

As an aside, it is worth noting that Richard Frasca's study of Koothu for his doctoral dissertation, was begun with the Purisai group but because of ego clashes among the Koothu artists he completed his study based on Perungattur Rajagopalan's group.[20] Hanne de Bruin continued her work on Koothu with the same group and eventually found her home and family with Perungattur Rajagopal.[21]

An interesting parallel to Muthusami's dramatic career is that of Purisai Kannappa Sambhandam. Sambhandam, son of Kannappa Thambiran, had almost given up the idea of pursuing Koothu and worked in the then Madras as an autorikshaw driver when he had the opportunity to attend an NSD workshop in Gandhigram in 1978. He had the lead role in Bansi Kaul's *Pinam Thinnum Sathirangal,* one of the earliest modern plays performed in Tamil. Later, Sambhandam went back to his family Koothu company and did not look back. Today, he leads the group. He is a regular resource person for many theatre groups. His father, Kannappa Tahmbiran, and Muthusami shared an amazing friendship. Sambhandan's play *Indrajit* was written as koothu and performed by the Purisai group and closely followed Muthusami's *Talai,* based on the same myth. Muthusami fondly recalls how they read the Kamba Ramayanam during a journey to Delhi. *Kandava Vana Thaganam (Burning of the Kandava Forest)*, a play dealing with deforestation was staged by Koothu-p-Pattarai with much assistance from the Purisai artists. Muthusami's *Dootha Gadothgajam* was performed with Karthik, a nephew of Sambhandam, in the lead role. More recently, in 2005, Palani, another nephew of Sambhandam, who has been trained in Koothu-p-Pattarai, debuted in a Koothu performance as Ravana.

Koothu pervades Muthusami's writing and direction in more ways than one. For him, Koothu is just not the external parameters of dance, music and drama rolled into one. In fact, Koothu appears in an abstract philosophic form in his works. Koothu-p-pattarai, with all its emphasis on rhythm, traditional forms and working with myths is never at home with a performance of dance, music and drama fused together. This has come under heated debate in Tamil Nadu, especially with Pathmanaathan, a theatre person from Sri Lanka, raising the issue of Koothu as representing Tamil identity. He has critiqued Muthusami's abstraction of Koothu, devoid of its physical language, as a middleclass attitude.

The Purisai group has also experimented with various texts due to the interaction with Muthusami and Koothu-p-Pattarai. The group performed Marquez's *An Old Man with Huge Wings* in Koothu form at the Bagota Theatre Festival in 1996. A post-modern moment struck the audience when, at the end of the play, a dead body is washed ashore and the Koothu group goes on to offer its regular *mangalam*, praying to Goddess Mariamma to grant enough rains that year. As part of the Brecht Birth Centenary, they performed the *Caucasian Chalk Circle* as *Vellai Vattam* in 1998. Sambhandam had already played the role of Azdec in K.S. Rajendran's production of the *Chalk Circle* for Koothu-p- Pattarai in 1987.[22] The Purisai group's *Vellai Vattam* is one of its kind in the whole country. There have been many plays from various countries adapted by urban playwrights or directors into a traditional form. Shakespeare in Kathakali or Gorky in Jatra are examples of such efforts. But for the first time a Koothu group, with exposure to contemporary theatre, wrote its own adaptation of *Chalk Circle* and performed it as an overnight Koothu performance. What could be a more befitting honour to Brecht and Koothu![23]

Muthusami's contribution to Tamil theatre has not been studied in depth as yet. His views and productions have been the cause of much heated debate. Chief among them are the comments of Venkat Swaminathan, the sole critic writing in English, till about five years ago, on Tamil Nadu politics, literature and drama. He was the first to recognise the importance of Muthusami's writings for and in Tamil theatre. He clubs him with Indira Parthasarathi, whose plays are in the style of western realism with some psychological undertones.[24] Swaminathan mounts a scathing attack on Muthusami in his summary article on Tamil theatre in the first issue of *Theatre India*.[25] Both his praise and critique are excessive.

The pan-Indian nationhood that was sought to be built, based on the various indigenous traditions of the different regions did not work smoothly in Tamil Nadu, owing to its troubled relationship with Indian nationalism. At the same time, the colonial legacy of constructing a selfhood that is universal in nature was distilled through the rationalist movements spearheaded by the Dravidians. Muthusami stands at the crossroads of culture, connecting himself to Koothu while at the same time articulating a kind of internationalism, if not universalism. The latter was a continuation of the modernist efforts in Tamil poetry and fiction. One cannot confidently say that the polarities of classical and folk did not exist in Muthusami. He was interested in the "classicalisation" of art and literature. He believed in aesthetics as a transcending power. The same dilemma prevailed in his conceptualization of caste and gender as well. He addresses these issues from his subjectivity. Therefore, there is much critique from an upper-caste, male perspective. A corresponding concern for the struggle of individuals and groups to undo the prevailing inequities does not seem to touch him.

His plays, performances, writings and theatrical activities cannot be ignored in studying the various modes by which modernity was constructed in India. By not giving a single, linear answer, he complicates our views. He is certainly a presence to be reckoned with. It is unfortunate that our cult/ canon-making mechanisms have not been able to allot him a space and therefore he is ignored in most discussions of contemporary Indian theatre.[26]

Notes

1 Sudhi Pradhan, *Marxist Cultural Movement in India: Chronicles and Documents (1936-1947)*, Calcutta: National Book Agency, 1979, Vasudha Dalmia, *Poetics, Plays, and Performance: The Politics of Modern Indian Theatre*, Delhi: Oxford University Press, 2006, Aparna Dharwadker, *Theatres of Independence: Drama, Theory, and Urban Performance in India Since 1947*, Delhi: Oxford University Press, 2005.

2 A. Mangai, and V. Arasu, *Ushering Changes: Constructing the History of Tamil Theatre During Colonial times through Drama Notices.* (Forthcoming Article).

3 Ananda Lal, ed., *The Oxford Companion to Indian Theatre,* Delhi: Oxford University Press, 2004, pp. 468-471.

4 K. Nambi Arooran, *Tamil Renaissance and Dravidian Nationalism (1905-1944)*, Madurai: Koodal Publishers, 1980.

5 Su Arangarasu, *Tamizh Pudukkavidhai: Oru Thiraangivu* (New Poetry in Tamil – A Study), Kovai : Moonram Ulaga Pathippagam, 1991. Many other scholars in Tamil have written insightfully on Tamil New Poetry, chief among them being Bala and Thamizhavan.

6 *Ezhuthu*, November 1967 and Jan-Feb 1968.

7 V. Geetha and S.V. Rajadurai., *Towards a Non-Brahmin Millenium: From Iyotheethass to Periyar,* Calcutta: Samya 1998.

8 C. Annamalai, ed., *Na. Muthusami Katturaigal*, Chennai: Kaavya, 2005, pp. 399-414.

9 Ibid., p. 402. All translations from Tamil texts are mine.

10 Ibid., p. 404.

11 Ibid., p. 406.

12 Ibid., p. 327-328.

13 Valarmathi, *Suya Mariyadhai Iyakka Veeranganaigal,* Chennai: International Institute of Tamil Studies, 2000.

14 A. Mangai, "'What Does She Want?': Female Identity in Indian Drama" *Theatre India*, No 2, November 2000, pp. 20-28.

15 Muthusami, *Padukalam*, Thanjavur: Annam, 2003, pp. 70-71.

16 For more on this see Rustom Bharucha, *The Politics of Cultural Practice*, Delhi: OUP, 2001.

17 Muthusami, *Andru Pootiya Vandi:* Ther-k-Koothu Patria Katturaigal, Sivagangai: Annam, 1982, p. 16.

18 Ibid., p. 17.

19 Ibid., p. 26.

20 See Richard A. Frasca, *The Theatre of the Mahabharata*: *Terukuttu* Performances *in South India,* Honolulu:University of Hawaii Press, 1990.

21 For details see Hanne de Bruin, *Kattaikuttu: The Flexibility of a South Indian Theatre Tradition*, Groningen:Egbert Forster,1999.

22 Pravin has confused the *Chalk Circle* production of Koothu-p-Pattarai, directed by K.S. Rajendran in 1987 and the Purisai group's Koothu production of *Chalk Circle* in 1998 as part of the Brecht Centenary in his recent article "Influences in Contemporary Tamil Theatre" in *Bring Down the Lights: 50 Years of the Madras Players,* ed. P.C. Ramakrishna, Chennai: the Madras Players, 2006, pp. 132-143.

23 A. Mangai, "Brecht in Tamil Nadu" in *Cultural Encounters in South India,* ed., Landwlier, M.Gabriele, Goethe Institute and Max Mueller Bhavan, Chennai,2007, pp. 86-96.

24 A. Mangai, 'What does she want?' pp. 20-28.

25 V. Swaminathan, "Post 1980 Plays: Tamil" in *Theatre India*, No 1, May 1999, pp 15-21.

26 Aparna Dharwadker's recent book on post-independent drama in India has Subbanna, Karanth and K.N. Panikker representing South India. There is hardly any discussion of Tamil Nadu, a state which has raised disturbing issues with the Centre about identity, language and the arts thereby complicating post-independent India's notions of nationalism.

5
Tamasha Theatre and Sushma Deshpande's *Teechya Aeechi Goshta*

Lata Singh

Middle class formation during the colonial period in India has been linked with the notion of "female". In fact, re-definition of the notion of "female" was a crucial feature of the hegemony that brought the middle class into power and ascendancy. In middle class discourse a "new" and "ideal" woman was constructed, subject to a new patriarchy and in opposition to the notion of the "other" woman. The "other" woman represented common women, considered to be coarse, vulgar, loud, morally degraded and sexually promiscuous. Having greater access to the public sphere, these women were relatively independent, outside rigid formations and not clearly contained by caste, class, gender or a demarcated space and were hence considered to be threatening. These "other" women have remained excluded from and marginalized in mainstream discourse. Most studies, too, have focused on middle class women for bringing marginalized women to the forefront as a subject would unsettle the middle class hegemonic discourse. Representation of women was an important site for the emergent middle class discourse on ideal female behaviour. The representation of women as public entertainers and the locus of male desire no longer served the interests of the English educated elite, which put in her place the *sugrihini* or the good housewife. Performers were part of popular culture which had a wide female audience. Having a rich repertoire of women's popular songs with a robust sense of humour and frank sensuality, popular culture was considered threatening to the new ideal of domestic order. The association of elite women with female performers was restricted as female performers were stigmatized as "prostitutes" and came under attack. The middle class erased and negated the creative aspect of performing women in its quest for a respectable nation. They were to be kept out of the frame of the nation-in-the-making.

A female performer is perhaps the most unsettling of figures, precisely because of her unsettledness – her seemingly excessive mobility in the public sphere which disrupts the foundational moral distinction between the home and the world. One of the dimensions of the stigma that accrues to actresses is their publicity as well as their mobility as they move about conducting their business. The form of this mobility – the very public nature of the actress's line of work – threatens to expose the fragility of the culturally naturalized division of the gendered sphere into the home and the world, as actresses move onto the public stage to enact what is meant to be the most private of relations. Middle class reforms undertaken on behalf of women were tied up with the self-definition of the class embedded in the new division of the private from the public sphere, that is, the home/world dichotomy, home being a sacred site for women. Enclosure is conceived as necessary to preserve a woman's chastity and, by extension, her men folk's honour. Since the social construction of gender places "good women" in seclusion, women who appear in public spaces (such as on stage) are defined as "bad", that is, as prostitutes. Unlike the chaste loyalty of the good wife who reveals herself to only one man, the actress's profession requires that she willingly expose herself to the gaze of many unfamiliar men.[1]

This paper is based on the play, *Teechya Aeechi Goshta* (Her Mother's Story), which highlights one such section of women performers, the tamasha women. The play, written and directed by Sushma Deshpande was first performed on 12 September 1995. By bringing to the forefront tamasha women's voices, which have been marginalized in mainstream discourse, Deshpande unsettles the mainstream hegemonic claim. While there have been occasional feminist explorations of Marathi theatre the life histories of tamasha performers, considered to be "loose" women, have remained largely invisible.[2] The play celebrates the spirit of the tamasha woman, who speaks confidently of her identity and what it means to her. In fact, by foregrounding the tamasha women performer, who is neither the "respectable" wife nor mother, the quintessential inspirational figures in mainstream discourse, Deshpande disrupts and ruptures the dominant bourgeois nationalist discourse, the trope of "Mother India" that has dominated middle class discourse.

Women performers come to the forefront only when they bag an award. The irony is that nobody sees their struggle before they get the award. Deshpande's play highlights how tamasha artist Hirabai's daughter, who had distanced herself from her mother because of her profession, wants to interview her when Hirabai gets a national award. But Hirabai does not want her daughter to tell her story. She wants to tell her own story in her own voice, not give the credit to others: "my memories are my own; they are very precious to me. Why should I tell them to Ratna? Why should I give my life in her hand? ... If Ratna narrates my story she will become well known at my cost. She will put her flag up. But I am holding my own flag. I know the colours and shades of my flag because I have coloured it on my own."[3]

2

Sushma Deshpande's work, which is an attempt to give agency and subjectivity to women performers, can be seen in the context of the development of the broader tradition where some women dramatists have gradually and quietly started asserting their individual identity by taking up themes and issues that centre on women's lives.[4]

In the play *Teechya Aeechi Goshta* too the strength of Hirabai, a Tamasha artist, in dealing with social humiliation and breakdowns in personal relationships is sensitively brought out by Deshpande. A survivor, Hirabai refuses sympathy and proudly makes her independence clear. In fact for a long time even before she staged *Whay Mee Savitribai,* (Here I am, Savitribai), written, directed and enacted solo by Deshpande, she had been thinking of doing a play on tamasha women's lives. Initially, when she started writing the script of tamasha women, she felt it came out sounding sad in a middle class kind of way. Deshpande felt that tamasha women and sentiment did not go together and that however terrible their lives were, they did not ask for anybody's sympathy. Unable to catch the right tone Deshpande put aside the idea and started working on *Savitri*. After *Savitri's* production she again went back to writing the script on the life of tamasha women. She wanted to be true to the women and their lives as she saw them. She interviewed these women, stayed with them, started attending their functions and became one of them. She says that her struggle was to try and include as much as she could from the huge amounts of materials that she had gathered.

The play *Teechya Aeechi Goshta* (Her Mother's Story) is based on the lives of the artists of the sangeetbari form of tamasha art, specializing in song and dance entertainment. Sangeetbari basically consists of a number of "lavanis". A lavani is a musical performance which unravels various shades inherent in a man-woman relationship. It is a one actor play in which the life and times of the Tamasha women are depicted. They play centres around Hira, a Tamasha performer and her daughter Ratna. Hira, going against society had provided Ratna with a good education and, as a result, Ratna is a journalist today. Ratna, who has despised the very idea of Tamasha since her childhood, comes to interview her mother regarding her life and art. Hira asks Ratna the reason for her sudden curiosity in the life of a Tamasha performer. Ratna explains that after seeing the world she has understood the value of Tamasha as an art and now admires the immense courage and determination of a Tamasha performer. Hira refuses to give the interview. She says, "I am a woman….that too unmarried, but one whose business is related solely to men. Such a story will indeed appeal to the people… and if you write on my life…you will achieve fame overnight. Why should you receive such fame because of the hardships that I bore through my life? So you work hard to achieve success…I won't give it to you." Ratna becomes furious and accuses Hira of being cowardly by refusing to bring before the people the complete story of her life – especially now that she has been honoured with an award by the government. Hira laughs and says that she has never feared anyone in her life for she has lived her life on her own terms. So, rather than talking to her daughter, Hira starts talking to the audience, saying that she has come to tell the people directly the story of her life. She starts, "So people…listen…her mother's story that is, my memories". Hira first talks about her relationship with her mother who was also a Tamasha dancer. Then she reflects on her father, some of her mother's clients, her childhood, and how she became a Tamasha dancer. Then she turns to talk about her clients, her colleagues, then a man in her life and the way the relationship developed. While describing her numerous relationship, she also interjects a few lavani performances in between.

Hira addresses Ratna as if Ratna were part of the audience. The development of the play is based on her relationship and the ongoing conflict with Ratna and her son, Gaja. Ratna is smart, determined and dashing, whereas Gaja is a product of the male dominated society with a strong chauvinist ego which leads to a cowardliness in his mannerisms. Hira admires the father of her children, who respects her art. While talking about his death she remembers that she was denied the right to attend his funeral and even her children could not understand her agony. After his death, eventually, another man enters her life. She explains that to survive the kind of life she leads such relationships are necessary. As the play develops, she comments on society and her way of life. She ends, by recalling the death of her mother. A fine was demanded to allow the funeral rituals to proceed, as her mother and her profession was held in contempt by society. She ends with an appeal to the people – "After my death…do not leave my body to these so-called leaders of society. Please…please perform the rituals yourself and do not let them lay a hand on me".

The play forms a base for a critical inquiry into the caste and gender complexities underlying the erotic lavani genre in Maharashtra. The lavani is a kind of erotic song in the folk genre of Maharashtra. The public performance of the lavani was a part of the tamasha or folk theatre. A typical tamasha performance begins with "gan" (devotional offerings to Ganesha) and a gavlan (a comical act performed by male artistes through exaggerated feminine gestures). This is followed by the female performance of the shringarik lavani and mujra or collection of rewards. The satirical vag (or spontaneous theatre) – is a later addition. There are now at least two kinds of tamashas: the "dholki-phad" tamasha in which the vag or the spontaneous theatre is central and the "sangeet barees" which centre on the performance of the erotic lavani. Men manage the dholki-phad tamasha while the sangeet barees are planned, financed and organized mainly by the women of the Kolhati caste.

The majority of the tamasha artistes come from the untouchable castes, mainly the Mang and Mahar castes, while the female dancers of the sangeet barees are from the Kolhati caste. The Mangs were known to be village musicians and songsters, while the Mahars were village watchmen and carriers of dead cattle. They had little land of their own and were the first among the untouchable castes to seek employment in urban centres. The Kolhati have two main divisions, the Dulkar Kolhati and the Kham or Bhatu Kolhati. The Kham Kolhati men do not work and are listed as subsisting on the "immoral" pursuits of their women. Their caste-based profession was entertainment and they constituted a travelling or nomadic group. Dancing has been recorded as their caste-based profession. The women were known to be the breadwinners of the family. The Kham Kolhati women are not permitted to marry by the caste panchayat while the women of the dholki-phad tamasha are most often married to troupe members and are relatively more subject to familial patriarchal regulatory controls. They look down upon the sangeet barees as "immoral" and as not being representative of the "true tamasha tradition".

The sangeet baree form articulates female desire in explicit sexual terms and is composed almost entirely by males and is performed by women before an almost entirely male audience. It marks the articulation of female desire as constructed through the male gaze. It is difficult to arrive at any conclusion regarding the origins of the erotic or shringarik lavani. It is only in the later Peshwa period (1796-1818) that clear references are found to the female performers of shringarik lavani.

Shringarik lavani can be viewed in the overall perspective of the intersection of caste and gender. It became one of the modes of constructing the sexuality of the women of the lower castes. The bodies of lower caste women were constructed in the lavani as either arousing or satiating male desire. Sharmila Rege's work has highlighted how such construction was crucial to the pre-colonial Peshwa state in the appropriation of the labour of lower caste women through the institution of slavery. The Peshwa state's involvement in the trade of female slaves was an important source of revenue. The prominent feature of the slavery of the period was the predominance of female slaves. Conventionally, there were two major means of procuring slaves; one by abducting women in wars and the other by enslaving lower caste women charged with adultery. A majority of the female slaves were lower caste women charged with adultery which was the major ground on which their sexual and productive labour was appropriated and the lavani of the period was one important mode of constructing them as adulterous. It also became the ideological justification of the enslavement of the women of the lower castes.[5]

Thus, within the context of the interrelationship of caste and gender, some loosely connecting ideas regarding the *kasbi* or entertainer castes like the Kolhatis, the sexual and caste-based division of labour may be put forward. Women's sexual insatiability was seen as the root of all problems and the lower castes' failure to control their women's sexuality was deemed to be partly the cause of their impurity. In such a context, gender divisions reinforced caste divisions and gender ideology legitimated both the structures of patriarchy and the organization of caste. Caste ideology, which ordered the division of labour, also ordered the division of sexual labour. By appropriating the sexual and erotic labour of the *kasbi* castes and constructing their women as *kabnurkarin* or pigeons, the Kolhati women are located in the space of the erotic (albeit as in the male gaze) and are denied material and familial spaces.[6]

The main patrons of shringarik lavani were the Peshwa rulers. But as the Peshwa rule came to an end, tamasha was forced to seek new sources of patronage. By the 1840s the lavani tamasha had shifted to the rural areas. Many of the lavani composers and their troupes moved to the princely state of Baroda in search of patronage. The troupes that stayed back in Maharashtra were at the mercy of the zamindars, inamdars and jagirdars. Colonial power and the emergence of bourgeois theatre, with the rise of the middle class, affected the fate of the lavani tamasha and its construction of female sexuality. The history of Marathi theatre during this period records attempts by women of the lower castes (probably displaced tamasha performers) to start theatre companies in which women enacted both male and female roles.[7] Such attempts, by popular artistes, to stake their claim to the newly emergent Marathi theatre, were severely criticized and ridiculed. It is possible, therefore, that the sangeet barees, a reformulated version of the tamasha, emerged as an offshoot of these companies.[8] By the early 1890s, tamasha theatres had been established in Mumbai and Pune and a contract system had emerged, as theatre owners became middlemen employing the troupe members on salaries or against an advance payment.

Sangeet baree troupes, owned by Kolhati women, include at least three or four male members as musicians, a *songadya* or male comedian and the main *nachee* with five to seven chorus girls and dancers. The main *nachee* (sometimes the mother or aunt) is the owner of the troupe and is known as *bai*. Every Diwali, the *bai* signs a contract with the theatre owner for an amount which varies with the popularity of the troupe. She then pays to the other artistes per programme in the troupe. A troupe generally plays at a theatre for two years before it moves to other cities and towns. Sangeet baree artistes perform every evening between 8.00 and 11.30 p.m. All the troupes perform every evening and are allotted 20 to 25 minutes each. The audience at these public performances comes from varied economic backgrounds. As each troupe begins to perform, the *daulat jadda* (the practice of bidding by the audience to have a lavani of their choice performed) assumes prime importance. *Daulat jadda* also includes *baksheesh* given by the audience to the *nachees*. The highest bidder (often the one who pays in hundred-rupee notes) places the money between his lips, from where the *nachee* takes it with her lips. The money earned from this *daulat jadda* is placed on the harmonium and then divided between all the artists in the troupe. The earnings from the *nachees* sexual labour are not entirely hers since the unstated understanding is that her body and art belong to the troupe. The theatres also organize *baithaks*, or private sittings, audiences for which are regulated by the contractors. These *baithaks*, each lasting for an hour, go on to the early hours of the morning, with charges ranging from Rs.500 to Rs.1,000 per *baithak*.[9]

3

The appropriation of "high" culture by the middle class was reinforced by indigenous social reform organizations which pushed the indigenous and folk theatre to the margins of respectability. In Bengal, the Brahmo Samaj epitomized the trend toward Puritanism. According to Meredith Borthwick, "It uncompromisingly condemned gambling, going to prostitutes, smoking, drinking, and the theatre".[10] In North India, the Arya Samaj, similarly, abolished performances by dancing girls, introduced a purified form of the Holi festival and condemned local theatrical forms.[11] Literary figures like Bharatendu Harishchandra of Banaras declared most kinds of popular theatre "depraved" and lacking in theatricality. Like other figures of the Indian renaissance, he championed a refined form of drama limited largely to drawing rooms and school auditoriums, whose purpose would be to assist in the moral regeneration of the nation.[12] Sumanta Banerjee's research on the popular culture of nineteenth-century Calcutta indicates that the *bhadralok* (English-educated professional elite) increasingly associated popular forms with the "licentious and voluptuous tastes" of the "vulgar" populace, from whom they were at pains to differentiate themselves.[13]

However, the middle class co-opted many folk forms while condemning popular forms. Appropriation and othering happened simultaneously. Popular cultural forms were also marginalised precisely because of the participation of women in them. The subordinate social status of women and their associations with the body and with sexuality were used to define these forms as "other" and establish the dominant group's superiority in relation to them. The emergent elite theatre marked its distinction from the folk via a process of desexualisation so that male performers, who were considered to be more cerebral, dominated the stage.

All this led to considerable reformulation in the content and form of tamasha. The dichotomy between *nachee/nartaki* (dancing girls/dancer), *tamasgir/kalkaar* (folk-performer/artist) intensified as the lower castes began to be displaced from their hereditary sphere of the performing arts by the emergence of bourgeois theatre. The growing popularity of this theatre with its mark of morality lead to a series of changes in the structure of tamasha. The performance of "vag" which had been second only to the performance of lavani, now emerged as central to tamasha. The theatre of the male performers superseded the sensuous lavani.[14] Though the tamasha form has contributed a great deal to the birth and evolution of the professional urban (Marathi) theatre, today none of the earlier vivacity and charm of this art form remains.

Today most existing Tamasha centers in small cities like Pune and Nagpur have fallen into disrepute and even the art form has been vulgarized to the popular idiom of Hindi film songs. Old lavanis are sacrificed at the altar of raunchy Hindi film songs. In fact, cinema had been one of the mediums where the appropriation and othering of lavani performance happened simultaneously. In Maharashtra, in the post Second World War period, regional cinema sought to appropriate lavani and tamasha. However, the adaptation of the tamasha genre by Marathi cinema clearly marked the drain of sexuality of the female lavani dancers of the kolhati and other lower castes. Marathi cinema, dominated by Brahmins and Marathas, drew its raw material from the lavani tamasha of the Kolhatis, Mahars and Mangs, converted it into saleable goods and took it back to the audiences in the small towns at double the price. The film actresses in the tamasha genre most often came from outside the Kolhati caste, and only a few tamasha artists could find space for themselves in Marathi cinema. Marathi films constructed the lavani dancer as a native with wild and rustic sexuality who had to be tamed and reformed by the hero (always upper caste). This exaggerated sexualisation of lavani dancers and their construction as wild, too hot to handle or uncontrolled become ways of consolidating caste and gender hierarchies. The overt sexualization of lavani dancers in Marathi films had serious consequences for lavani performers in the *sangeet barees* and tamasha. Tamasha theatres faced the threat of closure, with the increasing encroachment by cinema, both regional and national. The contractors demanded that the *naachee* dance to the film lavani and add erotic and provocative dance steps, as in films. The raw material that went from the Kolhati women to the films came back to them, ironically, in a form that they could hardly recognize as their own. Some troupes were recast as musical orchestras, in which the lavani was absent. Lavani dancers, now attired in trousers and caps, danced to film numbers.[15]

Teechya Acchi Goshta brings out the dominant position of Hirabai as an active subject of the art form she practices and believes in. Hirabai says that she wants "to write because this traditional art form should not die or fade away". Hirabai has accepted her profession wholeheartedly and will not compromise with her talent. Deshpande portrays Hirabai as an artist. Hirabai says "dancing is in my blood, if you were to examine my blood under a microscope, you will find my blood dancing, bouncing, not merely flowing. Right from the time I started walking – my mother put anklets round my feet. So I learned to walk with the rhythm of the ghunghrus in my anklets." Kolhati girls have to pick up the fine nuances of the art from an early age. A daughter stayed with her mother from childhood to learn the art. As a performing artist the mother wielded a significant influence over the young girl.

Their strong commitment to art is brought out in the incident Hirabai narrates about her mother. Just after the assassination of Mahatma Gandhi, an enraged group comes to burn the *madi* where her mother was performing. Her mother comes out to face the irate crowd. As she stood bedecked, all eyes on her, someone from the group shouted, "an upper caste Hindu, a Brahmin has assassinated the national leader Mahatma Gandhi and we believe some Brahmins have come here to listen to songs. Tell them to come out otherwise we will burn your madi." Hirabai's mother replied very gently, "This is an entertainment centre. There is no distinction of colour, class or need here. We have only one class, one caste which is of art lovers…do not think of violence. The language of violence is not the language of this madi." It was commonly accepted that artistes are above sectarian affiliations. Compared to mainstream society, with its rigid patriarchal structure and values, the artists' community is sensitive and open. Living on the fringes of social norms, they are far more liberal as compared to their educated and "respectable" counterparts. They are keen on freedom, savouring the winds that blow in from all sides, more ready than most to acknowledge human needs, including the formation of heterodox relationships.

Deshpande has also foregrounded lavani performers as professionals.

Their status as workers has not been highlighted in mainstream discourse. Hirabai says in the play that she has taken the financial responsibility for all her blood relations. She feels she has rented herself to earn money to provide for her daughter's education, hostel fees and clothes. She bought land for her brother and gave money for his children's education. Her natal family lived out of her money.

The social system acknowledged that some women would devote their lives to being breadwinners. Marked off as unmarriageable, their primary allegiance was expected to remain with the parental family. They were trained from earliest childhood to believe that they had a moral duty to provide for the entire family. They gave all their earnings to their parental family, feeling duty bound to support and provide for their younger siblings. Their brothers' education and luxury was dependent on their income.[16]

Their prime years for earning were in the age group 15 to 35. Despite hard work and high earnings, in the later phase of their lives the tamasha women did not have any money for the family had siphoned all their earnings. These women would buy land for their men-folk thinking that the men would work and earn something but the men usually blew up the money. Their fathers squandered much of this steady flow of cash in wasteful expenses, merry making and the like.[17]

Lavani is a performance based on the man-woman relationship, which is performed by a woman. Hence the woman in fact flirts with the audience which usually consists of men. Flirting of such kind is their business. This is their mode of performance. Due to the fundamental structures of these performances, the performers inevitably get emotionally involved with their clients. Relationships develop and these single performers do have children of their own. Men clients are central to their business. A Lavani performer knows her business well and what it demands. Hirabai says, "we can read men in and out, we are well versed with the male psyche. We are experts in handling men. My mother taught me…communicate properly to stay in the business". However, there is also the awareness amongst them that a man always looks at a woman as an object of entertainment and that art is overlooked and gratification becomes the primary focus.

Even though the tamasha women considered their work to be primarily the entertainment of men they did not consider themselves to be prostitutes. They led unconventional sexual lives and had children, though not married, but their society did not look upon them as "loose" and women of disrepute. In fact, these women walked a tightrope between making independent sexual choices on the one hand and being "available" on the other. They did not marry but entered into relationships with men. Hirabai says that "a man is bound to be interested in having a relationship with another women and this is our profession; we cannot shirk it". Hirabai also says "if you want to be in the profession, you should be fresh all the time and to keep fresh you need to have such relationships". Hirabai had one such relationship with a politician. Though he was not married to her he treated her with love and respect and introduced her to his friends. She travelled a lot with him and he also took her to the Assembly. She never felt used by him.

However, her feelings towards married women run the whole gamut from wistfulness to contempt. Deshpande says that shades of these feelings were bound to enter her script. However a number of women's groups saw this as creating a schism between women and objected to the occasional line indicating how Tamasha women feel towards "respectable" married women. Deshpande's answer was that she did not deliberately set out to underline this difference. "Such were the Tamasha women's lived experiences. What right did I have to erase them? One must remember that the married woman represents the opposite pole to them – it attracts as well as repels".

Deshpande looks upon tamasha women as fully empowered women. Deshpande says that "the Tamasha woman's strength lies in her knowledge that she is exploited. Armed with this knowledge, she can use the situation to her advantage. And she does, quite ruthlessly. She knows, for instance, that she must fleece the patron who has fallen for her charms. She is not hampered by sentiment. Some patrons ask the women to give up their business and 'stay home'. A patron sets up a home for a woman in order to have exclusive rights over her. So far so good, many of them say. But what if the man decides to withdraw from the arrangement? Or dies on her? The woman has lost her place in the profession as well as the man for whom she lost it. Most women, therefore, refuse to accept such an alternative. They are hard as nails about this part of their lives".[18] The one thing, Deshpande feels, that they are vulnerable about is their children, who often grow up ashamed of them. Sometimes the children also exploit their mothers' love and guilt.

The tamasha women have usually been seen as victims. Deshpande gives them subjectivity and agency. But somewhere Deshpande slides towards the overt glorification of tamasha women artists, as a result failing to capture the complexity of their lives. There is a certain similarity in her work with Veena Oldenburg's work on courtesans. Oldenburg's study of the courtesans of Lucknow viewed the kotha as a lifestyle of "resistance" that mocks or inverts hegemonic constructions of gender.[19] There is a tendency in such writings to romanticize lower caste patriarchies as permissive, overlooking the specificities of patriarchy in the lower castes and their responses to patriarchy in the upper castes.

Sharmila Rege's work has brought out how day-to-day decision-making and management of the troupe by the *bai* gives an outward appearance of authority and independence which may be read as "resistance". What is lost in such a reading is the fact that the ultimate authority of employing and developing *nachees* rests with the caste panchayat, i.e., with the males of the Kolhati caste in consultation with some of the older retired *nachees*. Though the *nachees* are the bread-winners of their families, which generally reside in rural areas, all decisions concerning putting a girl out for business or "alliance with troupes" are taken by the local caste panchayats. A Kolhati woman – once she is put out for business in the *sangeet barees* – cannot marry and any transgression of this norm is punishable by the caste panchayat. All decisions about the employment and training of the *nachees* involve the kinship network and joining an alien troupe for economic reasons is looked down upon. This evidence points to the importance of relating factors of both caste and gender in reference to control over female sexuality. Most *nachees* express a wish to keep their daughters away from the theatre and invest heavily in the education of their children. The older generation of *sangeet baree nachees* revealed how, at the end of their careers, they were at the mercy of their brothers who compelled them to put their daughters out for business. In actual fact they have very limited choices in life.[20]

It is against this background that one can examine the role of the state and cultural institutions in post-independence India towards such popular forms of art. Revival of older forms of art has been a central pre-occupation in Independent India, resulting in a unique situation. State cultural organizations and academies emerged as the patrons of authentic Indian folk tradition. However, this resulted in the phoney valorization of what passed for folk tradition within the parameters/matrices predetermined by the metropolitan culture machine, cast in a nationalist lyrical mode. There was the orchestration of virtuosic ensembles for national festivals and melas incorporating the choreography of folk elements. The whole process led to the decontextualisation of popular forms which are linked to the social and material context of the low castes. People's art was delinked from the actual contexts in which people create and interpret the art for themselves. The living forms were suffocated at the source while being appropriated by the elite. Tearing them from their dalit roots, the elite class established ownership over these forms, displacing the traditional community and occupying their space. The forms themselves changed in the process, losing their earthy vibrancy, and ended up as hothouse plants in a rarefied atmosphere. A transnational upper class thus translated and captured popular cultural forms.

Orthodox Indian upper classes also tried to erase the linkages between cultural forms and the contexts from which they had emerged. Suppressing their "sordid" contexts, the forms are presented as if they have arisen from a social vacuum. The actual social history of these genres is virtually obliterated. Humiliated and belittled, the highly talented practitioners of many authentic forms have rarely been able to survive. This includes dalit-caste courtesans, ordinary minstrels or dancers from a number of traditional performing castes, sufi fakirs and bhakti poets.[21]

Middle class theatre persons and institutions generally ignore the thousands of such down-at-heel but superbly talented practitioners of popular theatre forms. Poverty, lack of schooling and modern sophistication has made it difficult for genuine traditional artists to compete. While these practitioners are fading into invisibility, a new generation of the elite is being trained for the stage. Popular theatre is being hailed as a folk art even as its "folk" are not valued. The form is still looked down upon, not respected enough.

National awards become one more attempt at whitewashing the identity and origins of the artist and the art form. In the larger context the award becomes part of the problem. One artist is chosen, brought under the patronage of the state, whereas in fact the same state, occupied with other priorities, negates and abandons the popular form itself. The moral universe the artist inhabited is barely acknowledged by the award givers and far less respected. Her entire identity is whitewashed to fit into the official definitions of an appropriate cultural ambassador. There is a marked reluctance to acknowledge that an award winning artist can hail from a "smudgy" background and instead they pretend that all cultures have arisen from "pure" backgrounds. The background and contexts of the life of award winning artists are deftly blotted out. At most, their impoverished childhood is mentioned, only to glorify them as divinely talented – lotuses blossoming in dark cesspools.[22]

Providing such individual recognition is a token gesture. It serves to divert attention, and the state conveniently bypasses the much larger issue of providing substantial long-term support to help the form to survive. The government claims to support folk forms, quoting awards to popular artists as a case in point. Government institutions bask in reflected glory – championing locally rooted, accomplished artists. By the time the awards came, popular theatre was clearly a dying art. The Indian state and its elite cultural institutions did not really do what was required in order to stem the tide. The demand for popular performances kept dwindling. Government policies and priorities remained fundamentally insensitive to the plight of popular theatre and its practitioners. Bitter truths were swept under the carpet. Nasty caste, gender and cultural politics continued to infiltrate local and regional arts. Thousands of artistes keen to perform good popular theatre were unable to eke out a livelihood. Their plight was ignored and neglected. This is part of the wider politics that affected most folk art, music and theatre forms in twentieth century India.[23]

Notes

1. Susan Seizer, *Stigmas of the Tamil Stage: An Ethnography of Special Drama Artists in South India*, Duke University Press, Durham and London, 2005 and Kumkum Sangari and Sudesh Vaid, eds, *Recasting Women Essays in Colonial History*, Kali for Women, 1989, pp. 1-26.
2. See Neera Adarkar, "In Search of Women in History of Marathi Theatre, 1843 to 1933" in *EPW*, October 26, 1991.
3. I am thankful to Sushma Deshpande for giving me her English translation of her play *Teechya Aeechi Goshta* (Her Mother's Story) on which this paper is based. The English translation is yet unpublished.
4. See, for instance, Lakshmi Subramanyam ed. *Muffled Voices: Women in Modern Indian Theatre*, New Delhi: Har-Anand Publication, 2002.
5. Sharmila Rege, "Conceptualising Popular Culture, 'Lavani' and 'Powda' in Maharashtra," in *EPW*, 6 March 2002.
6. Ibid.
7. Neera Adarkar, "In Search of Women in History of Marathi Theatre, 1843 to 1933" in *EPW*, October 26, 1991.
8. Ibid.
9. Sharmila Rege, "The hegemonic appropriation of sexuality: The caste of the lavani performers of Maharashtra" in *Contribution to Indian Sociology* (n.s.) 29, 1 & 2 (1995), pp 32-5.
10. Meredith Borthwick, *The Changing Role of Women in Bengal, 1849-1905*, Princeton University Press, 1984, p. 117.
11. Kenneth W. Jones, *Arya Dharm: Hindu Consciousness in Nineteenth Century Punjab*,, University of California Press, 1976, pp 95,99.
12. Kathryn Hansen, "The Birth of Hindi Drama in Banaras", in Freitag, Sandria B., ed., *Culture and Power in Banaras: Community, Performance and Environment, 1800-1980*, University of California Press, 1989, p. 86.
13. Sumanta Banerjee, "Marginalization of Women's Popular Culture in Nineteenth-Century Bengal", in Kumkum Sangari and Sudesh Vaid, eds., *Recasting Women, Essays in Colonial History*, Kali for Women, 1989, pp. 130-32.
14. Sharmila Rege, "Conceptualising Popular Culture, 'Lavani' and 'Powda' in Maharashtra", in *EPW*, 6 March 2002.
15. Ibid.
16. Shantabai Kishore Kale, *Against All Odds*, translated from the Marathi by Sandhya Pandey, Penguin, New Delhi: 2000.

17. Ibid.
18. Quoted in Shanta Gokhale, *Playwright in the Centre, Marathi Drama from 1843 to the present*, Calcutta: Seagull 2000, pp. 358-59.
19. Veena Talwar Oldenburg, "Lifestyles as Resistance: The case of the Courtesans of Lucknow", in Douglas Haynes and Gyan Prakash(eds) *Contesting Power: Resistance and Everyday Social Relations in South Asia,* Berkeley: University of California Press, 1991, pp. 23-61.
20. Sharmila Rege, "The hegemonic appropriation of sexuality: The case of the lavani performers of Maharashtra" in *Contribution to Indian Sociology* (n.s.) 29, 1 &2 (1995), pp. 32-5.
21. Deepti Priya Malhotra, *Gulab Bai – The Queen of Nautanki Theatre*, Delhi: Penguin, 2006, pp. 220-32.
22. Ibid.
23. Ibid.

6
Theatre Between Cultures*

H.S. Shiva Prakash

1

The famous African poet and activist Aime Caeser said that no culture could survive without exchanges and that cultures which ceased to exchange became extinct. Colonialism was also an exchange but it was an unequal exchange between cultures and therefore needed to be fought. This paper seeks to examine the exchange of theatres between cultures in the light of Caesar's statement. Unequal exchange, according to Caesar, is the defining feature of colonialism. However, unequal exchange can also happen between nations, regions and cultures unevenly matched in terms of material and political power as in the case of mainstream cultures and marginalized cultures, of countries of the north and the south. This paper intends to examine some patterns of unequal exchange of theatres between different regions within India on the one hand, and between India and other countries with greater economic, political and military might on the other. It is

* This is a revised version of a paper presented at the international seminar on *Theatre:Making / Remaking Tradition* on the occasion of the ninth Bharat Rang Mahotsav, organized by the National School of Drama in New Delhi from January 6-20, 2007.

based on the assumption that exchange processes are for the most part, determined and directed by institutions of patronage and funding and the pulls and pressures exercised by socio-political movements—all these provide the matrices in which the creative freedom of theatre people function.

A Sufi parable tells of how Mullah Nasiruddin, having lost his keys in a dark room, was looking for them in the broad daylight on the royal road. His logic was that there was light on the road, not in the dark room. A good deal of writing on Indian theatre reminds me of this tale. We are looking for the keys of understanding in areas of theatre already well documented. It is inconvenient and more difficult to search for keys in the dark room. The dark rooms are our bewilderingly large numbers of regional and sub-regional theatres. In the present state of knowledge about the "dark rooms" in India, it is impossible to build up a comprehensive picture of Indian theatre practices today. The books that pretend to any kind of omniscience about the area arrive at conclusions that fly in the face of ground realities. Most often, facts are twisted to suit neat theoretical formulations. Another obstacle is our inability to know all the languages of our theatres. The observations in this paper make no pretence to any kind of omniscience. They are at best tentative. The colossal glass house of theories built in areas of culture with enormous, scholarly labour—like, for instance, Sheldon Pollack's hypothesis about the evolution of South Asian cultures and languages—can be easily smashed with a handful of stones of counter-examples.

Translation is an important form of cultural exchange. I am here using the term translation as a very broad, cultural category, following Octavio Paz, the famous Mexican poet and cultural historian. By translation he means, apart from linguistic translations, the exchange of religions, philosophies, ideologies, arts, customs, dressing habits, and cuisine. Modernism represents a period resulting from the intensification of this form of cultural exchange, or translation. I would like to point out the crucial role played by such translations in the histories of our theatre—the site of metamorphosis and transformations—during different stages. The reaction against traditional theatres in the nineteenth century in different language milieus coincided with translations from Sanskrit, on the one hand and, western classics through the language of the colonizer, on the other. The West mostly meant Shakespeare. The Kannada poet, scholar and courtier at the court of the benevolent Mysore kings who ruled with the blessings of the colonial masters, Basavappa Shastri, came out with a remarkable translation of Kalidasa's *Shakuntalam.* The language of this translation was *champu*, the mixture of prose and verse characteristic of Sanskrit drama. The verse passages were subjected to two parallel translations in the same text—first, into the classical Kannada dear to the court and second, into less formal Kannada that could work in theatre. What is more interesting is his translation of *Othello* from English, a language he did not know, into *Shurasena Charite* in the late nineteenth century. It should be pointed out in passing that the "original" plays themselves, like those translated by Shastri, were examples of inter-semiotic translation. He had *Othello* read out to him by a Brahmin courtier, Subba Rao, and translated it also into *champu,* the language of Sankrit drama. He ran into great difficulty while trying to translate Desdemona's chastity into the Indian wifely virtue of *paativratya.* Desdemona's physical intimacy (holding hands, allowing another man to kiss her hands) was quite consistent with the Christian concept of chastity, but not with an Indian *pativrata.* So he had to edit such details from the stage directions, thus making the Othello-figure's jealousy completely baseless. This shows how daunting the task of translating a text from a language and culture unintelligible to the translator was. Basavappa Shastri was completely at home with Sanskrit and Kannada but not with English. Several adaptations of Shakespeare fall between two stools because of their inability to see that translation is an imaginative, recumbent work, to borrow a term from bio-technology. What Basavappa Shastri had produced was a failed grafting. It takes the genius of Kuvempu, the greatest Kannada poet and playwright of the twentieth century, to produce a remarkable adaptation of *Hamlet* into *Raktakshi*, in which the action is transplanted into the tragic period of the Bidnur kingdom in medieval Karnataka. Here the hapless and passive Ophelia is transformed into a rebellious and energetic Rudrambe and Hamlet into a goody-goody victim. The result is an eminently stage-worthy play of great power, which matches the strength of the source text.

These two experiments in translation suggest two different possibilities of translating across cultures with varying degrees of freedom and limitation. This is clearly discernible in Indian avatars of Shakespeare in particular—a fact that became clear to me when I was asked to be the Director of the National Theatre Festival organized by the Kerala Sangeet Natak Akademi in 2001 at Kasaragodu. Nearly 12 Indian translations and adaptations of Shakespearean plays from far-flung regions of India were invited. Broadly the productions fell into two groups. Only a small number of them were direct translations of Shakespearean texts. These included the Marathi translation of *King Lear* by the eminent poet Vinda Karandikar. In spite of the good quality of translation, the production based on it did not work, for, it went for English costumes and music. Other translations whose productions used local costumes, like the Assamese and Manipuri versions, fared better. But the productions that fascinated the audience most were those that took complete liberty with source texts and changed them beyond recognition, particularly Indira Parthasarathi's *Irudiattam* (King

Lear) and my own Kannadisation of *Macbeth* into *Maranayakana Drshtanthakathe.*

What this suggests is that transplanting a foreign play into the soil of one's own culture brings it closer to audiences than the mere transposition through verbatim translations. This also seems to be true of translations of theatrical forms and styles across different languages, regions and epochs. When Brecht watched the performance of the Beijing Opera in Moscow, the concept of Epic Theatre took shape. He adapted the technique of Chinese performers to suit the needs of his theatre praxis.

At different stages of the evolution of modern Indian theatre, adaptation of techniques and forms has played a decisive role. Disgusted with the éclat and grandeur, the sound and fury of Parsi theatre signifying nothing, the practitioners of non-professional theatre turned to other cultures for inspiration. The impact of western realist texts and techniques was discernible in the productions of IPTA, which was the cultural wing of the Communist Party. Their attempt was to replace mythology with history, entertainment with edification. But the most influential productions of the Progressive Theatre had to go beyond this simple formulation. The historic Bengali production of Bijon Bhattacharya's *Nabanna (*1942*)* is one such instance. *Ningalenne Communist Aakki*, a Malayalam play written by Thoppil Bhasi and produced in 1952 by Kerala People's Art Club, was a phenomenal success. An amalgam of the traditional *sangeeta natakam* and realism, this production was characterized by melodrama and haunting music. It became a paradigm for the professional theatre of Kerala. The socio-political impact of this play was so enormous that, according to some, it paved the way for the rise of the first-ever elected Communist Party government. A great stalwart of Bengali theatre, the actor-director-playwright Utpal Dutt, had to go on extending the form of his theatre by creating new wholes through the combination of styles as diverse as realist theatre and Bengali Jatra.

Drama and theatre are often said to be the confluence of tradition and modernity, the old and the new. The most memorable plays I have read and productions I have watched, rise out of such binaries. The resultant products are something unexpected, the avatars of the principle of *chamatkara,* which Sanskrit poetics holds to be the essence of aesthetic creation.

The electrifying performances of Telugu revolutionary poet Gaddar are a remarkable example of one-man theatre enterprises. Reminiscent of folk forms like the *jogera ata* of Karnataka, they were a rich translation of folk singing and performance into the context of revolutionary praxis. He has disproved the orthodox Marxist view that feudal forms have only feudal content. By translating old forms into a new context, he has imbued them with new meanings.

Why do theatre people not take his experiments seriously? The exchange of texts and forms does not happen in a socio-political vacuum. Let me attempt some answers in the next section.

3

Though politically part of India, the North-Eastern states are beset with problems very different from those in the mainland. The state of Manipur, whose contribution to Indian theatre is invaluable, is now the bleeding wound of the sub-continent. Though the state is always represented in all-India festivals and any exchanges of theatre, both at home and abroad, any visitor to the state can see how the local people agonize over the violence between Indian forces and several warring factions of insurgent groups demanding autonomy. Lokendra Arambam, the well-known Manipuri theatre director and civil society activist, advanced powerful and convincing arguments regarding the unequal exchange of theatre between Manipur and the rest of India in a presentation made at a seminar on contemporary theatre, which was part of the Kerala Sangeet Natak Akademi Festival at Kochi in 2000. This presentation can be described as an elegy on political theatre in India. He locates his arguments about the unequal exchange in the context of the two stages of the history of post-Independence theatre. The first stage coincided with the emergence of national institutions like the Sangeet Natak Akademi and the National School of Drama in pursuit of the Nehruvian agenda of culture and with the work of stalwarts like Alkazi and Karnad. This period was characterized by the search for the universals of the new Indian, modernistic aesthetic. Artists of this period profiting from Nehruvian largesse did not suffer even a tinge of anguish or engage in any self-criticism as had been practiced by their predecessors in the colonial framework. However, this period, he adds, led to some of the finest experiments in playwriting by playwrights like Mohan Rakesh, Badal Sircar and Mahesh Elkunchwar and brilliant theatre work by Alkazi and Shambhu Mitra. The second phase corresponds with the "back to the roots" movement presided over by Suresh Awasthi of the Sangeet Natak Akademi and B V Karanth of the National School of Drama that led to the rise of regional theatres, bereft of the social ideology of the progressive theatres and the brilliant self-consciousness of early modernism. While the early modernists were engaged in an intensely individual search, the later "back of the roots" people sought to justify the ideology of their official patrons. This was the generation of directors like B V Karanth, K N Panikkar, Ratan Thiyam and M Ramaswami. "The resultant works of theatre art gained an identity separate from their creators and gained an exchange value as distinct from use value." This was, interestingly enough, also the period of the rise of sales persons of Indian spirituality and karma cola to the West.

Arambam sums up the ambivalent attitude of the mainland to Manipur against the framework in which the plays of Girish Karnad, Vijay Tendulkar, Chandrashekhar Kambar and Satish Alekar circulated all over India through translations into Hindi and other Indian languages for they, in spite of being regional, did not undermine the national. He asks:

"How about Ratan Thiyam and Kanhailal? Can *Chakravyuh* and *Pebet* be translated and produced in other regional languages and idioms? Will they have the same presence as the works of other playwrights? Why has this not been tried? Here lies the deep cultural contradiction which the present writer would like to probe further...Ratan Thiyam's plays elicit the same response as Manipuri products do in the Indian market. Manipuri handlooms are in great demand here, because they are finely crafted, exotic, strange and mysterious to Indian eyes. Here lies the essential contradiction of the Manipuri presence in India."

Having cautioned that the efforts of the likes of Ratan Thiyam and Kanhailal will never bear fruit, he goes on to create an oppositional structure through his own theatre of resistance. But this story of irreconcilability between India and Manipur has another ironic twist. In his entry on Manipuri theatre in the *Oxford Companion to Indian Theatre,* Arambam has this to say:

> At Aryan theatre, Lokendra Arambam(1939-) developed "theatre of resistance" to counter both these modes, but the establishment appropriated him by featuring his *Macbeth-Stage of Blood* (1997), an environmental production on a lake, in the celebration of fifty years of Indian Independence in London![1]

No matter what turn the story of Indo-Manipuri relationship takes in the future, Arambam's analysis highlights some deep contradictions in the unequal exchange of theatre between the two regions.

4

Arambam argues that the exchange of theatre between the Indian mainland and Manipur are determined by socio-political equations outside theatre. But how about the exchange, circulation and dissemination of theatre within the mainland itself? In one of his essays, "Cultural Colonialism", Nemichandra Jain bemoans the sad fate Hindi drama and theatre have suffered at the hands of other languages:

> ....it must be remembered that playwrights in various languages got national recognition and honour mainly because their plays were staged in Hindi in numerous theatre centres all over the country, and were translated into other languages, frequently from their Hindi translations. In a large number of cases, if their plays had not been staged only in their own languages and not in Hindi in metropolitan cities, they would have remained just regional playwrights, and it would have been much more difficult to get the countrywide or national recognition which they got....Thus, while Hindi may have acquired the dubious distinction of being a 'clearing house' for regional drama, the process has both obstructed and distorted its own drama and theatre.[2]

In the same essay he laments the fact that Hindi drama is not taken seriously by the NSD.

There is also the diametrically opposite complaint that NSD has scant respect for regional classics as in:

> The arbitrariness of the choice of plays by the NSD repertory is evident from the NSD publication *Rangyatra*(1992), which reveals that NSD does not bother even about the classics of Indian theatre. There is no production of Tagore's *Raktakarabi*, of *Nabanna* and other plays by Bijon Bhattacharya, or the plays of Kalidasa. The trouble is, when one names a playwright or a theatre group or a director not yet canonized by the NSD, one's choice is attributed to personal bias; and when one criticizes someone sanctified by such institutions, one's opinion becomes personal prejudice. On the other hand, these institutions, working together, establish some public opinions which originate in the high priests' personal biases which are made to appear as the country's opinion.[3]

The above quotes taken from the official publications of the NSD and the SNA voice, from opposite angles, the arbitrariness of the canon set up by national institutions of theatre. The dissonance between accounts and annals of national theatre in prestigious publications and the ground realities of theatre can be viewed from other perspectives also.

Prasanna, the well-known theatre director, also comes down hard on the "back to the roots" phase of Indian theatre. He condemns the whole business of seeking the "Indian" in Indian theatre as a reactionary stunt. Sympathetic to the secular, Alkazian phase of modern Indian theatre, he critiques severely the Karanthian phase which tried to purge all progressive and democratic elements from theatre.[4]

While not completely disagreeing with Arambam and Prasanna, I would like to pose the issues involved, differently from both. They see a tension between the universal/secular modernism and the reactionary, nativist phase. However, the modernist project was never monolithic. Brecht and Becket, Lorca and Yeats represent the different stands of modernism which spoke in different dialects: metropolitan, regional, experimental and progressive. In my study of the Telugu poet, Sri Sri, I have argued that Indian literary modernism has two facets: the experimental/formalist aspect and the progressive/agit prop aspect. In theatre, Alkazi and Karnaḍ represent the first trend and Utpal Dutt, the second. However, over and above these, there was also tension in modernism between the metropolitan and the nativist, for example, between Karnad and Kambar, both eminent playwrights. A close reading of these two playwrights coupled with a dispassionate analysis of the differences in the dissemination of their works is revealing. Though Kambar's works have received a great deal of acclaim at the national level, his works have not been as frequently exported abroad as Karnad's. Nevertheless, there is ample recompense for him. His plays, deriving their energy from the still rooted folk cultures of north Karnataka, have travelled back to the masses and won great popularity in rural areas, which is not true of the plays of Karnad, who is more popular in urban centres. Kambar's *Jokumaraswamy (*1972*)* has been reconverted into *Sannata* form and performed by local troupes for over ten hours, all through the night. The nativist claims of the "back to the roots" movement, therefore, also needs to be re-examined from a more balanced angle.

I would agree with Praasanna and Arambam that there are quite a few instances in the productions of Karanth and Thiyam where the ethnic is used as the icing on the cake. I do not find any justification for Karnath's use of *yakshagana* in *Birnamvan (* the Hindi version of Shakespeare's *Macbeth),* or Prasanna's own use of *harikatha* in *Ondu Loka Kathe,* his Kannada production based on Mani Kaul's film *Duvidha.* In such cases the form used has no inherent connection with the text or plot. One can, of course, make a *yakshagana* out of Shakespeare. In the early part of the twentieth century traditional *yakshagana* performers had made *King Lear* into a very popular *yakshagana* in *badagatittu* style. But they had effected a sea-change in the source text. In Kerala, Parmashivan Ayyar did the same when he narrated Shakespeare in the immensely popular one-man theatre of *kathakalakashepam.*

Some of the uses of folk forms in theatre after the 70's went beyond the official agenda of the cultural pundits of the capital. In Karnataka, most of the talented directors who came to theatre after Karanth and Prasanna were not Brahmins; they were from the backward and scheduled castes. Their sensibilities were totally different from that of their predecessors. Please note, sensibilities, not ideas. Karnath and Prasanna were both rebel Brahmins. Still, their sensibilities could not have been shudra or panchama. This new group of directors, CGK, Gopal Krishna Nayari, Basavalingiah and Suresh Anagalli came from the most exploited castes and tribes and with a leftwing, political background. At the time when Dalit writers were breaking out of standard Kannada, they were trying to break out of the standard idiom of Kannada theatre, which was either realistic or absurdist.

Let me illustrate this by referring to a magnificent production of Bhasa's *Karnabharam* by Gopala Krishana Nayari. It was done in the late 80's for the Bangalore amateur troupe, Prayoga Ranga. A low-budget production, it was performed in a rehearsal shed. No artificial lights were used to heighten the ritualistic nature of the performance. The acting area was small (10" x 10"). This was meant to intensify and contract the action to the ritualistic sacred space.

Nayari was born into one of the smallest tribes of coastal Karnataka, having not more than 2000 people. This tribe has not yet figured in any one of the Backward Caste Reports of the State. The members of this community have to go through a ritual from sunrise to sunset, in which they are given the sacred thread and initiated into Brahminhood. The plight of Karna was that he was abandoned by his Kshatriya mother, brought up by fishing people and promoted to Kshatriyahood by Duryodhana to pursue his own agenda. The indeterminate caste identity of a Nayari initiate was similar to that of Karna, who was derided for his lowly origins in spite of becoming a king. So the director bracketed the action with the Nayari ritual—a technique that provided refreshingly new semiotics to the thematic concerns in a way different and, according to me, more convincing than in the other celebrated productions of the same text which are on the top of the export list of quality Indian theatre which address the international market and does not find it necessary to have a critical dialogue with the milieu of "forms." On occasions like this, the idiom of theatre went ethnic not because the new directors saw them as marketable ethnic stuff but because it was part of their anguished collective memory that stuck to them at a level deeper than their skin. It was their birthright to speak to the rest of the world in their cultural mother tongues.

This was the other side of what Safdar Hashmi termed "wave of traditionalism" on 13 October, 1985.

5

The late K V Subbanna, in his book *Theatre and Community*, argues that theatre is closely related to the community.[5]

To drive his point home, he invokes the famous mythological story of the quarrel between the two sons of god Shiva as to who should get the magical mango. Because neither of the sons wants to divide the precious mango, Shiva says that whoever goes round the world and returns first will win it. The younger son, the six-faced Shanmukha instantly sets off on his peacock-mount. But the elephant-faced and pot-bellied Ganapati (literally "the lord of the tribe") decides on another course. Because his parents Shiva and Parvati are also the primal parents of the cosmos, he goes round them and demands that he be given the mango and he succeeds.

Subbanna argues that theatre, the art rooted in the community, is more like Ganapati, who perceives the whole world from the vantage point of the community, than his globetrotting brother. I demur. For, most of the known theatre of the world is the gift of nomads who have lost their homes but carry their memories in their hearts. Historically, the rise of touring actors led to the birth of full-fledged theatre. Therefore, the patron deity of theatre people should be Shanmukha, who left the sacred Kailasa of his parents and made the much smaller Palani his home. His second abode gets its name from the Tamil word meaning "you are the fruit", for he realizes the essence of the fruit within his exiled self. Theatre, the art of nomads, has to travel both within and across regions. It cannot live, let alone develop, without making contacts. But what needs to be questioned is the mode of exchange where neo-capitalist market rules obtain.

So far I have dwelt mostly on how theatre in India travels intra-culturally. But the scholars I have quoted refer to intercultural transactions in the area of theatre. Arambam feels that theatre exchange in Independent India is the result of commodification in the contemporary world order. A thoroughgoing and erudite analysis of the phenomenon is found in the works of Rustom Barucha. The arbitrariness in the creation of the pantheon of "great Indian playwrights" and the unequal nature of theatre exchanges between regional cultures have elicited furious reactions in the context of an uneven society.

What is true of intra-cultural exchanges is also true of intercultural exchanges. Further, the character of intercultural exchanges, the arena of mightier players, also forces itself on intra-cultural exchanges. The rules of the bigger game alter the rules of the smaller game. In a hard-hitting article in the December 1999 issue of *Eminence,* M. Prabha writes about how one single luminary of Indian theatre is able to corner huge financial and other benefits from various institutions. Once enthroned, always enthroned. If one takes a look at the list of plays exported to festivals abroad, one cannot escape the fact that the same set of names tend to recur. The plays that rely least on regional factors are generally preferred. To get taste of what the expectations are, let me provide some quotes from material available on the internet, related to some of the international festivals where Indians figured.

Listen to how the 2006 Bonn Festival began, according to Varpuri Jain :

> 'The ground-work for the Biennale was done by a group of Germans visiting different parts of India over a period of time,' says Sudhanshu Pandey, Counsellor for Press, Information, Education and Culture at the Embassy of India in Berlin.
>
> On the opening day, Rajasthan was the popular flavour. The Kawa Brass Band, Jaipur which had come for playing with a local Jazz band, started a typical Indian procession from the Bonn Opera towards the City Town Hall in Bonn.
>
> Dressed in colourful Rajasthani costumes, the band played popular Bollywood tunes and on its way, stopped at several places while its star artists charmed the enthusiastic audience with their jugglery skills.

Is this not the invocation of Orientalist India, pure and simple?

This is what the organizers of the Festival of India have to say of Girish Karnad's play *The Fire and the Rain*: it "portrays the conflict between the world of knowledge/experience and that of innocence and goodness". The production is further described as "a theatrical treat rooted in ancient India".

One of the entries at the Edinburgh Fringe Festival was a Mumbai production, *Yeh Mumbai Meri Jaan.* This production, the organizers assure us, has "the unadulterated spicy flavour of Bollywood" in which "the characters shine with the authentic and true spirit of Bollywood". We are also informed that the playwright is Sohaila Kapoor "whose brother Shekhar has directed the Oscar-nominated film, *Elizabeth*".

These samples show how we are presented to western eyes. The ire of Arambam and Prasanna, therefore, is understandable. So is the refusal of radical artists like Gaddar to be tempted into any state-run institution. But the situation is not always as bad as this.

The following *Times of India* report about the Biennale Bonn gives some ground for hope:

> Naseeruddin Shah has just learnt a thing or two. At the recent Biennale Bonn, where the actor-director's Motley Theatre Company staged *Ismat Apa Ke Naam* before riveted local audiences, a roundabout exercise first required him to translate feminist writer Ismat Chugtai's trio of 1940s stories from the original Urdu to English.
>
> The lines were then reinterpreted in German for an engrossed house there. The experience stands the acid test of a long-held claim: theatre has its own special language.
>
> 'Lesson One is that theatrical language transcends physical language', Shah says. Anxious that theirs wasn't a spectacular machine-driven production with elaborate sets and a huge cast as Europeans might expect, he and wife

> Ratna Pathak, co-starring in the three-character play, were rewarded with rapt attention early into the performance.
>
> 'There are quiet audiences and quiet audiences. But we sensed attentive-quiet, not bored-quiet', Ratna remarks. What could possibly connect urban European sensibilities with small town-India foibles that Chugtai explored in works set in Meerut or Lucknow?
>
> 'It was like venturing into virgin territory', Naseeruddin admits. 'There arose another aspect the encounter taught: perform only to communicate, not worrying about laughs coming a little late or the tempo slackening. In fact it was a relief not to have instant and constant reaction. One gets more than one needs of this from familiar audiences understanding the same language.'

The lesson that the encounter taught – "perform only to communicate" – in the absence of "a spectacular machine driven production with elaborate sets and huge cast as Europeans may expect" is important not only for sponsors of intercultural exchange but also for all theatre workers stymied by lack of funding either by state or foreign organizations. For, it is ultimately human resources of the word and the body that give life to the art, not material and mechanical resources.

I am not making a plea for a "theatre of poverty" or abstinence from struggle, like the one my fellow theatre workers are engaged in, back in Karnataka, demanding that all Indian language theatres be recognized as National Theatres. We need to carry on our struggle, and through our work to make our demand for a greater-share and for participation in theatre exchanges at home and abroad. At the same time, there is a need to look for other innovative, inexpensive and practical ways of doing good theatre in small ways, independent of state or foreign support.

Another question that is rankling in my mind is: why are we bothering more about what the world should do for theatre and less about what theatre can do for the world in general, and our own culture in particular? It is high time we bestowed greater attention on our exchange with our own languages and cultural communities.

Bharata said that theatre is *saarvavarnika*, i.e., for all castes. The cursed descendants of Bharata cannot help exchanging it with all human gods and demons; notwithstanding the fact that the world today is uneven in much more complicated ways than in those days. That exchanges are now taking place in an uneven world is a fact which theatre alone is in no position to alter.

Notes

1 Ananda Lal, ed., *The Oxford Companion to Indian Theatre*, Delhi: OUP, 2004, p.253.

2 Nemichandra Jain, *Asides*, New Delhi : NSD, 2003, p.175.

3 Dilip Kumar Basu, "Movements and Institutions of Indian Theatre", *Sangeet Natak Akademi* Nos 137-138.

4 Prasanna, "Derailment and After" in *Theatre India*,(Number 12).

5 Subbanna, K.V., *Theatre and Community*, New Delhi: Sri Ram Centre for Performing Arts,2000.

7

Interrogating the "Postcolonial"– a Reading of Plays by Girish Karnad, Vijay Tendulkar and Mahesh Dattani

Angelie Multani

> *We will say to them, we also according to our ability are tragic poets, and our tragedy is the best and the noblest; for our whole state is an imitation of the best and noblest life; which we affirm to be indeed the very truth of tragedy. You are poets and we are poets, both makers of the same strain, rivals and antagonists in the noblest of dramas, which true law can alone perfect, as our hope is. Do not then suppose that we shall all in a moment allow you to erect your stage in the agora, or introduce the fair voices of your actors, speaking above our own, and permit you to harangue our women and children, and the common people, about our institutions, in language other than our own, and very often the opposite of our own.*
>
> [Plato 1976:VII, 52]

The above lines, quoted from Plato, make clear that the contentious relationship between authority and theatre is an ancient and established one. Plato clearly demonstrates here that he understands the very real threat posed to the state and its organisation by art, and other such subversive practices. The state appropriates the entire nation-state/community as its performance space, within which theatre negotiates its own space. Just as theatre and performers (including playwrights, directors, actors) try to move their audiences to a particular end – a feeling, a realisation, an aesthetic or material judgement, the state needs to manipulate its citizens towards its own desired goal. They both need to enact power.

In contemporary versions of states, theatre fulfils several roles simultaneously – it entertains, educates, informs, antagonises and subverts. Obviously, the political functions of theatre tend to be more overt in states where there exists an open confrontation or conflict between different sections of society and the centralised or dominant power structures. Through its very basic form of presenting alternative stories and voices, theatre is potentially a powerful and radical subversive medium. Theatre doesn't have to "tell" – it merely has to "show" – and in various ways, the "showing" can be far more disruptive to a dominant state of being than an overt piece of political propaganda.

In colonised states, for instance, the anti-colonial power and reach of theatre is a well-established fact. Theatre has been an important agent in several anti-colonial struggles, from Kenya to New Zealand to India. As Nandi Bhatia states, "Theatre's visual focus, emphasis on collective participation and representation of shared histories, mobility, potential for disruption and spatial manoeuvrability impart yet another layer to the cultural investments of colonial and postcolonial texts in framing, organizing and presenting alternative stories."[1]

Before we go into a specific analysis of what postcoloniality may mean in theatre and dramatic representations, let us examine the theoretical basis of what we mean by postcoloniality in this paper.

I

As Ellen Shohat points out in her essay "Notes on the 'Post-Colonial'" the important thing to do is to "situate the term geographically, historically, and institutionally, while raising doubts about its political agency."[2] Many theoreticians and critics refer to "post-colonial" and "postcolonial" as terms that are largely interchangeable. At one level, the brouhaha about the hyphen may seem to be yet another example of the petty hair-splitting nature of academics; yet, the hyphen occupies a central space in the negotiations of post colonialism. At the very least, the terms of the debate range from whether "post-colonial" denotes (or should denote) "simply" a historical period, as in "after colonialism", "after the end of the Empire", and so on, to "postcolonial", non hyphenated, denoting or suggesting disparate forms of representation, reading practices and values. These, in the latter sense, of course cut across temporal and spatial barriers of colonial rule and political independence. In this sense, postcolonialism is not limited or contained within neat categories of time and space, although it is inevitably tied up with historical experiences. Another term that has gained currency is the related one of "postcoloniality" which, as Shohat says, "marks a contemporary state, situation, condition or epoch." The preface "post", then, aligns "post-colonialism" with a series of other "posts" – "post-structuralism", "post-modernism", "post-marxism", "post-feminism", "post-deconstructionism" – all sharing the notion of a movement beyond. Further, as Ania Loomba avers , the term "post" itself may be looked at from two perspectives – temporal and ideological: "A country may be both postcolonial (in the sense of being formally independent) and neo-colonial (in the sense of remaining economically and/or culturally dependent) at the same time."[3]

Many critics have expressed reservations about the efficacy of a term that seeks to demonstrate all movements with reference to a single category or marker – that of the colonising experience. Obviously, the experience of colonisation is not a uniform or even necessarily similar one for the various nation-states that have lived through it. Again, as Shohat points out, "Does the 'post' indicate the perspective and location of the ex-colonized (Algerian), the ex-colonizer (French), the ex-colonial settler (Pied-Noir) or the displaced hybrid in First World Metropolitans (Algerians in France)? Since the experience of colonialism and imperialism is shared, albeit asymmetrically, by (ex) colonizer and (ex) colonized, it becomes an easy move to apply the 'post' also to First World European countries. Since most of the world is now living after the period of colonisation, the 'post-colonial' can easily become a universalising category which neutralizes significant geo-political differences between France and Algeria, Britain and Iraq, or the U.S. and Brazil since they are all living in a 'post-colonial epoch'."[4] Following from this argument, would it be possible then, to speak of post-colonialsim in terms of the British Empire, or the experience of being English in the 1950s? Can it be stated that the loss of identity and the complex political and cultural crossroad that Jimmy Porter confronts in *Look Back in Anger* is descriptive of a post-colonial experience? Can we assert that in many senses, *Look Back in Anger* is, in fact, a post-colonial text?

If we accept that there is something wrong with this statement, then taking the position further, would it be possible to state that Vijay Tendulkar's *Ghashiram Kotwal*, Girish Karnad's *Tughlaq* and Mahesh Dattani's *Clearing the Rubble* are all equally postcolonial texts, representing or expressing a similar state of being or socio – cultural politics in that they are all dramatic texts written (written/translated) in English by Indian playwrights in post 1947 India? If, on the other hand, we do accept the statement, then it is possible to take the argument in a completely different direction.

II

First, let us begin with the assumption that we cannot or do not accept that a text by a former colonial power can be said to be postcolonial in the sense in which we use the term currently, that is, to describe the experience of post-colonialism from the standpoint of the state that was colonised, rather than from the perspective of the coloniser. The question that follows, then, is clear – does the term "postcolonialism" imply a static situation, that is, once a nation has been colonised, must it always remain postcolonised?

If, as Shohat and others point out, the concept of the "post-colonial" must be "interrogated and contextualised historically, geopolitically and culturally", we need to situate these different texts in the different spatio-temporal contexts they were written/staged in. Tendulkar's *Ghashiram Kotwal* was first performed in 1972 and along with Karnad's *Tughlaq* (1964) forms the core of the canon of modern Indian theatre. *Ghashiram Kotwal*, originally written in Marathi and later translated into English and various other Indian languages, has been performed all over India and in many parts of the world to tremendous commercial and critical acclaim. *Ghashiram*, is of course, a political play – both in terms of its content and "message" as well as in its controversial performative history. While the main aim of *Ghashiram* is to expose the machinations of power and the creation and destruction of "Ghashirams", the representation of the corruption and decadence of the Peshwas and the Brahmins of Pune has attracted tremendous critical (in all senses of the term) attention in the play's history of more than a thousand performances.

Ghashiram is a play about the title figure – Ghashiram Kotwal. Ghashiram is an outsider, a Brahmin from Kannauj, who rises to a position of almost supreme power – that of Kotwal in Pune — by pandering his daughter to Nana Phadnavis, the late eighteenth century Maratha ruler. *Ghashiram* is a play about the workings of power. As Samik Bandyopadhyay says, in "*Ghasiram* power is defined 'horizontally', (in the sense in which Maurice Duverger uses it in *The Idea of Politics*, London 1966), in terms of individuals against individuals; from humiliation, to revenge in assertion, to eventual victimization; played out against a background of political and moral decadence and degeneracy, with sexuality impinging on strategies of power."[5]

While the play has been extensively commented on for its representation of power, authority structures, the Maharashtrian Tamasha form in which it is cast and its gender roles, this study will concentrate on the "shadowy" figure of the white man who hovers at the fringe of the action; an actor on stage but never a direct participant in the action itself. As I have said elsewhere, Tendulkar's main concern in this play seems to be to represent the workings of power, that is, to show how power operates in a society, rather than to examine the consequences or implications or even sources of that power.[6] *Ghashiram Kotwal* represents how an outsider from Kannauj rises to a position of almost supreme authority in the closed and tightly knit community of Pune; how he abuses his power, only to be brought down, not as "punishment" for his tyrannous actions, but because he tried to appropriate the ultimate power which belonged to the Peshwa himself.

The very form of the play, set in a Tamasha format is itself an important comment. Many critics, notably Suresh Awasthi,(Theatre of Roots) have commented on the postcolonial enterprise of "returning" to traditional forms and structures as evidence of the attempt to re-locate a "lost" history and of forging links with a past that was disrupted by the fact of colonisation. Whether this project, of (re)establishing a "national" or (pre colonial) theatre, is a valid and practical one is something which has been refuted by several other notable critics and commentators, including Rustom Bharucha and Aparna Bhargava Dharwadker. As Dharwadker points out, "In fact, the 'new' traditional theatre is a commodity for the same predominantly middle-class urban audience as other forms of contemporary theatre. Its materials and conventions of representation are different; its location and modes of consumption are not. It is simply a new kind of urban theatrical experience mediated by large scale state patronage and dependant on the institutions both of print and performance."[7] Bharucha also has commented extensively on this phenomenon of inventing a cultural tradition. The invention of this cultural identity is usually achieved by putting together, in an apparently seamless whole, various characteristics and features of different performative traditions, in order to construct a monolithic image of one country with one history, one heritage, one culture and mostly, one language. This "Indian" atmosphere is constructed, in the words of Bharucha, "whereby the 'Indian' tradition is affirmed, not necessarily as people in India would understand it, but as our government would like to represent it to the world." Further, Bharucha states:

> 'Folk drama' is essentially an urban construct that cannot claim to be entirely 'indigenous' [and therefore, 'authentic']. It is a simulation of the 'folk form', sufficiently 'indigenous' (yet not entirely 'desi') to win the approval of urban audiences. The clientele of 'folk drama' is not the 'folk', but city people who need to be reminded of their 'roots' and 'native places' from which they are irrevocably displaced.[8]

Bharucha's comments suggest that when an urban theatre follows a pattern of stripping various "indigenous" performative traditions of their specificity and presents them on an urban a-historical proscenium stage, it may also be catering those performative traditions for easy consumption of those who need to see themselves as "Indian" despite their "urban" Western' identities that may have been formed from a variety of factors, including, of course, the aftermath of an engagement with the process of colonisation and the initiation of a process of increasing cultural imperialism and globalisation.

Returning to the actual text of Tendulkar's play, it seems clear that *Ghashiram Kotwal*, though set in a specific historical context, engages with the present in numerous ways. The decadence and corruption of the ruling class in eighteenth century Pune is inextricably linked with the degeneration of all political and social ethics in contemporary society. From a gendered perspective, the representation of the female protagonists comments on the unequal balance of power that operated and continue to operate against women in both pre as well as post colonial India.

The presence of the white man in *Ghashiram Kotwal*, as I have already stated, is the obvious marker of the vulnerability of a society rife with internal conflicts and riddled with caste and class hierarchies. This kind of symbolism is rife in all forms of popular culture in post 1947 India, from mainstream Hindi cinema to advertisements on television. The instances are well known, and really require no further clarification, but to name at least one of the most famous examples, I would like to mention the film *Mr India*, (directed by Shekhar Kapoor, 1987). The key idea, of course, is that when a society is unable to support its own contradictions and begins to be fractured with internal dissonances, it becomes easy prey to outside aggression. The symbolism of the white man in *Ghashiram Kotwal* is clear in the historical context of the play, in the fact of it being located, temporally, in the pre-colonial era.

There are other instances where popular culture has posited similar, if not the same, antagonisms and schisms between the ruling and ruled classes in post 1947 India as existed between the colonisers and the freedom fighters. Examples of this perspective also abound. The first popular film to clearly state this position was *Phir Bhi Dil hai Hindustani* (directed by Aziz Mirza, produced by "Dreamz Unlimited", 2000) and the latest one is *Rang de Basanti* (directed by Raykesh Mehra, produced by UTV, 2006)). This is an interesting perspective as it reinforces the question asked by many scholars today, as to whether it can really be said to be a post colonial age, or would it be more accurate to refer to it as a neo colonial or neo imperial age, where merely the actors have changed, but the roles and rules of exploitation remain the same? The colour and race of the exploiters may be different today but the imbalances and the sources as well as the enactments of power remain frighteningly unchanged in most instances.

The white man in *Ghashiram Kotwal* first appears just after the debauchery of the Brahmans as well as of Nana Phadnavis has been established. The Brahmans (several of them individually and all collectively) have been accosted by the Sutradhar while on their way to the courtesan, Gulabi's dance. They, of course, pretend they have other, more "respectable" pursuits – one says he is going to the graveyard, others to the temple, and so on. This episode highlights not only the carnal decadence of the ruling elite of Pune but also the fact that it is very thinly disguised and, more importantly, that the high social position of the Brahmins cannot be questioned. Their abuse of power is questioned by the text, but not the "fact" of their high caste. The protagonist Ghashiram is also implicated in the same corrupt structure, as is made clear from the very first move he makes on stage.

This occurs in the very first scene of the play, where the characters and the atmosphere are still being established. As Nana dances with the courtesans, he suddenly sprains his ankle – the questioning of the Sutradhar is full of puns and innuendoes linking the sprained foot with the sexual metaphor of "falling". In this "falling", it is Ghashiram who seizes the opportunity to curry favour with Nana and rushes forward offering his back to Nana for support. It is Ghashiram who literally carries Nana's sexual follies on his back. In this primary instance it is over Gulabi the courtesan; later, of course, it will be over his own daughter.

It is directly after this scene, when Ghashiram has been beaten by thugs and robbed of the necklace awarded to him as a "prize" by the Nana that the white man appears on stage. Ghashiram is wiping the dust off his face and is engulfed with an "air of humiliation" when the palanquin carrying the white man comes on stage. The Pune Brahmans then kick Ghashiram aside and abuse each other in order to be able to "serve" the white man, for a fee, of course.

> ...*To the beat of the drum, the palanquin of a white man comes on the stage. Two Brahmans walk alongside and talk to the Sahib. In front a Brahman with ash on his forehead, shouts: 'The Sahib is coming. Get aside.' A Brahman makes way for the palanquin.*
>
> BRAHMAN: get aside, you dog. Can't you see the Sahib is coming? You shapeless piece of shit! Sleeping on the street! (*Turns to the Sahib.*) The natives of this country have lost all their manners nowadays, sir. I swear, no one has any self-respect or pride. Come on, come on, sir. Now you'll get to see the ceremony of giving royal gifts to the Brahmans, from the inside. I'll sneak you in. Only three silver rupees, sir.

ANOTHER BRAHMAN: Go away, Rambhata. Give *me* two! Let's go, sir, I'll get you in.

THIRD BRAHMAN: Give me just one rupee! Come on, come on. (*To the others.*) Misbegotten bastards! Shut up![9]

This ironic exchange of the Brahmans literally selling themselves to the white man for the lowest price is followed by Ghashiram being questioned by the soldiers at the entrance to Nana's palace. When the white man comes out, Ghashiram has been accused of stealing a Brahman's money and is being beaten by the soldiers. At this point the "Sahib" intervenes directly in the action and after telling the Brahman who had accused Ghashiram that somebody else picked his pocket, the "Sahib" gives the man money to compensate him for the loss. Several other Brahmins run off after the white man and the stage is left for Ghashiram to be dragged in, bruised and bleeding.

The Englishman comes on stage again in the procession of Nana's seventh wedding, the prelude to Gauri's death and Ghashiram's downfall [41]. When the group of "foreign Brahmans" enter, presumably from South India, one of them misunderstands the Sutradhar's comment of "brutish city" and repeats it as "British city" [47].

If *Ghashiram Kotwal* is overtly a post colonial text in its form and mode of representation, because it deliberately adopts a "traditional" dramatic structure for performance on an urban stage and positions the coloniser figure on the fringes of its action, how about a play like *Tughlaq*, written in 1964 and set in the 14th Century, drawing parallels between Muhammed bin Tughlaq and modern Indian leaders like Jawaharlal Nehru and Indira Gandhi? Aparna Dharwadker discusses the changing and always fluid understanding that different audiences/ readers will bring to the play, as attitudes towards and understanding of historical events are not constant, but change over time. Quoting

Herbert Lindenberger's concept of historical drama, Dharwadker says that the Western attitude to historical drama seems to depend on a sense of the "continuity between past and present". However, as Dharwadker points out, the Indian audience's "knowledge of history is both discontinuous and heavily mediated."

After Dharwadker and U.R. Anantha Murthy, it is extremely easy to read contemporary parallels into the story of Tughlaq and his ill fated decisions. The understanding of the play has, naturally enough, evolved and changed over the decades, depending on the socio-political contexts prevailing at the time. When the play was first performed it was read as expressing the disillusionment and disenchantment of the "60s as the glory and hope of Nehruvian optimism crumbled. Later, it was seen as being an uncanny prediction of the draconian authority exerted by Indira Gandhi and the corruption and "Licence Raj" that flourished in the "70s and "80s. Today, more than fifty years after independence, according to Dharwadker,

> *Tughlaq* seems concerned less with specific figures than with two general political issues that have become dominant in the public sphere. The first is the untenability of the idealistic and visionary politics that Nehru and Gandhi practiced as national leaders and valorized in their respective meditations on political action – *The Discovery of India* and *The Story of My Experiments with Truth*. The second is the politics of power relations between groups that are separated by religious or racial difference, in a society that is poised between secular and fundamentalist ideologies.[10]

It is entirely possible to trace actual co-relations between the text of *Tughlaq* and specific historical events in the political histories of both

Mahatma Gandhi and Jawaharlal Nehru, and Dharwadker has done this. For the purposes of this argument, however, it is more important to focus on the idea of looking at history from a post colonial perspective, of interpreting current events and histories from a deliberately pre-colonial point of view. Is this inevitable in a country whose history as a modern nation state is so very recent, so inextricably linked with the project of colonialism?

III

Karnad has most often and most commonly been described as "a highly complex postcolonial intellectual temper".[11] This description probably has a great deal to do with the re-workings of myths and folk tales in Karnad's plays. *Yayati, Hayavadana*, *Tale-Danda*, *The Fire and the Rain* and, of course, *Nagamandala* all focus on "restoring a mythical and historical dimension to our literary consciousness".[12] This "return to the roots", of going back to a tradition of "Indian" theatre which predates colonialism and the Western European intervention of the proscenium stage is clearly oppositional in its definition of what constitutes modern "Indian" theatre to those who are proponents of an urban based, realistic representation of contemporary social life in India. These playwrights, most notably Mahesh Dattani, Manjula Padmanabhan and Mahesh Elkunchwar are not only writing and being performed in English, but in other Indian languages as well as being translated into and from English into other Indian languages. Obviously, the contention of these practitioners is that in our contemporary experience and position in history, representations of modern urban life in "borrowed" forms or even in languages which may not be "indigenous", are not less "authentic" or "Indian" today than folk forms or pre-colonial myths and legends.

The experience of these playwrights and practitioners naturally enough suggests a different understanding of "postcolonialism" from one that is derived from the work of Karnad or even Tendulkar (particularly in *Ghashiram Kotwal*). The question that emerges here is a simple one: must all post Independence narratives and representations in relatively newly formed nation states that were once colonised necessarily be either national allegories, or re-evoke a pre colonial past or even be post colonially constituted in a political or subjective sense?

Of course, not all of Karnad's plays themselves fall into this category. *Hayavadana* or *Nagamandala* cannot really be construed as national allegories, even if they do comment on the current nation-state and attempt to root themselves in a mythic past. The uneasy (for some critics) marriage of a constructed mythic representation with an urban stage creates its own set of problems. The pandering to an urban audience's sense of allegiance to an imagined past peacefully co-existing with a globalised postcolonial world is a problematic enterprise. The "Indian" English of these texts also raises questions of "authenticity" as does the patronising attitude of a western educated playwright and audience imagining that this will "of course" be the way in which a village woman or a rural iron smith speak. The fact that it is "translated" into English is "merely a convenience", much like subtitles in a foreign language film. An original English text then, becomes "less Indian" and more postcolonial in a negative sense, of being derivative, rather than ideologically supplanting.

IV

The work of Dattani is not easy to slot into a postcolonial paradigm simply on the basis of language, for Dattani's plays cannot be described as "national allegory" or as "re-constructing a past". Mahesh Dattani is a contemporary playwright, actor, director and producer of theatrical and cinematic narratives. His plays focus on contemporary situations found in his own context of urban metropolitan, and definitely English speaking India. He is a product of a particular and specific historical process, one which has formed him into a subject that uses English as his language of creative and intellectual expression. His texts focus on the urban middle-class Indian family, one which is not defined only by regional affiliation or community. Dattani's families are usually multi-cultural – either mixed communities or migrant ones – a Gujarati married to a Tamilian, a Kannadiga married to a Patel, Gujarati parents arranging matrimonial alliances with Gowdas, families located in Bombay, Bangalore, or moving from Bombay to Bangalore. The myths incorporated by Dattani are modern urban legends; the issues are contemporary and urban, clearly and overtly so. His rituals are urban, theatrical and dramatic rituals, courtship and dating rituals.

The realist structure, which is a favourite of Dattani's, may be "borrowed" from a Western European tradition but it has been assimilated into a very identifiable and recognizable Indian framework If we live in a multi-cultural context today, can we perpetuate the "ownership" and privileging of historical concepts depending on where they have originated from, regardless of the appropriation and assimilation they may have undergone?

Dattani's characters are all identifiably urban Indians, whether they are mothers-in-law, daughters, sons, prospective sons-in-law, friends, or any other social or filial role one may care to name. In his plays the issues range from sexual preferences to gender discrimination, from living conventional lives to breaking boundaries of tradition and history, from murder mysteries to art and culture. The common theme that runs through all these plays is that of being rooted in an identifiable and recognizable Indian urban context. The men and women who people these plays are "real" to the audience that watches them; they "belong" firmly to the milieu in which they are being performed and the representations are equally located in a firm and local site.

The contention here is not that this is the only kind of theatre possible or desirable, but simply that perhaps it is time that our definitions of "national" or "post colonial" or "borrowed" or even "derivative" should and must change. Elsewhere I have described Dattani's *Clearing The Rubble* as a perfect postcolonial text for a variety of reasons, and perhaps, for those very reasons, it challenges us to re-consider our easy acceptance of the postcolonial status of our contemporary literature.

V

Clearing the Rubble, interestingly enough, was written as a radio play for the BBC, the year after an earthquake devastated Gujarat on 26th January 2001. The play was performed for the first time in Delhi in 2004, directed by Dattani himself. If we look at the plot of the play, it is simple enough. It opens with a British journalist, Jeffrey, on the Kutch Express, "going back" to Gujarat one year after the earthquake. The text then moves into the past in one of Dattani's well known chronological "flashbacks", and we hear/see/read of Jeffrey's first arrival in Gujarat and encounter the devastation that he sees as he walks to the village. Jeffrey becomes the via media, the bridge between us and the other characters that Jeffrey encounters, the state of bureaucracy as well as the attitudes to the devastation around him.

Jeffrey sees the villagers trying to clear the rubble of the village hospital but without a crane it is an impossible task. As the men walk away, a young boy calls out for them to not give up – the only person to respond to this call is Jeffrey. The young boy is Salim whose mother and sisters are also trapped under the rubble. Jeffrey, too, realises that the rubble cannot be cleared without a crane so he decides to bring a crane back from the nearest town. The villagers eager to accept Jeffrey's help, walk with him to the town of Bhuj where, as Jeffrey says,

> "It is quite a different picture that greets me. There are vans full of relief material everywhere. There is enough activity going on to show that all efforts are being made to rescue people or to rehabilitate displaced families. Or to simply offer food and clothing. We go to the Red Cross and I speak to a German woman in charge of the operations. ..."[13]

Jeffrey does, indeed, manage to get a crane along with other relief material and returns to rescue Salim's family who are still trapped under the rubble. The rescue operation is successful and Salim's mother is found sitting next to the dead bodies of her children.

The other voices in the play are Salim's, and his mother Fatima's. Fatima explains to her daughters Mumtaz and Saira why it was imperative that their desires be sacrificed in order to enable Salim to get an education, have better food and a more comfortable present since he was the only one who could assure them all a better future. Salim then goes back with Jeffrey to England, to help Jeffrey battle with the ghosts in his life, and eventually, as we have been told at the start of the play, both of them return to the village to set Fatima free from the ghosts of her children and to enable all – the dead and the living-to carry on.

Why do I think that this is the "perfect" postcolonial text? Apart from the obvious issues of language and setting, the text brings to light some of the problems of contemporary India. We are all trapped under the various layers of rubble which must be cleared one after another, for those crushed to be set free, to see the light of day and which, ironically enough, can only be seen clearly by an outsider, a "foreigner". These layers are issues of community, class, caste, gender and, of course, of race or, in more contemporary terms, of developed economies and not-so-developed economies. The devastation has occurred in India and the rescue work, the "reporting of human conditions" is being carried out by international organisations and foreign journalists. The older imbalances of power still operate, whether of class, caste, gender or even social status, together with the newer imbalances of the rural/urban divide and of the "globalised" First World against the "poor Third World".

Clearing the Rubble works at different levels and brings to light successive layers of the post-colonial paradigm – it is Jeffrey, the "foreigner", the white man, who is essential to get the crane to the village just as it takes the Red Cross team, headed by a German woman who "lends" them the truck with the crane. The Indian government official stops the truck and is the one who tries to frustrate the rescue operation. He backs off only when Jeffrey threatens him with international media coverage –

> 'I am a journalist and I am writing on the communal and caste based nature of your relief operations.' I continue to shoot him with my camera. 'Are you preventing equipment and supplies from reaching Muslim and Dalit populations?' I try to sound like Tim Sebastian in one of his attack modes. 'No. No! That is not true. We are a very tolerant people.' Suddenly he yells to some people to grab my camera.

The alliances delineated in the text are clear – human beings, whatever their colour or nationality, are on one side and against the "government" or state bodies. But by raising the communal or caste line obliquely, in an attempt to scare the official, the impact is not diminished – the same question had emerged in the minds of the reader when Jeffrey was the only one to respond to the young Salim's cries for help.

As the text approaches its climax, the secret is revealed – Salim is no longer alive. He had died in the earthquake and was buried with his sisters under the rubble of the hospital. It was his debt to his mother and sisters that wouldn't allow Salim to leave the land of the living. He needed to have earned his existence, to have lived, before he could allow himself to die. His life had to be worth something, even if that something was the official compensation from the government to his mother, in recognition of the fact that she had three children and that all of them had died.

Thus, the relationship between Jeffrey and Salim is not unequal – Salim needs Jeffrey to help him settle the debts of his lifetime, to resolve the issues of the living in Salim's family, while Jeffrey needs the young boy/ghost to help him settle his own demons, to overcome his inability to communicate with the living by communicating with the dead.

The older relationship of servitude or enslavement or exploitation is thus side-stepped (within the text) by one of mutual need or dependency. The Red Cross vehicles are the mediums of relief and help, transcending barriers of nationality and obstructed by local bureaucracy and red tape at best, and communal and caste biases at worst. Jeffrey, as the contemporary "white man", becomes "part" of the village community on equal terms, through an act which only he, as a white man, could have committed. "We men did succeed in saving our village. We men of the village. I helped save the village. I am a man."

Being accepted as part of the village community, participating in the rescue operations, Jeffrey manages to transcend the barriers of "otherness" which had marked him out as an outsider in the beginning.

When Jeffrey first arrived in Gujarat, he is completely the alien figure, the outsider, the familiar "foreign visitor". As the local village headman attempts to strike up a conversation with Jeffrey we, the educated urban audience, recognise the familiarity with which the head man approaches Jeffrey even as we recognise (and legitimise) the discomfort with which Jeffrey relates to this familiarity.

> A man on the bus asks me why I am not with the official rescue workers all around Bhuj, the epicentre of the earthquake. I reply that I am not a rescue worker. I am a journalist. He replies. Did you come all the way from England to write about us? But why? He persists. I tell him that it means a lot to me, to write about the condition of humanity in other parts of the world. He asks me whether I am married and have children. I say no. He looks at me with sympathy as if he had got an answer to his first question…

Jeffrey literally remains on the outskirts of the village before he makes contact with Salim, and somehow, in his strangeness, in his unfamiliarity with the space and the people, and because he is the via media, as I have already said, this alienation of Jeffrey reinforces and underlines the urban audience/reader's own "strangeness" vis-à-vis the village in Gujarat.

VI

On the theme of postcolonialism Ania Loomba in her book *Colonialism/ Postcolonialism*, writes: "Food, objects or clothes (and perhaps ideas) from my part of the world become 'ethnic' in Europe or North America; within India, 'ethnic' applies to the cultures and objects of tribal or rural folk, especially when they are displayed in trendy markets."[14] It is this experience, the disconnection between rural and urban India that allows, and in fact enables, an urban Indian audience watching the play being performed in a Delhi theatre to so easily allow Jeffrey, the "colonial" figure in the play, to become the one character they can identity with. Years ago, when Vijay Tendulkar wrote *Ghashiram Kotwal*, there was a shadowy figure of a white man hovering on the fringes of the action. This figure clearly represented the colonial powers and their interest in the corruption and decadence of the Indian state at the time as it provided them the opportunity to step in and appropriate power for themselves. Today, in Dattani's play, the white man steps onto centre stage and rather than being hostile or antagonistic, is presented in a mutually dependant relationship with the other characters. What, then, is postcolonialism? Is it that we are finally overcoming the unequal relationship, or is this a different discourse of a new kind of complicity with a neo-imperial structure?

Looking at older texts, texts such as *Tughlaq, Nagamandala* and *Ghashiram Kotwal,* it becomes easier to trace the differences in outlook or perspective. Perhaps the anxiety of Indianness expressed in older literature is being slowly replaced by more confident or more comfortable subjectivity. The question that remains however is: does the new comfort zone of literature in English in India still remain trapped within similar paradigms of inequality and neo-imperialism?

If it is possible to see *Tughlaq*, as a text which interrogates the past (whether pre or post colonial) and, simultaneously evokes more general political and social issues pertaining to our current situation as subjects in a post colonial (in the temporal and ideological sense), milieu, then why is it not possible to see Dattani's plays about gay and eunuch identities, men who want to dance and women who don't want to raise families, as equally Indian, interrogating contemporary power imbalances and hierarchies? Does the language issue emerge again in an understanding or approach towards this play originally written in English, vis-à-vis a play "translated" into English?

When, in an interview, Dattani was asked if his film, *Morning Raaga,* had missed being the official Government of India entry to the 2005 Oscars on account of its language (English), his reply was that he thought the language was an excuse, that more Indians spoke English than the British and that the film was "Indian" in every sense of the term. Further, he was asked whether Aparna Sen's *36, Chowringhee Lane* (which was also in English) and had been selected as the official entry was somehow "more Indian" than *Morning Raaga.*[15] The question may be an ironical one, but the crucial point here is that somehow, in almost every seminar, every forum, every interview, Dattani, has invariably faced the language/identity question. He is constantly being put in the position of having to defend/justify his choice of language and to reconcile it with being "Indian".

There are several interesting questions that arise from this position. One, of course, is that somehow it is mostly playwrights/film makers who are asked to defend their choice of English as a medium of creative expression. Novelists, and even poets, are no longer asked to show evidence of their patriotism on account of writing in English. Is it the overt performativity of the theatrical or cinematic medium that makes us uncomfortable about the space English occupies in our lives as urban Indians? Despite the fact that most people who watch English language Indian made plays or films are quite comfortable with the use of English in different registers and discourses in their everyday personal and professional lives, somehow, the use of English as a "reflection" of life seems to make audiences a little uncomfortable. The other point is: will we ever be able to look at/study/judge/discuss Indian theatre in English as simply "Indian theatre"? Perhaps the same colonial cringe that made earlier generation identify Karnad and Tendulkar as unquestionably Indian because they used "folk" forms, "indigenous" dramatic devices and were "originally" written in "Indian" languages is at work here, defining Dattani as "less Indian" because of the fact that Roopa or Salim or Latha speak in English and because his plays are written for the context they are produced in – the proscenium stage in an Indian city.

VII

Girish Karnad's new play, *A Heap of Broken Images* opened in Bangalore on 22 March 2005. Hailed by both audiences and critics, this play attracted a great deal of attention for several reasons, including the "extra-textual" facts that it was a new play by Karnad after many years and that this particular production was directed by Karnad himself. It was also premiered in two versions – the Kannada version and the English one. One of the interesting points made by a review of the play in the newspaper *Deccan Herald* was that "Technology [was] playing such a major role for the first time in Kannada theatre, as a character."[16] Interesting, because this comment was made specifically in the context of the Kannada version of the play, although both language versions were being reviewed in the article.

Apart from the "technology" aspect of the play, where the television or digitized image of the writer/protagonist becomes the "Other"; in effect, his double and acquires a life and identity of its own, the sub text of the play focuses on the divide between the regional languages of India and English. One of the most important issues in the play revolves around the main protagonist, a woman who has written a very successful novel in English, marking a departure from her earlier creative work which was in Kannada. She is now attacked and castigated as a "sell-out" by her friends who continue to write in Kannada. For those who thought the language issue was by now settled, here it surfaces again. Many writers feel that the unequal divide between the payment received for creative work in English and other Indian languages is partly responsible for the bitterness. If the issue at stake is largely economic, then the terms of the argument have certainly changed. The charges made against those who write in English, however remain the same – they are seen as a "sell-out", because it is assumed that it is impossible to express one's thoughts in a language not one's own.

But is the language truly not our own? One of the main arguments of N'gugi' wa Thiong'o's path breaking argument in *Decolonising the Mind* centers around the issue of language and the cultural worlds it offers access to; what it privileges and what it marginalises or disempowers.[17] By speaking/reading/writing/expressing ourselves in English, are we still betraying or colouring our "Indian" identities? Or, to over turn the argument, have we managed to Indianise English enough to twist it, to mould it to our own realities, or have we moulded our realities to fit into English?

VIII

We can now return to the question of the difference between the white protagonist of Dattani's *Clearing the Rubble* and Tendulkar's white man in *Ghashiram Kotwal.* Is to ignore the language politics to be complicit with a neo-imperialism? At the root of the debate lies the issue of language – is English a functional skill, one which we, in urban India can and should exploit to gain and maintain our ascendancy in the global Mcworld today, or is it more than that? Is it possible or desirable to separate English from its colonial past and elitist present in this country? As Leela Gandhi points out is writing a way of political liberation, a path towards rewriting political positions or a way of side stepping politics? Is it "more" liberating to see the text in its own or in its present context? The next question that follows is, what is that context for an English text written by an Indian?

In our society today, English is seen as the passport to a well paying job and to a role on the global stage. It is seen as "empowering" young Indians in the realms of business outsourcing, information technology, and so on and so forth. We have all heard these arguments many times before, and no doubt shall continue to hear them in the future. As Gurcharan Das puts it, perhaps on behalf of those who espouse this side of the debate, "At the root of the dispute is ownership of the English language. Today's confident young Indians view English as a functional skill, not unlike Windows or learning to write an invoice. When they speak English, they feel they own it – it's another Indian language…"[18]

The question that comes up, then, is: is it possible (or desirable) to view a language as a "functional skill", thus completely erasing the historical and political structures that remain implicated in the choice of using that particular skill? Can we disassociate the English learnt or practised for call centres jobs and Pizza Huts from the English used all around us, in our daily lives, administrative, official and academic? And then, can we separate the so called "post colonial" question of language from the literary texts that are written in an allegedly postcolonial language?

This is not an easy question to answer, or even perhaps frame honestly. The fact that for some of us English remains the language we think in and express ourselves in, both intellectually as well as emotionally, is sometimes a matter of embarrassment and sometimes not. Perhaps the time has come when we can truly think of doing away with colonialism – the "post" included. If we are to forge our own identities, make the break with the markers of colonialism, temporal, ideological and intellectual, we should face it as one more event in the history of our political and social space, in the framing of our lives. There can be no further apologies or reversals.

Perhaps it is time to get "past the post" as the title of a seminar held in Delhi University recently declared, or rather asked. Whether it is Dattani or Karnad or Tendulkar or even a young film maker who decides to make a *My Brother Nikhil* or a *Being Cyrus* – they are creativity expressing the experience of Indians, rooted and located in a specific socio-politcal-cultural context. Let us look at these texts as simply texts by Indians, about their experience of being Indian, without bringing in degrees or qualities of what defines "Indian", who or what is "more" or "less" Indian. Whatever language we use, the accents and thoughts should be ours – without justifiers and without qualifiers.

Notes

1 Nandi Bhatia, *Acts of Authority/Acts of Resistance – Theatre and Politics in Colonial and Postcolonial India*, New Delhi, Oxford University Press, 2004, p. 3.

2 Ellen Shohat, *Notes on the "Post-Colonial". Social Text,* No. 31/32, *Third World and Post-Colonial Issues.* (1992), pp. 99-113. *http://links.jstor.org/sici?sici=01642472%281992%290%3A31%2F32%3C99%3ANOT%22%3E2.0.CO%3B2-E*

3 Ania Loomba, *Colonialism/Postcolonialism*, London: Routledge, 1998, p. 7.

4 Ellen Shohat, Ibid., p. 103.

5 Samik Bandyopadhyay, "Introduction", *Ghashiram Kotwal*, Vijay Tendulkar, [trans.] Jayant Karve and Eleanor Zelliot, Calcutta: Seagull Books, 1999, p. 3.

6 Angelie Multani, "Off-Centre: The Displacement of Women Characters in *Ghashiram Kotwal* and *Tara*" in *Muffled Voices: Women in Modern Indian Theatre*, Lakshmi Subramanyam, ed. (New Delhi: Har- Anand Publications, 2002).

7 Aparna Bhargava Dharwadker, *Theatres of Independence : Drama, Theory and Urban Performance in India since 1947,* New Delhi: Oxford University Press, 2005. pp. 144-5.

8 Rustom Bharucha, *Theatre and The World – Essays on Performance and the Politics of Culture*, New Delhi: Manohar Publications, 1990, p.250 and p. 261.

9 Vijay Tendulkar, *Ghashiram Kotwal*, Ibid., pp. 12-13.

10 Dharwadker, pp. 250-251.

11 Vanashree Tripathi, "Introduction", *Three Plays of Girish Karnad – A Study in Poetics and Culture* New Delhi:Prestige Books, 2004, p. 7.

12 Ibid., p. 10.

13 Mahesh Dattani, *Clearing the Rubble* . All quotations are from an unpublished text version of the play provided by Dattani.

14 Loomba, Ibid., p. xiii.

15 http://123india.santabanta.com/cinema.asp?pid=9193, accessed on 19/04/2006.

16 http://www.deccanherald.com/deccanherald/mar272005/ac1.asp

17 *Decolonising the Mind: The Politics of Language in African Literature*, London: James Currey, Nairobi; Heinemann Kenya, New Hampshire: Heinemann, 1986.

18 Gurcharan Das, "Cyber Coolies or Cyber Sahibs?" *The Times of India*, Sept. 7, 2003.

Charan's death in *Charandas chor*, directed by Habib Tanvir Photo: Courtesy Jana Natya Manch and Sudhanva Deshpande.

Habib Tanvir in *Charandas chor*
Photo: Courtesy Jana Natya Manch.

Rehearsal of *Dakghar*, Directed by Kanhailal. Photo by Jadumani Singh
Courtesy Kanhailal.

Habib Tanvir rehearses in *Zaharili Hawa*
Photo: Courtesy Jana Natya Manch.

Rehearsal of the Opening Scene of Tripurari Sharma's *Teen Betiyan* with basic sets.In the centre is Asha, well known Nautanki actor and Gulab Bai's daughter. Photo: Courtesy Alarippu.

A Scene from Muthusami's *Prahaladha Charithram*
Photo: Courtesy Koothu-p-Pattarai.

Sabitri in *Dakghar*, Directed by Kanhailal.
Photo by Pranab Basu Courtesy Kanhailal.

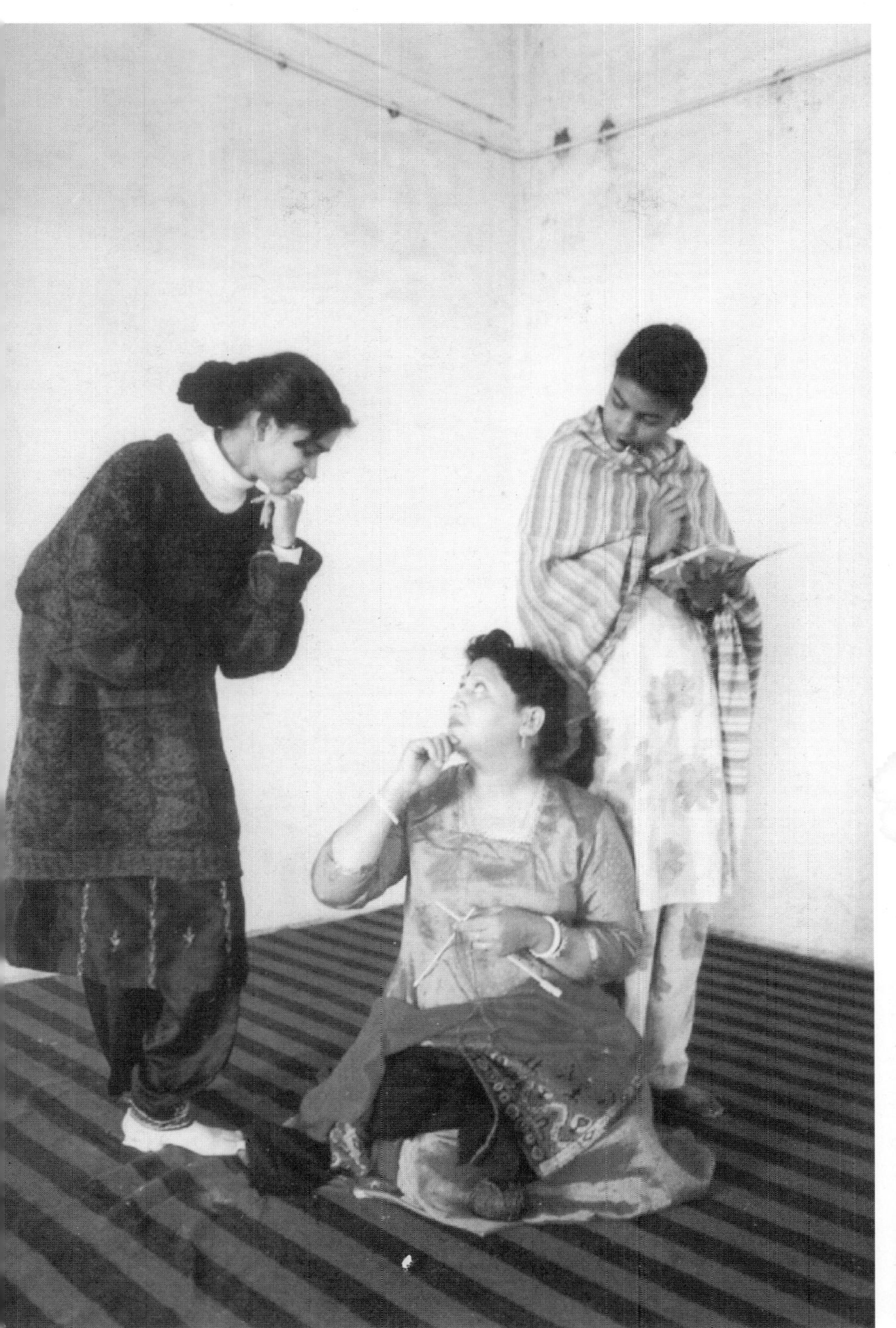

Rehearsal process of Tripurari Sharma's *Teen Betiyan* at Kanpur.
Photo: Courtesy Alarippu.

Rehearsal process of Tripurari Sharma's *Teen Betiyan* at Kanpur .
Photo: Courtesy Alarippu.

Jana Natya Manch performs *Samrath Ko Nahi Dosh Gosain*, early 1980s. Photo: courtesy Jana Natya Manch.

a Natya Manch performs *Samrath Ko Nahi Dosh Gosain*, Guwahati, early 1980s. Photo:Courtesy Jana Natya Manch.

दा ग्रेट गुलाब थियेट्रिकल कं0 की प्रस्तुत

प्रसिद्ध कानपुरी शैली में नौटंकी

दहलीज़ के पार

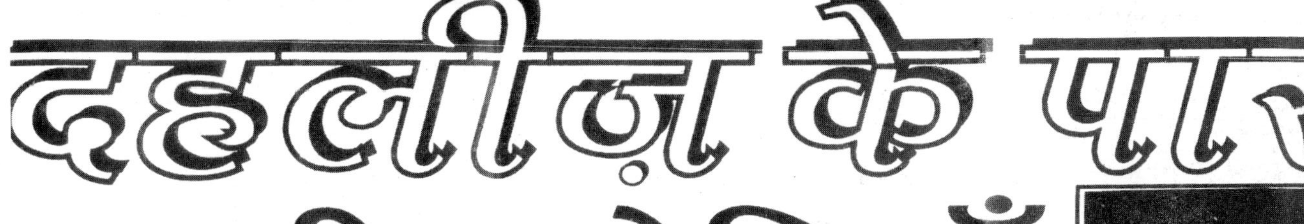

उर्फ तीन बेटियाँ

आलेख
त्रिपुरारी शर्मा

नौटंकीकरण
सिद्धेश्वर अवस्थी

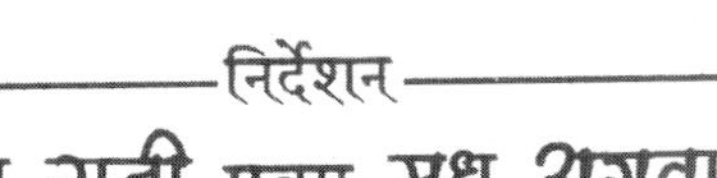

सहयोग : भँवर गोपाल

निर्देशन
आशा रानी एवम् मधु अग्रवाल

सौजन्य से – "अलारिप्पू", नई दिल्ल

8
Karnad, *Tughlaq*

GJV Prasad

Girish Karnad is perhaps the best living playwright in India; he definitely is the best in English, different from and having a more varied oeuvre than the distinguished Mahesh Dattani. I know that considering Karnad an Indian English playwright may sound a trifle controversial, but I am not judging his capability in Kannada here, only saying that since he "translates" his plays into English himself, self-avowedly re-writing and taking some of the changes back into Kannada, it seems to me best to look at his plays in English as originally written in English (his last few plays *are* written originally in English). In any case Karnad's original ambition was to write poetry in English. Hence, it is of interest to see how and why he came to write in Kannada instead.

There is nothing "natural" in a postcolonial situation like ours about language choice, especially for creative writing. Karnad was born in a Konkani speaking family in Marathi speaking Maharashtra (which too he learnt to speak and read). He grew up in Karnataka, where he learnt Kannada but has always spoken English in familial situations. So what was it that impelled Karnad to write plays in Kannada rather than (poetry) in English? There are a number of reasons for this. First, Karnad was used to theatre, having watched plays and performances from an early age. Secondly, he wrote his first play, *Yayati* (1961), on the eve of his first voyage out of India, to England, almost in reaction to the pressure he was under from his family to come back even before he had left, and thus discovered his creative roots in Indian mythology. The success of this play led to further dramatic writing. He also continued with plays because this was the right moment for it. India was being seriously written on to the stage with state patronage, during this decade and the beginning of the next.

Like Karnad, other playwrights too looked to the past because of the need to create a modern nation out of a sense of the history that informed the nation in terms of cultural continuity. Contemporary dramatists had discovered that there was a past waiting to be mined, to form the foundation of a new India, a literary and cultural past that could be used to enact, construct, and represent the modern. The mythic and the folk (along with the historical) would be used in the performance of modern India for quite a while by Karnad and his contemporaries. Thus, even if it was the success of *Yayati* that kept him in theatre and brought him back to India, he knew he had to come back to India because he and his craft had a past here, and the present had to be created here as well – Indian narratives had to be explored within reinvented western structures. (If he had taken avatar as a novelist two decades later, he could have stayed on wherever he was in the western world and continued to write India in English!) You could say that India had to be born into the world or that the western stage had to be ethnicised. It is because of this *raison d'être*, the ethnicisation of western dramatic structures in India to stage the modern nation, that these playwrights had to write in Indian languages, stake their claim in their Indian language theatre, not in English, even if, like Karnad, they were completely at home in the latter. Ethnicity ruled in their world, and they constituted the festival of India, for consumption both in and outside the country

Suffice it to say that at a particular historical moment Karnad was among a clutch of playwrights and theatre practitioners who fashioned modern Indian drama, staging the Indian nation in the nineteen sixties and seventies. As Karnad himself said on the occasion of his being conferred the Jnanpith award in 1999, "I see a legacy of my generation... I am happy to belong to a generation that had a Dharmaveer Bharti, a Mohan Rakesh, a Vijay Tendulkar and I. Together we can claim that we did create a national theatre for modern India."[1] Obviously, these playwrights would be translated into various Indian languages and would use similar techniques, and have similar concerns during that period, and write and be read in relationship to each other, as playwrights of the nation.

But it was not his first play, *Yayati*, which made Karnad the iconic playwright of the times; it was *Tughlaq* (1964) that made him a force to reckon with in Indian theatre. A play that expressed the sense of disillusionment of a whole generation at the end of the Nehruvian era, *Tughlaq* has the capacity to be read and enacted at any moment in our history, seemingly interacting with our changing times at all times. No one who was in Delhi at that time and witnessed the production can forget the staging of *Tughlaq* (as of *Razia Sultan*) at Purana Qila in 1974. Having watched different productions of *Tughlaq* at different times, I can vouch for the extraordinary impact of the play and the way in which it seems to address contemporary issues. A play about Nehru was already a play about Indira Gandhi when I watched it for the first time, and soon became a play about the Emergency and then about the loss of all faith in political figures and institutions. A historical play about history-making, *Tughlaq* will be read and performed for decades to come. Even if he had written no other play, Karnad would have made a name for himself in Indian theatre.

Tughlaq had its genesis in England, where Karnad did all his research for the play. Just as Bankim Chandra Chatterjee, who said that Bengal had no history and set about creating a history of Hindu valour Karnad, in reaction to a statement by Kirtinath Kurtkoti that Kannada theatre had "only costume plays and no historical plays ... which could appeal to modern sensibilities"[2] set about reading history books and found the delightful Muhammad bin Tughlaq in an elementary school text book. Karnad was perhaps looking for a Muslim king to write about since he felt that while Hindus treated history as myth it "was used as a positive concept to analyse life and society by the Muslim historians."[3] We now distrust the "science" of historiography and believe in the narrative nature of all history writing. However, there are certain facts that all historians agree upon: That Muhammad bin Tughlaq existed, that he ruled between 1325 and 1351, that he may have murdered his father and brother, and that he changed the capital of his kingdom from Delhi to Daulatabad. It is also well documented that he introduced copper currency, and that he tried to create laws that were equitable to all citizens regardless of their religion. The creative reading and writing is in what is made of these facts, how we read the times and how we read the character. It is here that Karnad intervenes, otherwise sticking closely to the history written by Ziauddin Barani, who was at Tughlaq's court and was privy to all that went on. Barani is a character in the play, a seemingly naïve observer and an Islamic historian who is a humanist and cannot accept the inherent violence of human beings or the inherent cynicism of statecraft. While Barani's history is critical of Muhammad bin Tughlaq, Karnad isn't necessarily so.

UR Ananthamurthy however, feels that "Although the theme of the play is from history – there are many such plays in Kannada – Karnad's theme is not historical."[4] Both the qualifications are interesting for us

– that there are many such plays in Kannada and that the theme is not historical. Ananthamurthy means that the play shows the "inner drama of Tughlaq" and hence is not strictly historical. He doesn't give us instances of the many plays from history, so we have to take his word for it. As we have seen, Karnad has gone on record to state that he was told that there were no good history plays in Kannada, which is why he wrote *Tughlaq*. Obviously, Karnad was interested in the story of Tughlaq not just because the Sultan's life and times tell us significant facts about the early Muslim period in India, though it does that as well, but because he found some echoes of contemporary issues in this ancient piece of history.

Karnad's comments on Tughlaq are worth noting:

> What struck me absolutely about Tughlaq's history was that it was contemporary. The fact that here was the most idealistic, the most intelligent king ever to come on the throne of Delhi … and one of the greatest failures also. And within a span of twenty years this tremendously capable man had gone to pieces. This seemed to be both due to his idealism as well as the shortcomings within him, such as his impatience, his cruelty, his feeling that he had the only correct answer. And I felt in the early sixties India had also come very far in the same direction – the twenty-year period seemed to me very much a striking parallel.[5]

The historical play was always meant to be the study of the protagonist because it was in his idealism and his failures that the course of history was to be charted. As Karnad says elsewhere, the play "reflected the slow disillusionment my generation felt with the new politics of independent India: the gradual erosion of … ethical norms… and the coming to terms with cynicism and realpolitik."[6]

The parallels are evident from the first lines of the play, which is set in 1327 Delhi, two years after Tughlaq's accession to the throne. Of course there have always been people in all ages who have lamented, "God what's the country coming to!" What I am pointing to is the changing nature of leadership – the king "isn't afraid to be human". Here is a king who wants to lead from the front but by asserting his oneness with the people, subject to the same laws that they are (which may seem to be quite an alien concept to our democratic politicians now!), a democratic despot! However, unlike Nehru, he is a religious person, one who prays five times a day and has decreed that his Islamic subjects do so as well or face punishment:

> Young Man: … Now you pray five times a day because that is the law and if you break it, you'll have the officers on your neck. Can you mention one earlier Sultan in whose time people read the Koran in the streets like now? Just one?[7]

Thus, Tughlaq ensures religiosity through fear – this dialogue immediately signalling that he presides over a kingdom that can only be a sham of a moral state, a distortion of the ideal of Ram-Rajya, which Gandhi envisioned for independent India. The Sultan also has the task of keeping the Hindus happy and loyal, and has discontinued the jizia, the religious tax that the Hindus had to pay. This arouses the anger of his Muslim subjects as well as the suspicion of the Hindus – secularism in this deeply religious and religiously divided country is an alien and threatening concept. Having established all this within minutes, Karnad shows us the Sultan's laws in action. A Hindu brahmin has just won a case against Tughlaq, who is ultimately responsible for the actions of his officers, for the illegal seizure of his lands. While the Kazi orders that Vishnu Prasad, the brahmin, should receive five hundred silver dinars in compensation, Tughlaq goes further and offers him a post in the civil service as well. This is a public gesture to accommodate and win over the Hindus but is again received with suspicion by the Hindu on stage and with alarm by the old Muslim. Tughlaq's soon professed aim is to create a secular kingdom that will work "towards greater justice, equality, progress and peace..." (7). All these are good aims, the aims in fact of the modern Indian state, but how are they to be achieved in an era of deep divides and suspicion, an era of cynical manipulation of the very processes that are set in motion to achieve the vision and ambition of the ruler and the state, a manipulation that is being enacted in the course of this very case, the brahmin being actually a Muslim dhobi in disguise?

What is immediately apparent is that Karnad wants to take Tughlaq seriously, as some one who genuinely desires an equitable and just state, but who is unwilling to take the time or make the effort to convince his subjects about the viability or even the desirability of his aims. This is underscored in the first scene itself when Tughlaq, having commented on the recent judgement in favour of the Brahmin and established himself as a model king who does what he says for the benefit of all his subjects, declares that he is shifting the capital from Delhi to Daulatabad. He does give logical reasons for the shift – from Daulatabad lying at the heart of his expanded kingdom, to the vulnerability of Delhi due to its proximity to the border, to the need to strengthening the bonds between Hindus and Muslims by moving his capital to a Hindu city – but he is not really bothered about whether the inhabitants of Delhi understand or appreciate his decision. Though he invites them all to accompany him to Daulatabad, assuring them that it is not an order, and asking only those with faith in him to make the shift, it is clear that he is asking for personal loyalty rather than a consensus or the acceptance of the rationality of his decision. As the

Old Man says immediately, "You can go to the Kazi-i-Mumalik for small offences. But who do you appeal to against such madness?" (8). This should have jogged the memory of the audience reminding them that Muhammad bin Tughlaq was also known as Muhammad the Mad.

But there was a method in his madness. As the ensuing dialogue shows, people suspect that Muhammad had his father and brother killed in what was made to seem like an accident. Tughlaq has many enemies, including Sheikh Imam-ud-din who preaches against him, accusing him of murder to capture the throne, and who seems to be leading a popular revolt against him. Tughlaq's kingdom doesn't seem to be holding well, with his very legitimacy to occupy the throne in doubt, but the end of the scene demonstrates a greater problem – Tughlaq himself is sowing the seeds for the hollowing of his vision, for the exploitation of the legal processes he is so proud of, by his eagerness to seem just and equitable to all subjects regardless of their religious affiliations, by simply not carrying out background checks! The brahmin who wins the case against him turns out to be a trickster, Aziz, a Muslim dhobi who realised that there was money to be made here. He and Aazam, a petty pickpocket, will now embark on a career of subversion, preying on every vision of the Sultan's and they are fit to do so. As Aziz says in his disguise as a brahmin when he offers a job to Aazam: "You know a Brahmin and a Muslim friend – the Sultan will like that" (12). The vision of a secular state is to be cast in the (false) coin of (false) tokenism.

This is seen as the essential weakness in Tughlaq. The fact that, visionary though he is, cultured though he is (he solves complex chess problems, knows his philosophy and poetry), he wants to enforce his dreams and schemes as quickly as possible, trying to convince his people through his actions that show his personal commitment to his projects. This need to display his commitment fully leads to his vulnerability to exploitation. Also, soon he would expect a similar commitment from his subjects, meeting out the cruelest of punishments in order to exact it. He may be an idealist, but he is shown to be always aware of realpolitik (and hence the chess – he thinks moves ahead of other people). He is also aware that he has the chance to make history , that he has a tryst with destiny and is impatient of all obstacles that seem to thwart the possibility of that appointment. But he has more than enough problems. While the Sheikh is stirring up trouble within his kingdom, his erstwhile friend, the Ain-ul-Mulk, is marching on Delhi with an army much larger than what the Sultan can hope to raise. Also, he is in Delhi where the Amirs are deeply suspicious of him. Almost every one seems to accept that he murdered his father and brother and that too during the time for prayer. And there is a deep divide not only between Hindus and Muslims, but also between "pure" Muslims and those who have converted recently from Hinduism – Barani's suspicions of Najib are an example of this divide. This is one reason the "real" Tughlaq liked to surround himself with courtiers of West Asian origin, including the famous Ibn Batuta (who doesn't appear in this play), and why Tughlaq, in the play, looks for endorsement from Ghiyas-ud-din Abbasid, a descendant of the Khalif.

However, if Tughlaq looks to be the master of intrigues, he needs to be. Apart from others, his step-mother is shown, by the end of the second scene, to be very interested in matters of court and state and quite confident of her ability to manipulate matters. She has no liking for the Vizier, Najib, and serves notice to Barani (who is shown to be pious and on the side of the forces of Islam but naïve in matters of statecraft) that she will take care of Najib if she can't counter his influence on Tughlaq: "If he goes on like this, I won't wish his fate even on a dog!" (23). She will try to win over both Barani and Shihab-ud-din, a prince who takes care of Delhi during the Sultan's absence. Her aim seems to be to have complete influence over Tughlaq, to ensure that he listens to her only and is not influenced by any one else, so that she can rule the kingdom through him. This will lead ultimately to her death, when she over reaches herself in her quest for power over Tughlaq.

It is apparent that death is what awaits all those who oppose or act against the wishes of Tughlaq. A loaded remark by Najib that Sheikh Imam-ud-din resembles Tughlaq leads to the elaborate stratagem that results in the death of the Sheikh. First, the Sheikh is asked to address the people of Delhi, after evening prayers, to analyse Tughlaq's administration and to show where all he has gone wrong. It is said that Tughlaq will be present at the assembly to receive the Sheik's advice. When no one turns up for the assembly, the Sheikh is convinced by Tughlaq that he stands compromised in the eyes of the public. Tughlaq tells Imam-ud-din: "… they suspect you now. The moment they heard that I, the Sultan, was organizing a meeting in which you, my severest critic, was going to speak – they became suspicious. Why should the Sultan sponsor his worst critic? They have suspected a trap. And wisely they have stayed away" (28). Actually, the trap is being laid now but Imam-ud-din, though suspicious, cannot even begin to guess how and why he is being manipulated, nor can the audience.

However, there is an important exchange, a debate between the Sultan and the Sheikh before this happens. Imam-ud-din castigates Tughlaq for not being a good Islamic ruler. When Tughlaq claims that he has not gone against the tenets of Islam consciously, the Sheikh tells him that instead of seeking directions he had imprisoned the Sayyids and the Ulema. Muhammad's essential argument is on the need to separate religion from politics, from matters of state. He says that the state has to be secular, his "kingdom has millions – Muslims, Hindus, Jains" (26). He doesn't believe that one should subsume oneself to just one view of life and that to be holistic one cannot ignore philosophers or poets or wisdom from other creeds and times. He cannot deny the validity of other visions. He tells the Sheikh: "You are asking me to make myself complete by killing the Greek in me and you propose to unify my people by denying the visions which led Zarathustra or the Buddha" (27). Hence, even though he is religious, Muhammad bin Tughlaq wants to create a secular state (one that will have respect for all religions and not one that has no use for religions – a typical Indian definition of secularism), that will ensure equality and justice to all his subjects even if it is at the point of the sword and threats of imprisonment. It has to be so, since all his subjects are like cattle and he can hope to convince only a few of them!

In Scene IV we realise why the resemblance between Imam-ud-din and Tughlaq was so crucial. Tughlaq's stratagem to use the resemblance to have the Sheikh killed by the Ain-ul-Mulk is revealed by Sardar Ratansingh, the adopted brother of Shihab-ud-din, the Prince of Sampanshahr, who has been asked to take care of the affairs of the state in the absence of the Sultan (notice the Hindu-Muslim pairing paralleling the sham pairing of Aziz and Aazam; also the prince has been asked to step in order to propitiate his father and also because the Sultan doesn't trust any one in Delhi). Ratansingh tells Shihab-ud-din that the Sultan hadn't been too happy to see him and had therefore placed him in the front rank of the platoon that accompanied the Sheikh to his death. While the overall strategy works brilliantly and the Ain-ul-Mulk's army, thinking that the Sultan is dead, pursues the fleeing platoon right into the trap laid by Tughlaq and is massacred, Ratansingh himself lives to tell the tale. He has now been invited to join a conspiracy against the Sultan by the nobles of Delhi.

We see the conspirators in Scene V. As usual, there is a holy man amongst them who wants to save Islam. Sheikh Shams-ud-din is the one who actually persuades Shihab-ud-din to join the conspiracy. It is revealed here that no one in Delhi had attended Imam-ud-din's assembly because Tughlaq had ordered his soldiers to make sure everyone stayed home! However, if Shihab-ud-din is shown as a man with a conscience, a bit naïve and idealistic, Shams-ud-din is seen as the typical religious person who wants to dabble in realpolitik without getting his hands dirty. He cannot agree to the assassination attempt taking place at prayer time (an idea put forward by the Hindu Ratansingh, but then the Sultan too is said to have had his father and brother murdered during prayer). The vested interests of the Amirs of Delhi and of the Muslim priests is seen to coincide and they both need the removal of the Sultan who is weakening their power. The priests may be holier than others but they too want power, the power to enforce their vision of the world on others.

The actual attempt on Tughlaq's life is presented in scene vi where Tughlaq makes two announcements – the first being that he has invited a descendant of the last Khalif, Abbasid Ghiyas-ud-din Muhammad, to visit the new capital of Daulatabad. This visit, the Sultan feels, would give his rule the legitimacy it seems to lack in the eyes of many. He also announces the introduction of copper coins in his kingdom. Even as we listen to the exchanges between the characters, even as we think how farsighted Tughlaq was to introduce copper currency and how right he was to say that paper currency and copper coins will work if the people trust the state, in this case, if they trusted him, we are aware of the passage of time, of the clock ticking towards prayer time when the conspirators would be able to murder him. However, it becomes apparent that the Sultan is leading all of us on: he is aware of the conspiracy and has a simple strategy to crush it without acting against Islamic religious principles – he has a posse of Hindu soldiers hidden behind the throne. The rebels are defeated easily and we have one more treachery to contend with – the rebels have been betrayed by the very man who gave them the plan, Ratansingh. This is his revenge for the death of his father at the hands of Shihab-ud-din's father. There is no getting away from the ever quickening cycle of death in this world.

As Tughlaq and Najib plan how to clean up the mess, Tughlaq takes a major step towards tyranny by ordering the evacuation of Delhi. The play portrays this as the moment of complete change in Tughlaq when he goes against everything he has seemingly lived by so far. He says;

> … What hopes I had built up when I came to the throne! I had wanted every act in my kingdom to become a prayer, every prayer to become a further step in knowledge, every step to lead us nearer to God. But our prayers too are riddled with disease and must be exiled. There will be no more praying in the kingdom, Najib. Anyone caught praying will be severely punished. Henceforth, let the moment of prayer walk my streets in silence and leave without a trace. (53)

Najib's intervention leads to the decree being changed so that prayers are banned till the arrival of Ghiyas-ud-din Abbasid. The "beautiful little paradox" that Najib sets up here is actually the fruit of the initial paradox that Tughlaq has conjured up for Muslim rule – how to rule a Hindu majority kingdom with justice and equity, how to treat all subjects as equal and give them equality of opportunity in the eyes of the law, while remaining a pious Muslim ruler. The basic question, then, is how to negotiate between personal religion and public secularism, even while the "personal" religion is visible and well displayed in the public space – a crucial question for post-Independence India.

Scene VII shows us how the people are exploited on their forced march to Daulatabad. We are told about people dying on the way and we see Aazam and Aziz lording it over the populace. The man who comes in with a large family is a Kafir, one who guards "the dead bodies in the palace yard – those executed by the Sultan you know" (58). We are made to understand that the chaos and the misery that we see on the road are the result of a truly cruel streak in Tughlaq – a streak we have seen in action in Scene VI. Moreover, Scene VII shows us now that other grand scheme of Tughlaq's has been sabotaged – the use of copper coins. Aziz and scores of others have already spotted the weak point – since the Sultan was bound to honour the stated value of the coins all they had to do was to make counterfeit coins and exchange them for silver dinars.

We see Tughlaq next in Scene VIII, which is set in 1832, five years after the first scene, four years after the capital has been moved to Daulatabad. We see a Tughlaq who is besieged from all sides, one who reacts with increasing violence to all offences. Barani tells him that though he is fit for the company of learned men, he was living "in the market of corpses" (66). One more corpse will be added to this by the end of the scene – that of the Vizier, Najib. It is in this scene that Tughlaq admits that he and the state are one – the sick kingdom, "racked by fever and crazed by the fear of the enveloping vultures" (66), can't be separated from him. His dilemma is that to give up his course of action is to admit that his vision had been wrong all along. There is no escape from the path that he has chosen to tread. In fact, this path has led him into a labyrinth from which he cannot find the exit, where each turn leads to a more horrific dead end. Najib has been killed by Tughlaq's step mother, as she confesses in the almost climactic Scene X. It is in this scene that Tughlaq also accepts that he killed his father and brother. It seems almost as if Tughlaq and his step mother share an intimate relationship and in rebelling against him by killing Najib, she has broken her vows – is almost an adulteress. Tughlaq first says that he had only three friends in the world – Najib, Barani, and the step mother. Then he says, "I love you more than I have loved anyone in my life" (79). After ordering her to be stoned to death like an adulteress, Tughlaq falls to his knees to give voice to a heart- rending prayer to God:

> God, God in Heaven, please help me, Please, don't let go of my hand. My skin drips with blood and I don't know how much of it is mine and how much of others. I started in Your path, Lord, why am I wandering naked in this desert now? I started in search of You. Why am I become a pig rolling in this gory mud? Raise me. Clean me. Cover me with Your Infinite Mercy. I can only clutch at the hem of Your cloak with my bloody fingers and plead. I can only beg have pity on me. I have no one but You now. Only You. Only You… You….You… You… (79-80)

In an almost tragic twist of irony Barani enters with news of Ghiyas-ud-din Abbasid's arrival – it is prayer time once again in the kingdom but, as the audience already knows, there is no truth or substance to it as the "real" Ghiyas-ud-din has been murdered by Aziz and Aazam in the previous scene, and that Aziz plans to impersonate the Khalif's descendant.

This breakdown in the Sultan is mirrored in the chaos and rioting outside the fort. A starving people refuse the benefit of re-legitimised prayers even as Tughlaq and Aziz (Ghiyas-ud-din) embrace (Scene XI). Scene xii is used to tell us about the week long riots that have taken place in the city. This is done through a conversation between Aazam and Aziz, Aazam having gone into the town twice. Aazam wants to escape and Aziz lets him go, having himself decided to stay on.

But the end of this movement in Tughlaq's life is near. In the last scene of the play, we have Barani finding excuses to leave Tughlaq. Tughlaq is also told of the murder of Aazam and realises that a man who wants to escape from the comforts of the fort into the city must be an impostor. So he confronts Aziz, who tells Tughlaq that he is Tughlaq's truest disciple. He asks the Sultan, "which other man in India has spent five years of his life fitting every act, deed and thought to Your Majesty's words?" (95). Tughlaq sees the absurd comicality of it all and rewards Aziz with a position in the Deccan. He is now resolved to shift back to Delhi, and we finally see the insomniac King fall asleep but not before he has shown Barani the violence that every man is capable of. This is a vision of deep cynicism: not only are we all capable of infinite cruelty to each other, we will not invest in any construct that will not brings, immediate returns. The nation may buy us but we will never buy the nation if it is of no immediate profit to us. Aziz, who knows how to milk the Sultan's constructs for his own profit, is the one who finally invests in the Sultan's dreams; he is Tughlaq's truest disciple.

The role of Aziz is of further critical interest. While a historical play will have historical characters and our legitimate interest lies in examining how the playwright interprets their motives and actions, of equal importance are the fictive characters because they are introduced to give rise to a possible reading that is not available through the "real" characters. In this play, two such characters are Aziz and Aazam. While they make an appearance in the first scene itself, stealing it from the grandiose Sultan, their next appearance is in scene vii on the road to Daulatabad. You see them again, as highway robbers who then murder the "real" Ghiyas-ud-din Abbasid, in Scene IX. They then appear in scene xi, and have a scene to themselves in Scene XII. Aziz walks away alive and triumphant in the last scene, Scene XIII. What we immediately notice is the increasing frequency of their appearance as the play enters its second phase, Aziz appearing five times in the last seven scenes, as the kingdom deteriorates in front of the eyes of the Sultan and the audience. Aziz and Aazam breach the divide between the court and the common people, making their way to the very centre of power. If Aziz can be seen as the comic inversion of Tughlaq, a grotesque parody of the Sultan, then one must also concede that both play with the image, one to project the idea of ideal kingship, to sell a vision to his subjects, and the other to exploit it for personal advancement. Both end up as murderers but only one of them has believed in the image – and it is the Sultan who is guilty of this self-delusion, guilty of killing others for *their* own good. So the role of the invented characters, especially Aziz, is to show us the invented nature of Tughlaq's world, the theatrical nature of his statecraft, and to hold up a mirror to its inherent absurdity. The impartiality of the ruler is expressed in the universality of his tyranny, in his insistence that all his subjects play the roles he has assigned them in order to stage a beautiful life, or prepare to die.

What else can we make of the play? It is obviously an existential-historical play – an Indian *Caligula*. Once confronted, death has no further significance. Once he has killed Shihab-ud-din, Tughlaq realises that nothing has any meaning in life, that death by starvation, death by hanging, death through illness, and death through old age are all the same – the cessation of life, which is meaningless in itself because the finest of visions have no takers. When you begin your quest for truth and beauty and justice by meting out death (as Tughlaq does to his father and brother) you discover that all you arrive at is the reality of the inevitability and meaninglessness of death, thus endorsing the meaningless of life and relationships. Loneliness is the price of this knowledge. And there is no exit from this hell – Tughlaq will wake up looking lost and bewildered after every nap. And his reign will be "nothing more than a tortured scream which will stab the night and melt away in the silence" (52).

Notes

1. S Kalidas and Rehmat Merchant, "Profile: Girish Karnad, Renaissance Man", *India Today*, April 12th 1999.
2. Tutun Mukherjee, "A Conversation with Girish Karnad", in Tutun Mukherjee (ed.) *Girish Karnad's Plays: Performance and Critical Perspectives*, New Delhi, Pencraft International, 2006, p. 35.
3. Ibid.
4. U.R. Ananthamurthy, "Introduction", Girish Karnad's *Tughlaq*, OUP, 1977, p. ix.
5. Rajinder Paul, "Girish Karnad Interviewed", *Enact* 54, June 1971, n.p.
6. Girish Karnad, "In Search of a New Theatre", in *Contemporary Indian Essays on the Use of Tradition*, edited by Carla Borden, Delhi, OUP, 1989, p. 98.
7. All references to the text are from Girish Karnad, *Collected Plays: Volume One*, OUP, 2005. Relevant page numbers are given in parenthesis at the end of each quotation.

9

Modernity and Hindi/Indian Theatre

Jaidev Taneja

The terms "modern" and "modernity" have been used in various ways in Hindi. Sometimes, "modernity" denotes "period-specificity"; at others, it is linked to the "present" or the contemporary. Some people use this term to "differentiate from the past" or in the sense of "novelty" to denote the modern phase of each period, whereas others take it to be thought-specific or viewpoint-specific. Some relate it to historicity, others use it to reject historicity. One accepts it as an extension of tradition, the other as its complete denial. This implies that "modernity" is not a set norm; it is complex and subtle. It does not have an obvious, established or fixed definition. "Modernity" is an eclectic notion which includes a number of factors. Broadly, we can take scientific developments and everything related to them as characteristics of "modernity" such as industrialization, literacy, freedom, urbanization , complex economic systems, gender equality, and the rejection of untouchability . As mentioned above, all these and many similar ideas are the markers of "modernity". Then the question is: what is "modernity" by itself? In fact, the impact of all the above mentioned factors on human beings is "modernity". Human nature, behaviour and thinking have been deeply affected by these factors and they have contributed significantly to changing human relationships and values. Undoubtedly, modernity is the outcome of science; but from the point of view of cause and effect, science, technology and industry themselves are the byproducts of the scientific outlook, which implies the desire to search for the truth with absolute objectivity. In this search the human mind leaves behind respect, faith, religion and tradition. In order to discover the truth, the scientific outlook does not hesitate to be sceptical and atheistic. This way modernity connects to intellectualism; and psychology, existentialism, evolutionism, dialectic materialism etc. intertwine with it. Because of this, probably, subconscious complexes such as frustration, loneliness, alienation, monotony, discordance, complexity of relationships, despondency and lack of communication etc. are also viewed as signs of modernity.

There is another significant side to modernity – an energetic relationship with its times, and also an intense realization of the moment of existence, acceptance of one's present circumstances and its unbiased artistic expression in the contemporary idiom.

Therefore, in the context of literature, modernity is related not to content but to the point of view which defines it. For instance, M F Hussain's paintings of mythological characters such as Rama, Sita, Hanuman etc. are not considered traditional or historical; likewise, a play written with a modern outlook but having a mythological story or ancient characters is also modern.

In the same manner, Dharmveer Bharati's *Andhayug*, which starts with the eighteenth evening of the Mahabharata war and ends with the death of (Lord) Krishna in *prabhas teerth*, can be considered as the first example of the post independence modern Hindi/Indian theatre. It meaningfully depicts the degradation of values and the crisis brought about by World War II as well as the partition of India and the trauma felt by a sensitive writer at this turn of events. At the level of playwriting, this was surely a unique theatrical experiment. For the first time, Dharmveer Bharati depicted the Kauravas and Pandavas, who had become age-old symbols of sin and virtue, in an absolutely unprejudiced and objective manner. He declared, in the very opening lines of the play:

> Torn and tattered, all codes scattered.
> Hammered by both, the order shattered.
> Somewhat less by the Pandavas; and by the Kauravas
> more.[1]

Based on the *Vishnu Puran*, the play paints an imaginary picture of the times after the Mahabharata. Who can say that it is not also an ugly but true picture of the modern times? Bharati had declared in 1954 that:

> They will wield power
> Who control the wealth. Imposters alone
> Shall command attention. Rulers shall be greedy
> And the people so oppressed
> Shall hide in caves dark and obscure.
> And thus abide by time.
> (obscure dark caves–real ones or the ones that lie deep
> within our frustrated selves?)

Despite the absence of values, the transgression of the boundaries of decorum, the greed for power, lack of integrity, cruelty, scepticism, hatred, self motivation, terror, the lack of a centre and being in the midst of a dark horror, the search for hope for human destiny takes this play a step ahead of today's modernity. Bharati's modern outlook is the basis of the subtle psychological analysis of the characters, unbiased probe into their motivations, the uncovering of their complexes and frustrations, their decaying personalities, tangled relationships, broken convictions. Bharati has given a human side to the unidimensional, good and the bad characters of the *Mahabharata* and has presented them in their three dimensional complexity. Modern scholars consider the analysis of psychological processes to be a basic condition of modern drama. Therefore, from the point of view of objective presentation of events and characters, *Andhayug* is a significant work of modern Hindi drama. Bridging the gap between the faith of the mythological times and the doubt of the modern age, the characters of *Andhayug* convey a reality which becomes a meeting point of past, present and future. This is the unique achievement of *Andhayug*. However even by the end of the 1960's, Hindi theatre was not ready to stage a multidimensional play such as *Andhayug*. It needed a talented and imaginative theatre personality like Ebrahim Alkazi to do so. Only after the National School of Drama came into existence and Alkazi became its Director and staged profound, poetic plays like *Ashadh Ka Ek Din*, *Andhayug* and *Tughlaq* on a large canvas that *Andhayug* achieved the distinction of becoming a significant dramatic text of the Hindi/Indian theatre.

The changes in social values and personal relationships witnessed in the sixties became the subject matter of dramatic texts in various Indian languages simultaneously. Playwrights such as Mohan Rakesh in Hindi, Badal Sircar in Bengali, Vijay Tendulkar in Marathi, Girish Karnad in Kannada and Madhu Rye in Guajrati exploded on the Indian theatre scene. Translation and the staging of theatrical texts in Hindi from various regional languages started a significant process of cultural exchange, which provided modern Indian theatre with a perspective full of diversity. It was the starting point of serious, meaningful and experimental theatre. A novel, theatrical consciousness spread out from the metropolises to other cities and towns.

New findings and theories from Galileo to Darwin, Freud, Marx, Nietzsche, Einstein etc. revolutionized the consciousness of the world. The value systems of the old gave way to the new and shook the culture and civilization of the whole world. Established ideals and value systems became hollow and meaningless. The world changed. But the Indian psyche and social structure was radically different from that of medieval Europe. Indian culture was deep rooted and also had a long history of having been colonized. It was torn between material progress and the glamour of technology on the one hand and love for its ancient and grand culture and history on the other. We negotiated modernity with skepticism. Our thoughts and sensibility could not become modern as fast as did our literature and arts. Even today we are not as modern and progressive in our dealings as we appear to be. Our society operates simultaneously at two extremes: ultra modern on the one hand and utterly conservative and primitive on the other. It is neither possible nor appropriate to generalize on the basis of these extremes since there are a number of other layers too. Yet, an attempt can be made, however limited.

Drama can be defined as an aesthetic expression of the conflict between human relations brought alive by a theatrical presentation. With the passage of time, human values and relations changed radically and these changes completely transformed the plot, characterization and the craft of theatre.

Human relations can be divided into two categories: horizontal and vertical. Feudal and bureaucratic systems give rise to vertical relations whereas socialism and democracy encourage horizontal relations. Whatever the reality, on a theoretical level, capitalism and an open economy also claim to support individual freedom and horizontal relationships. The history of politics, society and literature is, in fact, the story of the evolution of vertical relations into the horizontal; and the disintegration of autocratic, princely and feudal power centres is its outcome.

Modernity directly affected the individual, family relationships in the middle class and their social values. This disintegration of the joint family and the feudal system, the spread of education, women's liberation, individualism and other changing situations transformed the very basis of Indian society and family. In literature, the concept of a god-like, divine hero was replaced by an ordinary character with regular human weaknesses. The extra-ordinary qualities of the ordinary and the ordinary qualities of the extra-ordinary were highlighted. Established and pre-defined morality and relationships were interrogated on an individual-psychological scale. In the sixties and the seventies, these changes were almost simultaneously expressed in Hindi by Mohan Rakesh's *Ashadh Ka Ek Din* and *Aadhe Adhure*, in Bengali by Badal Sircar's *Evam Indrajit*, *Baki Itihas* and *Saari Raat*; in Marathi by Vijay Tendulkar's *Khamosh! Adalat Jari Hai* and *Giddh*; in Kannada by Girish Karnad's *Yayati* and *Hayavadana* and in Gujarati by Madhu Rye's *Kumar Ki Chhat Par* and *Kisi Ek Phool Ka Naam Lo*. These modern plays changed not only the form but also the way in which family relationships were viewed. Husband-wife became merely man-woman, and man and woman were reduced to male and female. In the 80s and 90s love was completely replaced by sex. The very foundations of the institution of family were shaken and the alternatives for the man-woman cohabitation were explored.

In Mohan Rakesh's plays, the primary concern was the search for "home" in the changing scenario. He kept searching for healthy and lasting equations in the man-woman relationship, both in his personal life and in his plays.

Plays dealing with different shades and dimensions of man-woman relationships became the main theme of Modern Hindi/Indian theatre.

In the realm of Indian society and family, modernity affected directly and extensively the undefined physical relationship between man and woman. In this respect, man and woman are moving increasingly towards pre-marital relationships, extra-marital relationships, live-in relationships, homosexuality, divorce and the single life. Day after day personal, family and social life and relationships are becoming more difficult and complex. The advancement of technology has made fantasies come true. The dividing line between dreams and reality is getting blurred. Traditional morality and virginity are gradually becoming outdated. Since time immemorial, man has dominated family and society. What is unprecedented and most significant is the fact that the modern enlightened woman, too, has openly joined the struggle for personal identity, rights, independence and space. In matters of sex, she has broken the age old barriers which had fettered her.

In this context it may be noted that it takes a while for the changing social tendencies to become effective, while in literature and art their signs begin to appear much earlier. The sensitive mind of the creative writer is able to feel the underlying current of unspoken reality and express it in his/her writings. The plays of the seventies and eighties prove this point.

In *Aadhe Adhure* Mohan Rakesh presents Savitri as a rebellious modern working woman. Not only does she handle her idle husband and a spoilt family, she also has the courage to do so single-handedly. Breaking the traditional image of a virtuous wife, she has a number of extra-marital relationships. She confronts her husband on an equal footing and actively shapes her own life after leaving him. She denounces traditional family values and the marital relationship. But there is another side to it. In the Indian society and family set up, such a so-called courageous and independent woman not only becomes occasionally, the victim of man's violence but is also forced to compromise with her husband and live with the family. One of the major limitations of Mohan Rakesh's life, milieu and thought is that he cannot even imagine husband and wife living separately or independently, away from home. All the women characters in Vijay Tendulkar's plays, too, are compelled or doomed to be the victims of cruel male sexual behaviour or violence, despite their independent and aggressive postures.

After *Aadhe Adhure*, the change and openness in the man-woman relationship can be seen in the plays of Surendra Verma and Ramesh Bakshi. Sex has, obviously, replaced love. Although its aggressive and startling side was seen in Surendra Verma's *Draupadi*, a woman's assertion of personal freedom and self-acquired space was seen for the first time in Sheelvati in *Surya Ki Antim Kiran Se Surya Ki Pehli Kiran Tak*. In this play, both sides of the Indian woman's personality are available. Like a faithful and devoted wife Sheelvati, despite her sexual dissatisfaction with her impotent husband Okkak, loves him with an exclusive loyalty. But when the state compels her to sleep with another man as *niyog*, in order to acquire a successor to the kingdom, she chooses to fly free of hollow traditions, morality and values. Instead of motherhood, she finds the unique sexual pleasure from cohabitation with a man to be the only meaningful purpose of a woman's body. Therefore, she invents new channels for extramarital relationships. Like the extremely independent woman of the modern West she tells her husband firmly, as a matter of right: "when one is running blindly after self-gratification – seeking personal pleasure … life becomes very complex, Okkak … and so are its demands … for fulfilment, you need more then one man … one for social status, another for physical possessions, one for emotional satisfaction … another for the gratification of the body." Sheelvati's self-centred philosophy of physicality completely destroys the traditional India concept (of woman) and opens the door for polyandry. In Surendra Verma's *Shakuntala ki Angoothi*, Kanak, the actress who plays the role of Shakuntala, unflinchingly chooses abortion when betrayed by Kumar, the actor who plays proxy for Dushyant. As soon as she gets back her ring from Kumar she gets ready to marry the highly-placed Sudarshan, who play the minor role of a fisherman, by putting the ring on his finger. One also finds many shades of extramarital relations in Surendra Verma's *Draupadi*, *Setubandh*, *Marnoparant*, *Ek Dhooni Ek* and *Qaid-e-Hayat*.

Assuming that the institution of marriage is irrelevant and insufficient in today's permissive social milieu Ramesh Bakshi, in search of an alternative, closely analyses marital relationships in his play *Devyani ka Kehna Hai*. Like Sheelvati, Devyani also unhesitatingly declares publically: "One apple is not enough for an entire lifetime, taste more." She prefers to marry Sadhan simply because "unmarried sex is more expensive and risky". Therefore, one day, the unmarried (?) Devyani and Sadhan decide to live in one room and tell their acquaintances and relatives that they have got married. On the first day, not quarrelling with each other like the traditional husband and wife they attempt, rather unsuccessfully, to arrive at some new live-in arrangement. On the second day Devyani again tries, unsuccessfully, by behaving like a prostitute, to define their relationship. On the third day, despite all her efforts, their "marriage reception" turns out to be their "farewell". Finding the relationship inconvenient and unacceptable to her, Devyani does not hesitate to walk out on her man/husband or the security of a home. Despite her dark and uncertain future she acts in a courageous and aggressive manner. Based on the mythological story of the *Mahabharata*, Bhisham Sahni's *Madhavi* also deals with the anomalous man-woman relationship. The story of man's use of woman for self-gratification has been repeated, albeit with minor modifications, since time immemorial. But the significant point is that Bhisham Sahni's modern Madhavi, after realising her lover Galav's extreme self-centredness, chooses to leave him and goes out into the wide world to find her time, place and identity, despite his earnest entreaties that she regain her virginity by observing a ceremony of his choice. Similarly, Vijay Tendulkar's woman of the sixties, Benare in *Khamosh! Adalat Jaari Hai*, keeps her protestations/clarifications to herself, while the woman of the nineties, Sarita in *Kamala* confidently declares: "A day will come when I will not be a slave anymore. Kaka sahib, I will not be something to use and throw away. I will live on my own terms and no one will be able to boss over me. That day will definitely come. I will face whatever be the consequences." They may be few in number but independent and courageous women like Savitri, Sheelvati, Kanak, Devyani, Madhavi, Benare, Sarita, and Shubha (*Hastinapur*) are no longer unusual or exceptional in Indian society today. Nowadays, sex, individuality, ambition and career have become more significant than family values and honour. According to a recent survey now women, rather than men, derive greater pleasure and satisfaction from their jobs than from their families.

Forbidden physical relationships are continuously on the increase. Although, in Indian drama, this issue has not been much written about yet playwrights have not ignored this characteristic of modern life. While Vijay Tendulkar's *Meeta Ki Kahani* and Mahesh Elkunchwar's *Sonata* explore the theme of lesbianism, Kewal Sood's *Murgikhana*, Mahesh Elkunchwar's *Holi* and Nandkishore Acharya's political play *Zille Subhani* can be cited for homosexuality. In Dr. Laxminarayan Lal's *Suryamukh*, an unrestrained love between Krishna's last wife *Venuvati* and their son *Pradyumn* has been depicted. Based on the life of the historically famous emperor Ashoka, Rameshwar Pran's *Antarang* depicts the forbidden love between the emperor's young wife, Tishyarakshita and son Kunal.

About forbidden physical relationship between brother and sister, Girish Karnad's Kannada play *Anju Mallige* and Mahesh Elkunchwar's Marathi play *Vaasanakaand* are noteworthy. In Badal Sircar's Bengali play *Evam Indrajit*, Manasi is Indrajit's sister as well as his love, muse and eternal woman. In Vijay Tendulkar's Marathi Play *Giddh*, Rajani Nath and Rama are brother and sister-in-law; in Madhu Rye's Gujarati play *Kumar Ki Chat Par* a forbidden sexual relationship has been depicted between Nisha and her son-like bachelor brother-in-law. In Tendulkar's *Khamosh! Adaalat Jari Hai*, Benare's first love affair is with her maternal uncle. In Mahesh Elkunchwar's *Aatmkatha* a child is born of the union of Rajadhyaksh and his sister-in-law, Vasanti. But then, the playwright has depicted the context in a natural and extremely convincing psychological manner. Dr. C. D. Siddhu's Hindi/Punjabi play *Ikkisveen Manzil* depicts the irony, tragedy and complexity of family relations due to Hardwai Lal Goel's illicit relations with his sister-in-law, Archana Bansal, and maid servant, Kesro.

In Girish Karnad's *Agni and Barkha*, Vishakha's father-in-law forcibly establishes a sexual relationship with her, while she surrenders to her brother-in-law Yavakri on her own. Based on mythological stories, Girish Karnad's *Yayati* and Nandkishore Acharya's *Dehantar*, depict extremely anomalous and complex relationships between a mother and her son and a father-in-law and his daughter in-law.. Modern man is depicted as a victim of doubts, uncertainly, conflict and divided sensibilities in adulterous relationships. Yayati's desire for a moment of true love is seen as the biggest delusion of modern man. Nandkishore Acharya's *Kimidam Yaksham* presents a complex but hazy version of a man-woman relationship as it minutely shifts between imagination and reality. The play deals with the impossibility of the discovery of the history of relations buried in the ruins of the past and appears rather complicated and mysterious.

With regard to self-realization through scepticism, intellectualism and personal experience, modern existentialists are akin, in many ways to Gautam Buddha's basic philosophy of *Atm Deepo Bhav,* "Be a light unto yourself". In the context of human existence, the attempt to deal with fundamental issues such as freedom, choice, loneliness, momentariness, alienation and suicide on the level of one's experience or lived reality is the basis of existentialism. Mohan Rakesh's *Lehron Ke Rajhans* emphasized finding one's own path instead of treading the beaten track or following what others believe. Nand and Sundari, though contemporaries of the Buddha, seem completely modern, in Rakesh's treatment. Nand's conflict, tension, loneliness, scepticism, instability, uneasiness, suffocation, attachment to worldly matters, each expression on his face, his body language are a testimony of modern man's predicament and his destiny.

The dividing moment between life and death unmasks a person and makes him realise the truth of his existence. Mudrarakshas's *Santola* and Mohan Rakesh's unfinished play, completed by Kamleshwar, *Pair Tale Ki Zamin* are existential plays dealing with such defining moments of self-realisation and self-acceptance. One of the major streams dealing with the illogicality and incoherence of human life is absurd theatre. In Hindi, Bhuvaneshwar's *Tambe Ke Keede* is the first absurd play, but most plays of this type were written and staged in the sixties and seventies only. Mani Madhukar and Mudrarakshas made an interesting use of this trend in their plays. But Vipin Agrawal in notable for using it comprehensively. Balraj Pandit's *Panchva Savaar* portrays the ennui of modern life and Vipin Agrawal's *Teen Apaahij* and *Lotan* are other significant plays influenced by the theatre of the absurd. Kashinath Singh's *Ghoas* is also noteworthy in this context. It portrays the inner boredom and anxiety-ridden meaningless life of today. Rameshwar Prem's *Ajatghar* deals with fear and the mutual humanity of persons caught in communal violence. B. M. Shah, too, has made interesting use of the absurd in *Trishanku, Sheh Ye Maat* and *YudhMann.*

Mani Madhukar is notable for creatively combining the elements of the Indian folk theatre and the theatre of the absurd. Making use of folk elements and realism and fantasy, his *Ras Gandharv* raises an effective voice against injustice. The play attacks the corrupt establishment from all sides and eventually becomes a testimony to the impotent struggle of the frightened and frustrated common man. Some Oriya playwrights like Manoranjan Das's (*Aranya Fasal, Kath Ka Ghoda*) and J. P. Das (*Asangat Naata*) were also influenced by this style of theatre. In Marathi, Mahesh Elkunchwar's *Garbo*, *Sultan*, *Holi* and *Pratibimb*; Satish Alekar's *Mahanirvana*, and *Begum Barve*; in Kannada Chandrashekhar Kambar's play *Aks Tamaasha*; in Bengali Badal Sircar's play *Evam Indrajit, Pagla Ghoda, Baki Itihas, Saari Raat* and Mohit Chatterjee's *Guinea Pig* make use of the same theatre tradition. In Hindi, almost all the plays of Krishna Baldev Vaid have been influenced by this style. They attempt to depict the conflicts, contradictions, frustrations, inconsistencies and meaningless life of today's man in a new idiom.

In search of a modern yet Indian theatre craft, many dramatists tried creative and multiple experiments with folk, traditional and Sanskrit drama to express the complex experiences of contemporary life. Girish Karnad's *Hayavadan* and *Nagamandala*, Vijay Tendulkar's *Ghashiram Kotwal*, Chandrashekhar Kambar's *Tota Bola,* Sarveshwar Dayal Saxena's *Bakri* and Mani Madhukar's *Naatak Polampur Ka* and their theatrical presentations are significant. Theatre directors like Habib Tanvir, B. V. Karanth, K. N. Panikkar, Rattan Thiyam, Bansi Kaul and Waman Kendre have been actively involved with this kind of theatre and have contributed significantly to it. Habib Tanvir in *Bahadur Kalarin* and Chandrashekhar Kambar in *Siri Sampige* have depicted complicated psychological constructions on the stage in their own original styles.

In the Indian context, the concept of modernity is riddled with a number of contradictions; its origin and evolution has witnessed a process of long struggle both within and outside, which still continues. Mahesh Elkunchwar, in a series of three plays *Viraasat, Taalab Ke Pass Khandhar* and *Yugant* has depicted the disintegration of the joint family under the pressure of a variety of new situations and the changing values arising out of a conflict between urban and rural cultures, through the life cycles of three generations of a family. This trilogy depicts the psychology, sociology, economic concerns and dramatic history of contradictions and conflicts that the Indian family and society undergoes in the process of becoming modern.

Writing a play, like any other literary activity, is a solitary affair, but theatre is a group activity. It requires hard work as well as finance. At the state level it is conducted and encouraged according to a defined cultural policy. As a serious, meaningful and powerful medium, it requires a great deal of assistance. In almost all developed and democratic countries of the world the government, under the right to freedom of expression, gives assistance to theatre, both supporting and opposing it. From this point of view in India, too, a number of government plans were made after independence to promote literature, culture and the arts. On the initiative of Prime Minister Pandit Jawahar Lal Nehru and many of his visionary advisors, the Kendriya Sangeet Natak Akademi was established in 1953 and by 1956 regional academies in many states had been established to encourage the all round development of music, dance and drama. The establishment of the Asian Natya Sansthan or the National School of Drama in 1958-59 was instrumental in bringing about a new theatre awareness as well as technical richness to serious Indian, especially Hindi, theatre.

In this context it is noteworthy that by the time the National School of Drama came up theatre groups such as Anamika in Kolkata, Theatre Unit in Mumbai and the Three Arts Club, Little Theatre Group, Delhi Art Theatre, Indraprastha Theatre and Yatrik in Delhi were already active in theatre. Apart from these, theatre groups such as the Rashtriya Natya Parishad in Lucknow, Allahabad Artists Association and Natya Kendra in Allahabad, Shri Natyan in Varanasi, Bhartiya Kala Mandir, Kala Natya Bharati and Performers in Kanpur were also quite active. In many regions and cities, branches of IPTA were engaged in some theatre work or the other. Therefore, from independence till the beginning of the sixties, the background to the revolution in Hindi theatre is provided by the scattered efforts of these big and small outfits in search of a modern stage-craft combining experiment with tradition and tireless hardwork with quiet dedication. In languages like Bengali, Marathi and Kannada also there were numerous theatre activities brimming with enthusiasm and dedication and continuously evolving. During this phase, apart from original Indian plays, translations/adaptations in Hindi/Urdu of the plays of renowned western playwrights played a decisive role in enriching our theatre. However, these translated/adapted plays also, to some extent, obstructed and limited our search for a modern Indian theatrical style. In our enthusiasm to become modern we ran blindly and with unbridled speed after the technique-rich theatre styles of the West. But besides the prominent realistic stream of theatre in Hindi and other Indian languages, the need for creative experimentation from Sanskrit, folk and traditional styles was also felt. This matter was prominently outlined in the third National Theatre Seminar in 1961, which was held under the auspices of the Bhartiya Natya Sangh founded by Kamladevi Chattopadhyaya in 1951.

Some talented theatre persons were already active in this direction. Habib Tanvir in *Agra Baazar* and *Mitti Ki Gadi* had already made a significant and historical beginning with his folk-based modern presentations.

As with drama, modern Indian theatre also has travelled a long and diverse path. A large number of theatre persons have struggled hard and for long to evolve and make it rich. Here we can mention the historical contribution of only some of the prominent theatre persons. Ebrahim Alkazi is the most significant theatre director amongst the senior generation of theatre persons. He created a niche for himself with his imaginative, creative and experimental outlook. His path breaking innovations in modern Hindi/Indian theatre used the technical excellence of realistic theatre, spectacular sets, poetic dramatization, skilled acting, well-thought out gestures and movements, artistic groupings with effective backstage coordination. As the Director of the National School of Drama, he produced a large group of talented theatre persons, who went on to create a country-wide revolution with their serious, meaningful, diverse and original theatrical experimentations. Today, his disciples man all the powerful mediums such as theatre, TV and cinema.

The living legend of contemporary Indian theatre and a celebrated personality of Bengali stage, Shombhu Mitra (1915-1997) was a distinguished actor, director, translator-adapter, playwright and theatre critic. His theatre depicts lively human emotions, intense feelings, sharp insights, the subtle complexities of modern life and the conflict ridden pressures of mind in an easy, effective and lively manner. His original theatre experiments and creativity achieved unprecedented success in showcasing the poetic beauty and dramatic achievements of Rabindranath Tagore's plays to the audience. He was a valuable contributor to modern Indian theatre.

After having thoroughly studied Western theatre practises, Habib Tanvir consciously rejected them and searched for a tradition-based style for his modern Indian theatre. On the strength of the famous folk style, "nacha", of Madhya Pradesh and the energetic singing and spontaneous and lively acting of Chhattisgarh folk artists, Habib Tanvir became famous all over the world by writing and staging not only plays based on folk tales but also the classical plays of Sanskrit as well as adaptations of Moliere, Shakespeare and Brecht.

B. V. Karanth (1929-2003) was a versatile theatre personality. He developed his own rich and multidimensional theatre perspective in which he combined, creatively and meaningfully, the folk theatre of Karnataka, company theatre and the realistic Western theatre-craft. He not only successfully presented Sanskrit, traditional, contemporary multi-lingual and multidimensional plays but also the treasures of world drama in his own unique theatre style. Apart from Kannada and Hindi, he also worked in other regional languages and dialects. Because of his innovative theatre talent, Karanth effectively staged the so far unstageable plays of the great Hindi dramatist, Jaishankar Prasad.

Kerala's extremely famous and important poet, dramatist and director Kavlam Narayan Panikker presented his own and classical Sanskrit plays from the modern perspective and created a new theatre style. He made use of Kudiyattam, Kalari and folk elements in an original and interesting manner. He produced a large number of excellent plays in Malayalam, Sanskrit and Hindi with the same creativity and effectiveness, both in India and abroad. Rapid dance movements, highly lyrical dialogue, sharp gestures, painted half curtains and ritualistic spectacles make his productions unique. He makes use of colours and form from Kerala in an interesting manner for dress-designing, decoration and stage equipment. Simplicity in stage settings and creative and meaningful use of traditional instruments in music give his productions a unique aesthetic touch.

Rattan Thiyam, is not only a much talked about theatre personality from Manipur bût also a highly creative and talented director, dramatist, translator, adapter, poet and painter. Having been born with a talent for theatre, he received his education in theatre technique at the National School of Drama. He also trained with the best of gurus in martial arts like nat-sankirtan, chalam, Thang-ta and music and also in the use of local musical instruments. In this manner Ratan Thiyam creatively combined the folk-tradition, conventional Parsi theatre and realistic theatre techniques and developed his own unique dance-drama style of theatre. Combining the Manipuri tradition of theatre and culture with western theatre techniques, he enchanted his audiences with his experimental productions. Many people prefer to term these productions "ballet" because of the abundance of dance movements and music in them.

Having been influenced by the modern world view and Western theatre styles and productions, Badal Sircar the established Bengali playwright, actor, director and dramaturgist produced not only numerous significant scripts, he also invented a very significant common-man-centric third theatre. In the early eighties, his expensive psycho-physical theatre activities influenced the open air and proscenium theatre work in all Indian languages in a big way. Badal Sircar has made a notable contribution to contemporary Indian theatre by his experimentations.

Today there are many theatre institutions, both governmental and non-governmental, which, apart from training artists, also produce plays. But the National School of Drama remains the biggest and most significant drama school in Asia. Satu Sen may have been its first Director, but it acquired its distinct identity and national recognition only when Ebrahim Alkazi became its Director. He prepared a definite curriculum for the school and implemented it with a variety of practical teaching and training methods. He motivated the students to have a strong belief in theatre activities and inspired them to pursue these with complete dedication. He taught them self-control, decorum and discipline. He created social respect and popularity for theatre work by producing high quality plays for the public. He established a repertory company for the graduates of the school. He also provided fascinating theatre experiences by producing plays like *Andhayug* and *Tughlaq*, which have a huge mythological and historical canvas, against the ruins of the Ferozshah Kotla, the Purana Quila and Talkatora. Visualisation of historical ruins as well as small studio theatres and open air theatres such as the "Meghdoot" were his ideas. He chose to produce world classics and contemporary plays at appropriate "stages", according to their individual nature and respective demands. In this way he communicated most effectively and created unparalleled records of aesthetic productions in modern Hindi/Indian theatre. Back in their own regions, his students experimented with new theatre styles in a variety of ways in regional languages with the help of their new theatre consciousness and modern techniques.

However, today the National School of Drama, which had pioneered a new theatre consciousness on an all India basis seems to have has lost sight of its goal. The fact is that the world has changed today and there are absolutely different kinds of challenges facing theatre. These challenges can be met only by finding new alternatives and breaking new paths and not by new escape routes or by pretending to fight on other frontiers.

Translated by Vijay K. Sharma and Archana Sharma

Note

1 All translations of *Andha Yug* are by me.

10

The Good Enough Mother: An Analysis of Vijay Tendulkar's *Baby*

Sonali Jain

In the course of my doctoral dissertation I had engaged with most of Tendulkar's works. I noticed that the titles of his plays tend to be quite direct. While *Kamala*, *Ghashiram Kotwal* and *Sakharam Binder* are titles about characters in their specificity, *Silence! The Court is in Session*, *Encounter in Embugland*, *A Friend's Story* and *Kanyadaan* set the pace for the narrative to follow. But what about the title of one of his most neglected plays *Baby*?[1]

Baby immediately brought to my mind the tender image of a newborn, and I wondered why this playwright so adept at writing about the human predicament chose this title and what he meant by it. How is a literary character different from an individual in real life? What goes into the creation of a literary character? A play combines two elements that enable the reader to enter and enjoy the fictional world: first, an image of a life, a story which is believable at least as long as we are reading the work; second an imaginative construction which organizes this story and creates a coherent artistic whole. Mental life may be simulated by the characters giving the appearance of being more than is described, of having a certain ambiguity, and acting as a consequence of motives which may or may not be clarified by the playwright.

I have chosen to provide a psychoanalytic interpretation of Vijay Tendulkar's play *Baby* as the play lends itself remarkably to psychoanalytic theory. It introduces a significant approach to what Paul Ricouer calls the hermeneutics of suspicion.[2]

According to Ricouer hermeneutics seems to be animated by a double motivation: willingness to suspect as well as a willingness to listen; a vow of rigour as well as a vow of obedience. This suggests that there are motives and meanings which are disguised by and work through other meanings. Psychoanalysis deals with motives, especially hidden or disguised motives; as such it helps clarify ***Baby*** on two levels, the level of the writing itself, and the level of character motivation within the text. It also opens up a realm of relationships of meaning and identity and what they are to the psychic and cultural forces which ground so much of the play. Tendulkar's body of writing is deeply suggestive of his fascination and preoccupation with the very origins of psychic life.

What Tendulkar strives to achieve in ***Baby*** , then, is a portrayal of psychic reality, not just the external reality of characters, which is revealed through speeches, gestures, actions, and thoughts, through comments made by other characters, and of course in the playwright's treatment of form. Where and how does thinking begin? At what point do human babies learn to distinguish subject from object, and therefore realize that they exist separately from the "other"? In this play Tendulkar gives credence to the intuition that madness runs through human affairs and plays a role in everyone's life. The playwright is extremely sensitive to issues of madness and sanity and captures the nuances of both in the play. He establishes that psychopathology is intrinsic to the way the human psyche works.

An infant is characterized by (a) the establishment of a symbiotic relationship with the primary caretaker (generally the mother) and (b) the subsequent dissolution of that relationship through processes of separation and individuation. There are symbiotic relationships in the cases of all the main characters - Baby, Shivapa and Raghav. Their processes of separation and individuation are extremely difficult and this is what makes the play so tragic.

The protagonist of the play is a young woman called Baby. The play opens with an array of images of separation with the arrival of Raghav, Baby's mad brother, at her house. Baby is introduced to us standing in front of a mirror looking at herself. Raghav begins with a wish to be well fed and well looked after by Baby. He laments his sister's lack of concern for him all the while he was in the madhouse and enquires after her persistently. Finally Baby reveals that she now works as an "extra" in films and is Shivapa's mistress. Shivapa had thrown Raghav into this madhouse after raping Baby, whom Raghav had tried to protect. Raghav is crestfallen at his sister's plight, and regrets not having assumed the responsibility of her welfare. He remembers his promise to his dying mother and his shock quickly turns into indignation and finally to a piteous despair.

Shivapa and Baby are in a queer sexual relationship. In spite of the horror of her situation, Baby lives on with an implicit faith in God and goodness. She stoically clings to a hope of a better future, believing that her virtue will be rewarded someday. Essentially a loner, Baby reads most of the time. She reads Bhushan Chanda's popular sentimental fiction and believes that like Bhushan Chanda's heroines, she, too, will be redeemed at last.

Karve is the assistant director in the same film unit in which Baby works. He displays some sexual interest in Baby and sells her the fantasy of being cast as the heroine in his adaptation of Bhushan Chanda's novel. While Baby obliges Karve, Shivapa comes, in grieving over his wife's death and in her moment of flickering protest, Baby confronts

Shivapa. She is soon kicked out of the house by Shivapa and of course abandoned by Karve. Her hopes are dashed. The play closes with a climactic streak of pathos in Raghav's laughter.

Shivapa's perversion expresses forbidden feminine strivings in the guise of masculine domination. Shivapa is cathected with aggression and violence. He embodies power in the play. He is the fear element, the aggressor. He has raped Baby, beaten up Raghav and forced him into the mental asylum. Shivapa comes to Baby every night. His behaviour with Baby is truly exploitative. He calls her "Bobby" and expects her to behave like a slut who must thrust her breasts and pose for him, dance for him and then behave like a bitch, not just metaphorically but literally, walking on all fours and panting and salivating like one.

Shivapa: Say again!

Baby: Chu-Chu!

Shivapa: Again, again.

Baby: Chu…Chu…Chu

Shivapa: [*Feels tickled and pulls out half his vest.*] Here…!

…Shivapa: Bobby, Gillas! Water!

[*Baby fetches everything, acting like a bitch. Is getting tired.]*

If we look closely at his unconscious patterns, the first thing that strikes us in the scene are huge processes of regression in Shivapa which must be acted out again and again via his perverse sexuality. While the whore excites him, the bitch can promise him unfailing loyalty over and over again. He must generate this excitement every night for himself to make himself believe that Baby belongs to him and that he is not alone.

[*Baby sings as she dances. It's very painful for her.*]

Baby: Enough.

Shivapa: Not enough. More! Sing! Dance! C'mon.

[*Baby is panting. Begins dancing again.*]

Shivapa: More…more…louder…more…!

[*Finally, Baby falls down tired.*]

Shivapa: [*Lapping it up.*] More…!

Baby: No…!

Shivapa: More, Bobby more! Little more! Some more, child, just a little more…

[*Baby gets up with difficulty. Dances, hums a tune, lies down. Is breathing hard.*]

Shivapa: Tch…tch…tchh…my Bobby tired. Come here my litt-tle one! Come here sweety…!

[*Baby crawls toward him on her knees.*]

Shivapa: [Grabbing her hair] O…O… darling…my pigeon…my little one…O…!

[*Purses her lips because of pain. Shrinks her body.*][3]

It is almost as if we see an infant at the mother's breast. Melanie Klein has observed that the infant harbours destructive tendencies towards the maternal object which are not dependent on environmental frustrations. This would mean that "the infant directs aggression to the mother in all circumstances, both when she deprives him and also when she fulfills him. This latter tendency to attack the fulfilling object would clearly point to anti-life, death instinct roots since by attacking the source of fulfilment the infant is attacking his own livelihood. This frustration is traced back to earliest infancy, and to a primitive frustrating environment. Separation would be one such frustration; an inappropriate response to the person of the baby can be another."[4] Fulfilment in this sense is something that the baby has failed to get from its environment at a crucial early stage. In Tendulkar's play, Baby is the maternal object for Shivapa. She is the good breast and the bad breast - both a depriving and gratifying object.

Shivapa: [*Leaving her.*] Get away, you two-penny whore.

[Baby tries to get up but cannot. Gives up and sits down]

Shivapa: [*Going close to her.] Does it hurt, my Bobby*?[5]

Heinz Kohut, in his work on narcissism, claimed that the infant experiences itself still in a state of limitless power and knowledge, a state that we as outsiders deprecatingly call the child's grandiosity, its grandiose self. If, for a variety of reasons, this infantile grandiose state of narcissism is prevented from maturing into healthy self-esteem we meet with what looks like an adult but really is a very shakily put together oversensitive and shame-prone narcissist.[6] In the play Shivapa is the shame-prone individual who responds with insatiable rage and violence to any situation that he cannot handle. Shivapa touches intense levels of sadism in the play with both Baby and Raghav. He cannot rest until he has blotted out Raghav who dared to oppose him. He beats him up and tickles him to the point of excruciating pain. The scene between Shivapa and Baby at the death of Shivapa's wife is quite complex. He begins by mourning the death of Gangamma to Baby. This is the only brief sequence in which one sees more of Shivapa the man and not the perpetrator. He cries at his insensitivity towards the mother of his children, a woman who perhaps mothered him most clearly: "Gangamma you were my ma". This time Baby speaks to him as an equal and rebukes him for his utter callousness towards her. However, as soon as Baby says that he is now to fend for himself, his sense of abandonment, his narcissistic injury and guilt becomes too much for him to bear. He reacts with extreme rage again because his own "badness" threatens him and he must compulsively block out guilt. He must exhibit power to counter his own helplessness. This archaic rage goes on and on and on. Primarily, there is a need to separate from internal objects through external violence. If we accept Freud's formulation that phantasies of violence in the primal scene are universal, in Shivapa this violence acquires actual belief.

The madhouse symbolizes stink, shit and filth. It is everything but a place to heal and it signifies castration – a loss of manhood. Raghav feels castrated and unable to experience himself as a man, capable of taking care of his sister. Like all young boys who have been metaphorically castrated by the father for desiring the mother sexually, all he can do is regress in order to cope. Raghav uses the defense of regression unconsciously but much more after he realizes the newness of violence and trauma, post asylum, and finds it impossible to deal with. Back in Baby's house now, he urges her to feed him, give him tea to drink. The first demand, to be fed, comes from Raghav. He needs nourishment and engulfment from Baby. He wishes Baby to hold him back, urge him to stay with her forever. To use Winnicotts's phrase, Raghav is quite in need of a "good enough mother"[7] and Baby's house provides the holding environment. He is the helpless one, the psychotic, the baby. Raghav gets a cruel shock when he discovers that Baby is living as Shivapa's mistress and that she must spend each night with Shivapa. At night Raghav is shunted out of the house by Baby. It is an oedipal situation. Raghav must not witness the primal scene. His shock turns into rage and finally to piteous despair. He cannot bear to be left alone and yet the phantasy of his mother (whom Baby has come to unconsciously represent) indulging in sex with the father is unbearable for him. He cannot bear the darkness because darkness brings with it the terrors of the primal scene.

I would like to refer to Freud's paper "A Child is Being Beaten". According to Freud: "the first phase of beating phantasies among girls, then, must belong to a very early period of childhood. The child being beaten is never the one producing the phantasy, but is invariably another child, most often a brother or a sister if there is any. This first phase of the beating phantasy is therefore completely represented by the phrase: *'My father is beating the child'*. I am betraying a great deal of what is to be brought forward later when instead of this I say '*My father is beating the child whom I hate*'."

Profound transformations have taken place between this first phase and the next. It is true that the person beating remains the same (that is, the father); but the child who is beaten has been changed into another one and is now invariably the child producing the phantasy. The phantasy is accompanied by a high degree of pleasure. Now, therefore the wording runs:

"*I am being beaten by my father*."

Freud adds that "if the child in question is a younger brother or sister, it is despised and hated: yet it attracts to itself the share of affection, and this is a spectacle the sight of which cannot be avoided. One soon learns that being beaten, even if it does not hurt very much, signifies a deprivation of love and a humiliation. The idea of the father beating this hateful child is therefore an agreeable one. It means '*My father does not love this other child, he loves only me.*'"[8] The pleasure attaching to this phantasy is both sadistic and masochistic. This infantile perversion persists throughout in Baby and Raghav both.

Baby and Raghav are both clearly in an oedipal crisis. There is an unconscious sense of guilt in Raghav which could be translated into an unconscious need for punishment by parental power that Shivapa connotes; the wish to be beaten by the father "stands very close to the ... wish to have a passive (feminine) sexual relation to him and is only a regressive distortion of it."[9] Thus, through morality it becomes sexualized once more, the Oedipus complex is revived and the way is opened for a regression from morality to the Oedipus complex. There is a double drama with both a homosexual and a heterosexual plot.

Raghav, like every child in its psychic bisexuality, wishes to possess both the parents.

Masochism is fundamentally an expression of forbidden sexual desire and it eroticizes power differentials modeled on those between father and child. This equation of masochism with oedipal sexuality has long been reinforced by both Freudian and Lacanian traditions.[10] Accordingly, Baby seems to be her own worst enemy. Her life is filled with decisions and actions that are antithetical to her own well being. Her behaviour is self defeating or masochistic in which she seems to say "if I suffer enough one way or the other, I will get love from my father."[11].

There is a clear demarcation between an outer and an inner in the play. The action is clearly divided between the outer room and the inner room. Baby keeps making this distinction between her soul and her body. Her response to her body is "not me", whereas the soul must remain pure. She is introduced standing in front of a mirror. In terms of Lacanian theory, this is Baby's mirror stage. As is well known, in the mirror stage the encounter with the imago of a whole, stable, autonomous self presents the infant with an ideal image of him- or herself. The mirror stage is the period when the child begins to draw rudimentary distinctions between self and other. In making a "connection" with this ideal image through identification, the infant enters a lifelong quest to correspond wholly with this ideal. Baby has a fantasy image of herself as Bhushan Chanda's heroine. The "mirror" in the play is at once self and not-self. A permanent split within Baby's self-image is thus suggested at the outset with the introduction of the mirror. Klein describes splitting as the way in which a child seeks to retain good feelings and introjects good objects, whilst expelling bad objects and projecting bad feelings onto an external object.[12]

Splitting and projection is integral to Baby's tragedy. The good and the bad objects are not external; they are feelings that lie within the psyche. Baby would like to retain good feelings and introject her good object Bhushan Chanda, who is the mother she is so much in need of. Baby reads to have her fill from her mother, and her psyche develops a kind of fantasy pump attempting to use fantasies with good affects to counteract bad ones. She devours quotations like a hungry baby. However, along with the good feelings, the sadism has also been deeply internalised. Shivapa is the perpetrator yet she protests about his good intentions. Baby is anxious throughout the play as if she does not really believe herself. Her staying with Shivapa is objectively more destructive and dangerous than her leaving him would be yet she continues to behave as if her ultimate well-being were contingent on her enduring mistreatment. Baby feels resentment and indignation on her own behalf. She sees herself as suffering miserably but unfairly; as ill starred, cursed through no fault of her own as she rails against her fate. She endures pain and suffering in the hope of some greater good. It could be argued that she suffers abuse as she tries to avert a more painful eventuality, that of abandonment. Baby's confusion regarding Shivapa is not consciously felt deeply by her. She cannot accept her own perversion and thus blames Shivapa out and out in the end. The good and the bad cannot lie together for Baby does not reach that maturity. Her self-image, maternally derived, is invested primarily with feelings of rejection experienced as coming from the mother, and secondarily with aggressive feelings first projected on to the mother and subsequently reintrojected and directed towards the self. When she is with this good part, her own bad part seems to laugh, scold and smirk at her which she quickly expels and projects on to Shivapa. Indeed, there has been external violation, but the subsequent sexual relationship could not have happened only through force on the part of Shivapa.

She must enact the sado- masochism repeatedly with Shivapa (and with Karve in a drunken state) in order to protect the good object from being contaminated by the bad object. These internal attempts to regulate bad feelings run amok in the case of Baby.

In keeping with the theme, the form of the play is also split. The stage directions to Act II Scene II begin like this:

> [*Afternoon. Half the stage is set as a film studio. In the remaining half is Baby's outer room and the space outside. An old poster or two. A piece of a palace set. Lower ground level is another part of a set.*
>
> *The sound of hammering.*
> *Karve at complete ease, sitting and smoking a cigarette.*
> *Raghav is pacing, agitated in the outer room in Baby's house. Gesticulates. Mutters. Holds his head once or twice. Gets up. Mutters excitedly. Sits down. Starts pacing again.]*[13]

The narrative spins with a visual and mental momentum as the stage is split and differently located events are depicted simultaneously. In the outer world, the studio, Baby is being doled out exciting fantasies by Karve whereas in the inner world, her home, Raghav is being beaten mercilessly by Shivapa. At the manifest level Raghav is being beaten but at the immanent level a vulnerable weak part, unable to resist violence, is being bruised and scarred. Baby's battered psyche is seen in Raghav. In this scene, the apparent and the immanent coalesce in Baby and Raghav.

Again, in the same scene, excitement is juxtaposed with deadness and death. Baby says *"I cannot take in so much of happiness..."*[14] and immediately the scene shifts to Shivapa sitting like a shadow next to his dying wife. Baby is with Karve at night. As Baby gets drunk, hysterical, and finally unconscious, Shivapa's chair is empty and his wife lies dead. A little later Baby spontaneously barks like a bitch even in that drunken state when she hears Shivapa's voice.

In juxtaposing these two scenes, Tendulkar reiterates the fact that too much splitting and projection of bad objects/bad feelings can thin the personality through dispersal, so that one passes from excitement/rage/dread through progressive phases of deadness. It is essential to keep the memory of loss.

It is also interesting to examine the way laughter has been used in the play. Each night Baby is forced to laugh by Shivapa. Laughter expresses complicated conscious and unconscious psychological meanings. Freud says "… laughter arises when the sum of psychic energy, formerly used for the occupation of certain psychic channels, has become unutilizable so that it can experience free discharge".[15] Unendurable psychic conflict can be recognized to be related to fear, hate, aggression or frank hostility. In the play Raghav, unable to express his aggression directly, expresses it indirectly in laughter. The sadism having been turned from great things to small, a laugh results. Unable to express their sadistic drive more directly, Raghav and Baby turn part of their own sadism as well as Shivapa's against themselves. Laughing, therefore, has a definite relationship to their sado-masochistic and compulsive dynamisms. Shivapa terrorizes Raghav into laughter, poking him and tickling him till Raghav can no longer bear it and has an epileptic fit. It is as though he hastens to laugh at everything for fear of being obliged to weep. The more normal person, who has learned to manage his hostilities and is unafraid of his aggressions, is capable of occasional laughter. The ending, too, builds up a contrast between horror and laughter. Tendulkar is quite remarkable in portraying the distortion of an emotion and its transformation into its opposite. He turns his characters' anxiety, grief and depression into laughter just the way it happens in life.

Laughter takes us to the theme of lost mourning which is also integral to ***Baby***. "Mourning" is used to denote the psychological processes that are set in train by the loss of a loved object and which commonly lead to the relinquishing of the object.[16] The responses seen in infants and young children to the loss of the mother are, at the descriptive level, substantially the same as those to be observed when the older child or adult loses a loved figure; and it has been argued that the underlying processes are probably similar.[17] All the three major characters in this play are people who have not accepted the reality of grief and mourning that occured in infancy. A normal part of the process of mourning is that the individual becomes depressed. Baby is depressed at the end of the play. When the mother-figure is believed to be temporarily absent the response of the baby is one of anxiety; when she appears to be permanently absent it is one of pain and mourning. It has been well established that anger with the lost object (often unconscious and directed elsewhere) plays a major role in pathological mourning. The process of weeping, or of anger, is always or nearly always present, a means for the recovery of the lost loved object. Both, it is noted, are apt to be evoked at an especially intense level in early childhood. "The anger appears to have two main objectives: anger against those believed to have been responsible for the loss, and anger against those who seem to impede reunion. Although there may be many other individuals (including himself) who seem to the bereaved to be guilty in one or other of these respects, it is plain that the lost object is almost always sensed as being in some degree responsible also."[18] This means that anger directed against the lost loved object is practically inevitable and universal. Baby's anger at Shivapa in the end and Shivapa's anger at Baby after his wife dies can be understood in terms of this theory.

In the play Tendulkar allows his characters to increase their feeling of freedom. They can and need not be good people. Baby can be a child at heart, sluttish with her men, caring with her infant brother; his setting allows enough space for her to be all. Similarly in the case of Raghav, his regression, his fears, his rage is given free play. He understands that the instincts of his characters seek representation. Almost like a psychoanalyst Tendulkar helps his characters to go as far as possible in the representation of their internal worlds and of their relationship to the external.

All three struggle hard with their internal and external worlds to live a life essentially without meaning. And that is where the irony of violence lies. At one level Baby, Shivapa and Raghav all seem like parts and projections of the same self. External reality is used as a psychic object by all the characters. Externalization as a defense is predominant. By concentrating on the various forms of physical violence in the play there is an attempt to create a mental space in relation to confusing internal primary objects, locked in a violent primal scene, particularly in relation to the mother. This is where I see the significance of the title of the play.

Tendulkar injects enormous violence into his texts. I have grappled long with the question as to why Tendulkar created a character like Shivapa and why he wrote a play like *Baby* in the first place. The violence in *Baby* seems to drive a point home: violence is endemic to the self. Tendulkar expresses ever so succinctly that the borders of normalcy and madness lie too close together in us, and our orientation depends on which one is tapped and built upon. Tendulkar's persistent occupation with incomprehensible levels of violence on stage is indeed his preoccupation with mental agony: agony which is relentless, which will not rid the human psyche.

Through the violence in the play the playwright asserts his sense of being alive. In *Baby* he does this, remarkably, without using the authorial voice through the entire text. The violence is a metaphor for aliveness because at the other end of the spectrum lies abandonment. And, of course, for all three characters abandonment carries an annhilatory anxiety that is too pervasive. Tendulkar tortures his readers to the point of madness by reducing them to scar tissue in search of an outlet. The audience is led into simultaneous positions of torturers and the tortured. There is a disconcerting, discomforting intimacy with the violence that they see on the stage and hence, must live. And, perhaps, this is where his sadistic and masochistic pleasures also lie.

Notes

1 Originally written in Marathi and translated into Hindi by Vasant Dev, New Delhi: Vidya Prakashan Mandir, 2002. *Baby* is one of the few plays of Tendulkar which is rarely performed and has not yet been translated into English.

2 Paul Ricoeur *Freud and Philosophy: An Essay on Interpretation* New Haven: Yale University Press, 1970, p. 27.

3 Tendulkar, *Baby*, pp. 30-31. Translation of the text in this esssay is mine.

4 Melanie Klein "Notes on Some Schizoid Mechanisms" in *Developments in Psycho-Analysis*, London: Hogarth Press, 1946 rpt. 1952.

5 Tendulkar, *Baby*, p. 69.

6\. Heinz Kohut "Thoughts on Narcissism and Narcissistic Rage" in *The Psychoanalytic Study of the Child* Vol. XXVII New York and Chicago: Quadrangle Books, 1972 pp. 360-400 . also Freud 1914 "On Narcissism: An Introduction" Standard Edition XIV London: Hogarth Press. pp. 73-102.

7 D W Winnicott, *Clinical Notes on the Disorders of Childhood*, London: William Heinemann, 1931.

8 Sigmund Freud, "A Child is Being Beaten" in Collected Papers II, London: Hogarth Press, 1919 rpt. 1924, pp. 184-185.

9 Ibid., pp. 185-6.

10 See Nancy McWilliams, *Psychoanalytic Diagnosis: Understanding Personality Structure in the Clinical Process*, London: The Guidford Press, 1994, pp. 267-75.

11 Ibid.

12 Melanie Klein, "Notes on Some Schizoid Mechanisms" in *Developments in Psycho-Analysis*, London: Hogarth Press, 1946 rpt. 1952.

13 See *Projection, Identification, Projective Identification* edited by Joseph Sandler, London: Karnac Books,1989

14 Tendulkar, *Baby* pp. 36-37.

15 Sigmund Freud, "Wit and its Relation to the Unconscious" in *The Basic Writings of Sigmund Freud*, New York: The Modern Library, 1938, p.733.

16 Sigmund Freud, "Mourning and Melancholia" in Standard Edition, Vol XIV, London: Hogarth Press, 1917.

17 John Bowlby, "Grief and Mourning in Infancy and Early Childhood" in *Psychoanalytic Study of a Child* Vol 15, Psycho-analtyic Electronic Publishing CD

18 John Bowlby, "Processes of Mourning" in International Journal of Psychoanalysis, Vol 42, Psychoanalytic Electronic Publishing CD.

11

Re-visioning the Family and Nation : A Critical Look at Dalit Theatre

Maya Pandit

If marginalization is an important theme in post colonial studies, it would be difficult to find a more telling example of this than the treatment meted out to Marathi Dalit theatre in the major discussions on theatre. In fact, theatre itself has been noted to occupy a dark corner of postcolonial studies, for a variety of reasons. In spite of the fact that Dalit theatre has come up with novel forms of resistance and protest, there have been few attempts to take a serious note of the issues addressed by Dalit theatre and the forms they have evolved, their ideological moorings and their concerns. The contribution of Dalit theatre to the debates on cultural practices, social institutions and struggles for equality in terms of their representation of the processes of interpellation of individuals in historical formations has not received the attention it deserves. In terms of the ideological re-visioning of cultural institutions, Dalit playwrights have often adopted a distinctively different approach, more compassionate and humane, to the treatment of social institutions like family and religion, caste and patriarchy, gender justice and a more egalitarian vision of the new utopias, that sets them apart from mainstream Marathi theatre. This is so because, by its very definition, Dalit theatre is a movement born out of the desire to bring about a radical transformation of society and reconstruct the nation. This is evident from the way cultural spaces in the public and private domain have come to be re-visioned in Dalit theatre.

One such space in the private domain is "home". Home has been the preoccupation of many playwrights in the post independence decades. As Aparna Dharwadkar has pointed out, Mohan Rakesh's *Adhe Adhure*, Girish Karnad's *Nagamandal*, Vijay Tendulkar's *Shrimant*, *Kanyadaan*, *Kamala* and *Gidhade*, Mahesh Elkunchwar's *Wada* trilogy — all plays from the sixties and seventies represent the disintegration of home on various levels- economic, socio-cultural and moral-ethical.[1] Home is obviously a trope for the newly emergent nation. However, the way Dalit theatre envisions "home" and recasts "family" is quite unique though it has not found any mention in the dominant critiques of Indian theatre. To understand the distinctiveness of their re-visioning, both of the domestic, private space, as well as of the nation, the space in the public domain, it is necessary to locate Dalit theatre in the history of Dalit theatre in Marathi and explore the genealogies of formation.

Dalit theatre, as an expression of protest and the angst of an entirely subjugated and oppressed community under the exploitative chaturvarna system, is not necessarily a postcolonial phenomenon, as it is very often assumed to be. The roots of Dalit theatre and the protest it has voiced go far back into history. It has links with the so-called "folk" forms such as Tamasha or Lokanatya and Gondhal, which were basically bahujan people's theatre and which gave expression to their protest against the hegemony of the upper classes and castes through their subversive humour.[2] The Batawani in the Tamasha is an excellent example of this.[3] This theatre, however, has been more subaltern, as distinct from "folk", and gives cultural expression to the politics of anti-caste ideology as it has evolved in our pre-colonial and colonial history and also in the generative context of the dynamics of decolonization. It has been a theatre of protest and, as I hope to demonstrate in the following pages, clearly maintains its own distinctiveness against the canons of established theatre practices. Historically, it also has very strong roots in the movement of cultural revolt spearheaded by Jotiba Phule in the nineteenth century.[4] Later on, it absorbed impulses from revolutionary ideologies and sought to express them in the revolutionary cultural practice represented by the IPTA through Annabhau Sathe, Amar Sheikh and their comrades. The Dalit movement spearheaded by Dr Babasaheb Ambedkar gave it a new life and creative vibrancy. Dalit theatre has produced some scintillating examples of theatre practitioners in Datta Bhagat, Sanjay Pawar and many others who have provided theatre discourse with a new idiom.

The term "Dalit" itself, however, poses problems of definition. The question of who constitutes a Dalit has been extensively debated. Is Dalit a term of reference for particular downtrodden castes, or does it refer to "the depressed and suppressed groups of various social formations living more often than not on the margins of society?"[5] Can anybody living on the margins of a society be called a Dalit? Zelliot claims that in the term and concept itself there is an inherent denial of dignity, a sense of pollution and an acceptance of the karma theory that justifies caste hierarchy and she defines Dalit in a very specific sense that involves only the caste and religious dimensions of Dalit exploitation.[6] If one looks at history, one does not find the word Dalit being used at all. In nineteenth century Maharashtra, Mahatma Jotiba Phule used the terms "Shudra" and "Atishudra" for people who were the lowest in, and outside of, the social hierarchy that was spelt out by the Brahminical chaturvarnya system, whereas Dr Babasaheb Ambedkar, in the twentieth century, used the term "Bahishkrit" (meaning excommunicated, ostracized) to account for the exploitation, suppression and marginalization of such people by the dominant Brahminical ideology. Thus, for him, the Bahishkrit were people subjected to a systemic cultural, social, economic, and political quarantine for ages in Indian society. However, radical Dalit thinkers like Baburao Bagul, who was the major ideologue of the Dalit Panthers movement in Maharashtra in the 1960s, constructs the category in such a way as to carry the history of the revolutionary struggles of all oppressed people, so that Dalit connotes all the lower castes, tribal people, toiling classes and women because the term represents those who have been broken and oppressed by those above them in the social hierarchy. Thus, it becomes a comprehensive revolutionary category, specifically designating all the culturally, socially and physically repressed sections of society, carrying within it the explanation of how these inequalities have been maintained by virtue of a traditional, hierarchical socio-cultural set up. Other scholars seek to understand the category along parallel lines, which allows the inclusion of converted untouchable Muslims or Christians and others into it. Bama, the Dalit Christian writer from Tamil Nadu, raises the same issue in her autobiography *Karakku*, published in 2000. If one considers the problems of identity of converted Muslims, Christians and even the "Kirvant" Brahmins, my point will be clear.[7] For the purposes of this discussion, I use the term Dalit on the lines of the Dalit Panther movement, signifying revolt, pride, militancy and sophisticated creativity.

Dalit theatre has generally not been an organic part of the major theatre discourse in Marathi or other languages. Most critical accounts stop after Tendulkar, Elkunchwar and Alekar when they talk about the new, experimental theatre. Even post Tendulkar criticism has not looked upon Dalit theatre as a major area of critical inquiry. Nonetheless, it has been an organic and significant part of the *political theatre* in

Maharashtra. If the post-independence theatre scenario in Maharashtra has seen theatre emerge as a space where relations between the political and social world of unequal relations of power and exploitative dominations of patriarchy, upper castes and class are contested, Dalit theatre has made a significant contribution to the redefining process.

In its earliest forms, one of the major preoccupations of Dalit theatre, nineteenth century onwards, has been to raise the consciousness of Dalits regarding the exploitation they have to face at the hands of the culturally dominant castes in the public domain. Mahatma Phule's ***Tritiya Ratna*** (1856) was the first protest play of this kind. The Tamasha, before Phule, did have scope for critical comments about oppressive customs and the subversive humour it employed did register that protest in diverse and enticing ways, yet Phule was the first playwright to write a whole play which addressed the issue of how the Shudra had to face exploitative practices at the hands of the Brahmins because of their lack of knowledge, literacy and poverty. Structured in the form of Plato's Dialogues, the play shows a Kunbi couple that is deceived and fleeced by a scheming and crafty Brahmin. Exploiting their ignorance and crapulent nature, the Brahmin priest strikes the fear of God in the heart of the poor Kunbi woman and her husband, filling them with superstitious dread and drives them to distraction by constantly demanding money "to appease the gods" in order to protect their yet-to-be-born child. Finally, a Christian priest comes and opens their eyes to their exploitation. The racy dialogues, everyday language, a neat plot and effective characterization were indeed a new development on the Marathi stage. The first Marathi play, by Vishnudas Bhave, was written in 1843 and 1860 onwards several translations of English plays (known as Bookish plays) were made and occasionally came to be staged. But Phule's play was thrown into oblivion. The real reason for this probably was, as G P Deshpande argues, that Phule's play was a very conscious attempt to present a political analysis of Hinduism in the public domain, as well as an attempt to point out the causes of why colonial powers managed to defeat the indigenous society here. Phule made a political statement about the caste system in the context of the colonial occupation of the country. His argument was that there were internal reasons for this defeat of Indian society and these were to be located in the public domain, in the way our society was hierarchically organized into various castes. That this political play was completely ignored by Marathi writers, scholars as well as British cultural ideologues in India is a telling fact. Even an august body like the Duxina Prize Committee (a prestigious and influential Government organization in the nineteenth century which had a tremendous impact on literary culture in Maharashtra) did not consider this play for any award though it bestowed awards on all kinds of books. And the main reason seems to be that it was a protest play, which launched a scathing attack on the "Brahmanshahi".

Kisan Phagu Bansode's play about the Shudra saint poet ***Chokha Mela***, was intended to educate the Dalits and "[our] upper caste brothers about reforming the society" by doing away with caste prejudices. It also went on to demolish the practice and ideology of pollution and untouchability by rationally analyzing the concepts, breaking them up into their component themes and, linking them with menstruating women also considered both polluted and untouchable.

It was, however, the Dalit protest movement led by Dr Babasaheb Bhimrao Ambedkar that truly utilized the theatre through the form called *jalsa,* a theatre that had music and songs in it. Bhimrao Kardak, an activist in the Dalit movement as well as the Dalit theatre movement, calls these *jalsas* " the detailed historical document of the struggle of the untouchable Dalits for human rights." The first major play in this respect came to be written by Principal M B Chitnis, ***Yuga Yatra***, which presented a series of scenes from history detailing Dalit exploitation, right from the killing of Jambuka in the Ramayana in the name of religion and God to the present day. It presented scenes from the Buddhist period, the era of Manu, saint poets, British rule to the satyagraha of the Chavadar Tale in Mahad under Dr Ambedkar's leadership for the right to drink from the common lake. This was first performed on 14th April 1955 in front of Dr Ambedkar himself and later it was performed in front of 6 lakh people after the Deekshanta ceremony at Nagpur.

Writers like Janoji Nakuji Dongare and activists like Keubuwa Gaikwad presented thousands of performances of similar plays in the 1940s and 50s, reaching the message of Dr Babasaheb Ambedkar and Dalit reawakening to the toiling multitudes. Suresh Wanjari (***Mrutyu Patra***, or *The Will*) Gangadhar Pantavne (***Manuskiche Banda*** or *The Revolt of Humanity*), and Baburao Gaikwad (***Nate*** or *The Relation*) were some other playwrights who wrote in a similar vein. Most of the plays located their theatre in the public domain.

This tradition was continued by writers like Texas Gaikwad. His play ***Amhi Dehsache Marekari***, or *We, The Murderers of The Nation*, has been praised as a revolutionary play that tried to expose the politics of fundamentalist organizations like the RSS. It was published in 1982, after it had been performed at several places for around 15-20 years. The play had a very explicit political message: beware of the RSS. Using the metaphor of a dharmashala, it tried to show how people running this dharmashala are least bothered about caste violence and how they themselves endorsed and even practiced it. Another play in the same vein but which was politically more mature and theatrically more sophisticated was Prakash Tribhuwan's ***Thamba Ramrajya Yetay or Wait***, *the Kingdom of Rama is Coming*. The play deals with the struggle a

Dalit activist, Anand, has to put up against the agencies of state power in independent India. He is an educated Dalit youth who aspires to the job of a Police Patil in a village through the policy of reservation. But this is not acceptable to upper caste leaders who manage to get him killed under the pretext of maintaining law and order as he dares to challenge the feudal lords in the village. Though it was a somewhat loud play, it displayed a deep understanding of the political power games the upper castes and classes play against the Dalits. The policy of reservation is shamelessly flouted by the state itself but even that is not enough; finally it crushes the voice that throws it a challenge.

If these two plays managed to vocalize Dalit protest against the oppression of the scheduled castes, a play called ***Karan*** by a non-Dalit writer, Tushar Bhadre, successfully exposed the complex web of superstition, feudal patriarchal power structure, caste based politics and the life of hardship and cruelty that nomadic tribes have to face. ***Karan*** was the first play within the dalit movement that visualized the domestic space as fraught with violence. Apart from a very strong and powerful plot, the play employed the nomadic community as a symbol of the marginalization of people and especially of women, who live beyond the boundary of the co-called civilized world of the upper castes and upper classes. Premanand Gajwi's ***Dev Navri*** or *God's Bride* dealt with the problems of both, Devadasis and bonded labourers, with the focus on the public domain and public institutions. Both these plays are attempts at a better understanding of the Dalit movement, which was trying to be more broad based as well as the complex reality which it sought to deal with through the plays. Another play, ***Zulwa***, by the non-Dalit writer, Chetan Datar, dealt with the problems of a Devadaasi's attempts at marriage. Based on a novel of the same name by a Dalit writer, Uttam Bandu Tupe, it tried to evolve a striking theatre idiom by mixing the elements of folk theatre (like music, dance) with the methods of experimental theatre in its presentation. However, in most of these plays, women do not have any agency. This, probably is true of the established theatre as well and in both women are usually portrayed as passive sufferers, objects of desire, and landscapes to be reviled and conquered.

It is with respect to this issue of agency that the most significant contribution has been made by two major playwrights: Datta Bhagat and Sanjay Pawar. They have produced a re-visioning of the domestic space which is charged with a utopian vision. Their cultural critique of dominant caste ideologies/ practices, which represent the public domain, and their re-visioning of family and marriage, which represent the private domain, are organically fused in their plays.

According to Dharwadkar, in the plays of the major playwrights of post independence India, like Mohan Rakesh, Girish Karnad, Tendulkar and Elkunchwar, "home" becomes a major trope representing an organic relationship between economic decline and emotional disintegration. (This phenomenon, however, is not confined to theatre alone. As Patricia Oberoi notes, the narrative structures of popular Indian films during this period are the collective and gendered projections of the anxieties generated by the changing social and cultural scenario, when a transition is made from the joint family to the nuclear family.)[8] However, what is lacking in most of the established, mainstream playwrights is the re-visioning of the space called "home". In playwrights such as Mohan Rakesh, Tendulkar and Elkunchwar, "home" becomes an allegory of both, disintegrating family and social life, as well as the new nation on the brink of disaster. In fact, in Tendulkar's dark vision in *Ghashiram Kotwal, Gidhade* and *Kanyadaan*, home becomes the symbol of destitution and bestiality and the victimization of gendered identities. According to Dharwadkar "home," in these playwrights, represents the condition of victimization, alienation from other family members, entrapment and the impossibility of release.[9]

The approach of Dalit playwrights like Bhagat and Pawar has been quite different because the kind of re-visioning these playwrights have attempted is distinctively different from that of the established playwrights. In fact, the various meanings of Dalit, which the political movement against caste oppression has created and endorsed, are evidenced in this act of re-visioning. The agony of understanding caste oppression, the pride in creatively redrawing the geography of the new space of a home where caste, class and gender tensions in the public domain are sorted out; the awareness of being a creative and positive agency of transformation - all these combine with the ideology of Marx and Ambedkar to open up possibilities of liberation of human relations as well as of private domains. These Dalit playwrights project home and family as the site on which the intricate patterns of caste and gendered relationships are teased out but at the same time they also present the family as a site on which new humane relationships can be crafted. Located within the divisive, hierarchically organized Indian society, this re-visioning is sought to be done in terms of the radical reorganization of family relations as an organic part of the transformative caste politics.

Let us look at *Routes and Escape Routes* and *Kon Mhanto Takka Dila* by Datta Bhagat and Sanjay Pawar respectively as a case in point. Both plays have established Dalit theatre as a rich field of cultural critique, through a more mature and realist representation of protest against exploitative caste politics. Both also evidence a spirit of critical self-reflexivity and experimentation that provides a strong alternative in the formulation of a new theatre idiom. Whereas Tendulkar is skillful and provocative in his critique of the so-called "intercaste marriages", his violent vision of caste politics within the family domain is essentially static. But Datta Bhagat and Sanjay Pawar, though less artistic, are more analytical and political and their dynamic, in some senses even utopian, re-visioning of the family domain does not end up in making their plays "cautionary tales" like Tendulkar's. This dynamism surges from their being located in radical caste politics that attempts to offer an alternative vision of both marriage and home.

Datta Bhagat's *Wata Palwata* or *Routes and Escape Routes is* a realistic play that centers on caste politics and inter-caste marriages through its portrayal of three generations of Dalit activists, represented by Kaka, Satish and Arjun. Kaka is an old Ambedkarite, an activist who has worked with stalwarts in Dr Ambedkar's movement. Satish, his educated and activist nephew is a professor in a college who has married a Brahmin girl, Hema, and Arjun is a fiery student leader in the Dalit organization, also in love with a Brahmin girl. They represent the three generations of Dalit politics and the major ideological debates within the Dalit movement regarding political struggles and citizenship. The distinctive feature of this representation of Dalit politics is that it is not perceived from outside, with the typically upper caste and static perspective of caste politics. It is a dynamic view from within, from below, from the perspective of activists directly engaged in the struggle against caste domination. Dasrao Guruji, a crafty, cunning and corrupt Brahmin teacher and a freedom fighter of yester years, represents the exploitative upper caste politics. The struggle begins in the public domain with the Dalits demanding the right to occupy the houses built for flood-affected people but seeps into the private domain of Satish Godghate's house in the Dalit locality. The house becomes metaphorically the street and the drawing room, the college compound and the battleground on which ideologies clash. Though the houses are actually built for those affected by the flood, people like Dasrao Guruji have already "managed" things from inside and got the houses allotted to upper caste people. Kaka and Arjun take a defiant stand and decide to forcefully occupy the homes so that they can shelter their own flood affected people who are homeless. Satish, who believes in the rule of the law, refuses to side with them. But he finds himself completely sidelined. The agitation turns violent and a poor Dalit widow dies. Kaka feels responsible for her death and finally dies from the shock of the betrayal. Arjun remains adamant as he also is a prisoner of the forces unleashed and cannot turn back even if the road he has chosen to walk involves bribery of government officials. Brahmins like Dasrao Guruji coolly continue to have their bread buttered on both sides. It is the home of Satish and Hema that emerges as the testing ground for their own political convictions and in the process the radical caste politics in the public domain obliterates the traditional boundaries of the four walls of the home as the private space. It emerges as the space that provides emotional bonding to the egalitarian forces in two diverse communities in the face of intense caste hatred and animosity.

The tensions in the Brahmin-Mahar marriage of Hema and Satish are obvious right from the beginning. Hema has been compelled to live in isolation from her own family, for quite a few years, as they are not happy with her choice of life partner solely because he is a Mahar, a low caste person. She is constantly at the receiving end of the barbs of Kaka, her father-in-law, who is angry with her for marrying his nephew and depriving an eligible Mahar girl of the opportunity of living a life of comfort and luxury. The Brahmins, he says, will have their cake and eat it too. They have always enjoyed privileges in society and now, when Dalits have started getting a small piece of the cake, through reservations, they want to usurp that as well! Arjun suspects Hema's belief in him and Sonal because she is a Brahmin. For Hema, both the terms "Dalit" and "Brahmin" are weapons to hurt. In one moment of uncontrollable outburst against this hounding, she exclaims:

" If you call someone a Mahar, that's an insult! And what if you call someone a Brahmin? Is that supposed to be an honour? I rejected my caste when I married you. It's a deliberate insult to me to be called a Brahmin! A downright affront! Everybody claws at me with their savage caste nails!"[10]

Hema has accepted the reality of caste with her eyes open, taking full responsibility for her actions. But this acceptance is qualitatively different from the acceptance of Tendulkar's Jyoti, the protagonist of *Kanyadaan.* Hema is quite unlike Jyoti. Jyoti ends up humiliated, beaten and broken, ready to submit to the violence meted out to her. Hema's marriage is not a disaster like Jyoti's because it is constructed along different lines altogether. The foundation for this marriage is human bonding. Nor is Satish cut along the same lines as Arun, the fiery Dalit rebel of *Kanyadaan*. Bhagat's Satish is a complete contrast to Tendulkar's Arun. Satish is sensitive, intelligent and an intellectual who has his roots in the Dalit movement. Arun also is shown to be an activist in the Dalit movement but the live sense of "movement", so strong in Bhagat's play is sadly lacking in Tendulkar. Tendulkar's Dalit rebel is basically a violent, bestial man whereas Bhagat's characters – Satish, Kaka, Arjun, are far more mature, responsible and humane. Their sense of human relationships has grown out of the suffering and contestation that the entire Dalit community and the Dalit movement has experienced. But it is not narrowly caste bound. On the contrary, it carries the larger meanings of "Dalit" in its underpinnings and that is probably why it is charged with a utopian vision.

Bhagat brings alive the conflicts and tensions in inter-caste relationships through many situations: from simple things such as how to respond to a call ("yes", the Brahmin way or "ji", the Dalit way?); to greeting each other ("Namaskar" or "Jai Bhim"?), the political implications of touch and pollution and the ideological representations of hegemony and counter politics, as it works out in the actual relations between Satish and Hema, Hema and Kaka, Sonal and Arjun, and between the Dalits and upper castes. The cultural scenario presented by the playwright brings alive the intricacies of the day-to-day life in a minutely nuanced manner. The escalating tensions in the struggle over possession of the houses; over Shewant's death and Dasrao's malicious dealings in the Sonal - Arjun affair get inserted into the very texture of familial relationships. The drawing room of Satish Godghate's house is transformed into an arena where oppositional ideologies within caste, class and gender politics clash with each other. The end result is, however, not the representation of home as a prison from where no release is possible. Relationships do not deteriorate to the level where no communication can take place. On the contrary, the re-visioned home evolves as a space with a tremendous potential to provide succour, security and emotional bonding to people who may not be related by blood or marriage alone, but who affirm their faith in values such as equality, respect for the old, responsibility, tolerance and mature self-reflexivity. This is how the family gets defined. And in the process it does away with the typically modernist vision of home and family. The four walls disappear to usher in the whole world outside.

If realism is the form chosen by Bhagat, Sanjay Pawar chooses to combine myth and realism to concoct a new brew. His play *Kon Mhanto Takka Dila*, (a title derived from a children's game of passing the buck), provides a caustic comment on the hypocritical upper caste ideologies and practices. It explodes the myth that there is no place for caste in our upper caste, upper class homes as well as our so-called secular and democratic state. The distinctively different use of the Mahabharata myth of Kacha and Devayani to focus on caste ideologies makes the play stand apart from earlier attempts like Dharamveer Bharati's *Andha Yug*. The satirical, comic, at times even farcical, and symbolic use of the myth in the play is just a camouflage for the politics of ideas which explosively bring into question the myths of a casteless society carefully built up by the upper castes in the social sphere. Pawar does not even spare the state, which waxes eloquent about how it protects the interests of Dalits in the political sphere. In actual practice, it is all hollow rhetoric. Pawar goes on to also explode another cultural-political strategy of the emergent New Right in India: to evoke selective memories of the past to substantiate their theory of a Hindu nation. Pawar makes this logic stand on its head by using the same strategy to counter their selective appropriation of mythology. He evokes the love story of Kacha and Devayani from the Puranas on which he predicates the caste politics in contemporary India.

The play begins with a prologue which radically re-casts the famous mythological story of Kacha and Devayani. The Gods send Kacha to steal "Sanjeevani", the knowledge of how to conquer death, from Shukracharya, the Guru of the Rakshasas. Kacha makes Devyani, Shukracharya's daughter, fall in love with him to achieve his devious objective but the Rakshasas get wind of his plan. They kill Kacha, burn him and mix his ashes in Shukracharya's liquor, who drinks his ashes off. Because his daughter is heartbroken, however, Shukracharya has to bring him back to life. But when Kacha comes back to life, like a true upper caste god, he refuses to marry Devyani. She is angry and curses him that he will be born in the twentieth century as a Dalit and made to stay in an upper caste household as a punishment for the fraud he has committed. The prologue is over.

Act one pans on to a Brahmin household in the twentieth century. The lady of the household is absolutely shaken by a new Government rule that every upper caste family must keep a Dalit person in their house in order to demonstrate to the whole world how Government policies have completely transformed the caste ridden Indian society and how caste has been ultimately cast off by the Indians. The government circular makes it clear that people can select a Dalit from the newly established "Equality Distribution Centres". People are warned that unless they fulfill this requirement they will not be entitled to benefits such as a gas connection or a, passport, symbols of the middle class / upper caste's aspirations for a better life for themselves.

The play goes on to hilariously portray the fall out of this impossible government policy in several upper caste households. The main focus, however, is on the household of one Mr. Kamalakar Aradhye, which consists of his wife Vimla, a typical, hypocritical Brahmin, their son Sudershan, an activist of the Hindu fundamentalist organization RSS, and their egalitarian daughter Sukanya. To most upper caste women, a Dalit is a pollutant of their sanitized, upper caste homes but soon having a Dalit or a Tribal in the house becomes another competition, meant to enhance the social prestige of the family.

In the ensuing chaos that follows, Pawar demonstrates how upper caste homes have become hotbeds of the caste "dis-ease" and the rot has reached to the very bones of the social structure till it is about to collapse. In spite of the industrial revolution and the concomitant prosperity it brought into the homes of the dominant castes, the condition of the poor people from the down trodden castes, the Dalits, hardly changed. In spite of the constitutional structure of democracy and the professed secularism of the state, the divisive and hierarchical structure of Indian society has hardly changed. The Dalits, who have had a long history of being uprooted and displaced, have been marginalized in more ways than one in post-independence India. As Kamalakar Arhdhye says in the play:

> I have realized that really we thrive on lies. Our thinking is essentially casteist, we pretend 'Where is casteism?' People from villages say, casteism exists in cities and city dwellers, it is thriving in villages. Then again somebody asks with fatigued innocence 'where is casteism?'

Sukanya supports him, saying:

> 'In your language Mummy, this is like saying, pass the buck on!'[11]

Mrs. Aradhye is the representative of the upper castes who believe that the Dalits are dirty, ignorant, polluting. "We are different" she says, "our culture is different, our way of life is different; cleanliness, purity…"(19). She is horrified at the idea of the Dalit man staying in the same house as her, eating, sleeping in the sanitized, pure space of her house but helpless against the Government directive, she tries to give her reactionary casteist ideology a whitewash of sophistication by buying him a separate bucket, soap etc. This apparently comic situation is a caustic critique on the hypocritical secularism and sham democracy we have in the country. In spite of the professed claims of having created an egalitarian society, what we have finally managed to create is a much more sophisticated version of the society in which the age old prejudices against the Dalits are still intact in both our thinking and practice.

Kachrya, the Dalit radical, whom the Aradhyes choose from the "stall" (the name clearly echoes Kacha, the spy of the Gods who had tried to steal Sanjeevani from the Rakshasa and means, literally, "born of dirt" in Marathi) is a metaphorical "re-presentation of the polluting and dirty people!"

Pawar launches a scathing attack on caste ideology through the confrontation of Kachrya and the right wing Sudershan. Right from placing his "stone god" next to the upper caste gods in the Puja room, to setting the record of Dalit oppression straight, Kachrya focuses the discussion on the reassessment of history and present practices. He argues:

> "If you really mean it, we will have to set the account right from the beginning! Then we will have to push you

> beyond the Khyber Pass. We are the original inhabitants, this place really belongs to us, you ass! We were just like the stones, like the gods we worship, when you came from outside and fucked us!" (21)

With each confrontation, Pawar's radical Dalit protagonist goes on to debunk the myth of the upper classes and castes' great show of being "casteless". As he says:

> "This is so strange! As this century advances, some people are not only compelled to accept that they are essentially inferior; they are also compelled to say that the essentially superior people have given up their tough stand about their superiority. And on top of it, we are also expected to praise the upper castes for their hypocritical stand!" (37)

The hypocritical acceptance of the tribals and Dalits as a "fashion statement" in the upper caste and upper class families and Sudarshan's increasing annoyance at Kachrya's constant demolition of his Hindutva ideology worsens when Sukanya falls in love with Kachrya and decides to marry him. The discussion is no longer on the vague and abstract terrain of "nation", it directly enters "family". Sudershan is hopeful that the policy will be scrapped by the Supreme Court (an obvious dig at the judicial and legal system) and keeping a Dalit in the house will only be a temporary arrangement. He believes that once Kachrya is legally made to leave the house, it can be washed with cow urine and purified as the sacred abode of the upper castes. But Sukanya's decision to marry Kachrya rips off the very foundations of the upper caste family.

For Sukanya, Kachrya is a revelation; to her, he is a human being who is completely transparent and clear; his conduct is a lesson in ideology without any limiting frames and labels. In other words, he is the antithesis of everything that she sees in her own elite, upper class, upper caste world. Her mother's reaction to her decision is of explosive anger but her father wishes her well and asks her to be a responsible person as she is taking this decision with her eyes open. The character of Kachrya as a humane, educated, balanced, radical individual who wants to transforms the world is a complete antithesis to the angry, young, violent Arun of Tendulkar's *Kanyadaan*. As Kachrya, the Kacha from the mythic past, eloquently explains at the end:

> "Thank you Devayani because it was through you that I could explain to the others the futile divinity of gods and the inhumanness of monsters. I do not want to give birth to either a god or a monster. Our child will be a human being, pure and simple, without the markings of any caste. Humanity will be his horizon and humanity will be his destination." (55)

The utopia of the Dalit movement, the blue dawn of a new world order, is enshrined in these dreams. It is through this marriage of Kachrya and Sukanya that the possibilities of the new home and family come alive. And it is through this re-visioning that the new nation will be crafted. Nation here does not remain a clautrophobic, hostile space which treats the downtrodden as secondary citizens but becomes a land of equal opportunities to all. It will not be the land from where people are either uprooted or displaced, it will be the sanctuary, the haven for all.

The distinctiveness of this re-visioning of the family and the nation is generated by the radical politics of the Dalit ideology. Even if, as Dharwadkar suggests, we treat *Kanyadaan* as a "political play of ideas", about the relationship between the political and personal, and of the public to the private, it is obvious that Tendulkar's vision and the underlying ideas are regressive and static rather than progressive and dynamic. He is not being apolitical here. To be apolitical also is politics of a certain kind. The two Dalit plays discussed above reveal a far more mature political understanding of the complex web of issues involved. *Wata Palwata* or *Routes and Escape Routes*, reveals self critically the contradictions within the Dalit movement and its equally complex relationship with the political structures represented by the new Nation state. It also highlights the terrible loneliness and alienation of sensitive individuals in both the upper and lower castes but the ideological underpinnings refuse to allow them to be the helpless victims of that loneliness and alienation. Human agency is important. And that is the politics of *Kon Mhanto Takka Dila* too. There are no easy solutions suggested in either of the plays. But these plays manage to open up the direction for a transformation in society on all levels of organization, including the family and home.

Thus, Dalit theatre today is an important landmark in post colonial Marathi theatre and provides a distinctively different dimension to the tradition of political plays in Marathi. The theatre idiom of these plays evolves out of a live grappling with issues of identity politics, and recognizes the futility of the easy solutions suggested by political leaders, for the nation state is occupied by feudal and capitalist powers and casteist ideologies. At the same time it also subjects its own politics and the contradictions within the movement to a critical scrutiny. The struggle is not only with the forces outside but also within itself. The point is to see how traditions, and alternatives, are constructed, modified and challenged, what preoccupations playwrights have and why.

Notes

1. For more details see Aparna Dharwadkar, *Theatres of Independence: Drama ,Theory and Urban Performance in India since 1947*. New Delhi: OUP, 2005 pp.268-309.

2 Gondhal is a very old, folk form of Maharashtra, which originated in ritualistic worship; it is performed at the home of a yajamana (host) by "Gondhali" artists after ceremonies like marriage, etc. it has two parts, the *purva ranga* and the *uttar ranga* and the latter contains a story from the Ramayana or the Mahabharata narrated through dialogues, song and dance sequences, jokes etc, with humorous comments provided on many contemporary events."Bahujan" literally means the majority and signifies the non-brahmin masses, "counterpublics" in the political movement of Ambedkar. For details see Maya Pandit's note on Gondhal and Tamasha in *The Oxford Companion to Indian Theatre* ed. Ananda Lal, OUP, New Delhi, 2004 pp 135-6 & pp. 466-7

3 Batawani is one of the elements of Tamasha, the Marathi folk theatre. It is generally presented after the Gana (prayer), Gaulana (a humorous scene between Krishna and the milkmaids of Gokula), and contains a humorous event, anecdote or jokes in which socially powerful people like brahmin priests, kings, politicians, merchants and even gods, etc are subjected to comic treatment. For details see Maya Pandit, Ibid.

4 Jotiba Phule was the most significant non-brahmin thinker in 19th century Maharashtra whose play *Tritiya Ratna* (The Third Jewel) launched a scathing attack on the way brahmin priests exploited the lower castes.

5 For more details see Guru, "Understanding the Category Dalit" in *Atrophy in Dalit Politics:* Intervention I Mumbai: Vikas Adhyayan Kendra, 1998.

6 Eleanor Zelliot, *From Untouchable to Dalit: Essays on Ambedkar Movement*, New Delhi: Manohar, 1992, p. 267.

7 Brahmins who are assigned the task of performing the last rites among the Hindus and who, because of the work they do, are treated as polluting and stay almost excommunicated and ostracized.

8 For more details see Patricia Oberoi, "Imagining the Family" in *Pleasure and the Nation: The History, Politics and Consumption of Public Culture in India*, ed. Tachel Dwayer & Christopher Pinney, New Delhi, OUP, 2001.

9 Aparna Dharwadkar, Ibid., pp.268-309.

10 Datta Bhagat, *Wata Palwata/Routes and Escape Routes* tr. Maya Pandit in *Drama Contemporary* ed. Erin B. Mee, Baltimore & London: The John Hopkins Univ. Press, 2001, p. 322.

11 Sanjay Pawar, *Kon Mhanto Takka Dila*, Pune: Neelkantha Prakashan, 1993, p.19. Translation into English is mine. All further references to the play indicate page no in brackets at the end of quotations.

12

Boundaries of Performance: Ritual and Street Theatre: A Case Study of Safdar Hashmi's *Samrath Ko Nahi Dosh Gosain*

Swati Pal

And you will ask : why doesn't his poetry
speak of dreams and leaves
and the great volcanoes of his native land?

Come and see the blood in the streets.
Come and see
the blood in the streets.
Come and see the blood
in the streets!

– Pablo Neruda *I'm Explaining a Few Things*

I

In an interview with Anjum Katyal in New Delhi on March 9, 1997, Moloyashree Hashmi, actress and convenor of Jana Natya Manch (JANAM), said, "Drama has to be created and crafted, even on the streets."[1] This truism is often forgotten as the general trend is to discredit street theatre, indeed any form of agitationist-propagandist (agit prop) theatre, as performances that are often cliché ridden with rehashed plots, weak story lines and unskilled acting. Perhaps the pejorative connotations of the word "propaganda", which connotes such misdeeds as false and misleading advertising or the broken campaign promises of a thousand politicians or the deceptively stated war aims of World Wars I and II and the operations of the Nazi Ministry of Public Enlightenment and Propaganda also contribute to the aspersions cast against such theatre. Even a brief look at theatre history, however, can prove that such theatre has stood in the vanguard of political and social change. And while the gurus of such theatre, such as Erwin Piscator, asserted that "any artistic intention must be subordinated to the revolutionary purpose of the whole",[2] any theatre activist involved in street theatre would echo Moloyashree Hashmi's words. Though many elements are involved in the art and craft of street theatre, this essay will foreground the aspect of "ritual" and how it is embedded in the creation of street plays, through a study of JANAM's play *Samrath Ko Nahi Dosh Gosain* (also known as *Mehengai Ki Maar*, *Madari Jamura*, etc), first performed in March 1980 and which has logged more than a thousand performances since.[3]

Why ritual? While the most obvious reason for the successful survival of street theatre is the very nature of such theatre i.e., its emotional appeal during a politically charged situation and time the question is, how is this emotional response elicited? If performance studies can be seen (primarily by cultural anthropologists such as Victor Turner and Richard Schechner) as synchronous with ritual studies, the answer to the question becomes more manifest.[4] Even a more reading of the text of street plays throws up certain clear patterns in the language, form and the themes. It is these elastic patterns that this essay will address as "rituals".

Since ritual studies have their root in disciplines as diverse as religion, sociology and cultural anthropology it is necessary to chart out the parameters within which this essay intends to use the term "ritual".

Even though the range of critical approaches to ritual studies is wide, there are certain points of convergence. To begin with, ritual is considered, on the one hand ,as a symbolic action which is temporarily discontinuous with routine activities, by enforcing itself spontaneously on the other hand, reveals a tremendous capacity for routinisation. At once the connection between this definition of ritual and theatre becomes clear. As Eugenio Barba says:

> It is the performance not the theatre which lasts only a short time. The theatre is made up of traditions, of conventions, of institutions, of habits which endure throughout time. The weight of this endurance is so heavy that it often prevents life from emerging and replaces it with routine. Routine is another of theatre's natural boundaries[5].

Hence "drama" or a "play", which can be defined as a mode of fiction represented on stage and constructed according to certain dramatic conventions may be replaced by another. But "theatre", which is a complex phenomena associated with the performer-audience transaction, i.e., with the production and communication of meaning in the performance itself and with the systems underlying it, endures conceptually.[6]

Such a definition of ritual ushers in notions of the "sacred" and the "profane". While "profane" embraces the routine aspects of a man's activities, the "sacred" is that aspect of a community's beliefs, myths and material objects that is set apart and sacrosanct. The function of ritual in the community is to provide the proper rules for action in the realm of the sacred as well as to supply a bridge for passing on into the realm of the profane. Van Gennep, in his *Les Rites de Passage*, speaks of the "pivoting of the sacred" meaning that nothing is inherently sacred or profane.[7] These are not substantive categories but rather situational or relational categories; mobile boundaries which shift according to the map being employed. There is nothing that is in itself sacred, only things sacred in relation to. It is perhaps easy to recognize this feature of ritual as an intrinsic characteristic of all theatre but especially of street theatre.

Ritual can also be studied as non-verbal communication based on its own structure and semantics.[8] The space, spatial orientation and location of the ritual setting are essential features of the semantics of ritual action. Examples of ritual time and ritual space orientation can be found in sacrificial rites in Indian Brahmanic ritual texts; codes for the building of a Hindu temple or a Christian Cathedral or for consecrating those structures that symbolize a definite space-time orientation in which rituals are enacted. Man's use of space in his architectural, domestic, urban, workplace and aesthetic activities is neither casual nor merely functional but represents a semiotically loaded choice, subject to powerful rules which generate a range of connotative cultural units. The three principal "syntactic" systems distinguished by the American anthropologist Edward T Hall, and which are an important basis for the study of drama and theatre, are the "fixed feature", the "semi fixed feature" and the "informal".[9] In Hall's own words the fixed feature space involves "static architectural configurations" which relate to the playhouse itself, be it the opera house, the proscenium arch theatre, the open square or the street—the shapes and dimensions of the stage and auditorium. The semi fixed feature space involves such movable but rather static subjects such as the furniture or the set and other auxiliary factors like the lighting. And the informal space is concerned with the ever shifting relations of proximity and distance between individuals in the theatre viz. actor-actor, actor-spectator and spectator-spectator. Such proxemic analysis can reveal how drama, and in this case street theatre, affects and transforms dramaturgic space.

While there are many conflicting views about whether ritual is prior to explanatory belief, or whether there is a priority of belief over ritual there can be no doubt that ritual can be seen as an expression of the urge for integration with the whole that transcends it and transfigures it. This "integration" [read variously as allegiance/ binding/affiliation and affinity] however, seeks not just to reinforce notions of collectivity but also serves to impart a sense of belief in individual identity to all the members within the collectivity because within it, the members have their own status and role. Ritual is thus oriented to the need dispositions of a collectivity and requires the participation of a community. Bearing this aspect of ritual in mind, the parallels between it and street theatre are not hard to discern for after all, the aim of street theatre is to integrate a community by propagating a certain ideology. As Kertzer says:

> *Ritual is a means by which we express our social dependence; what is important in ritual is our common participation and emotional involvement, not the specific rationalization by which we account for the rites.*[10]

It follows then that ritual has both a hierarchical as well as an egalitarian structure. It is hierarchical when the sacred is outside the person of the communicants who reach out to it as individuals approaching factual objects. And it is egalitarian when the sacred is inside the person of the individual communicants who listen within and join together in a group. Theatre may wield its power over spectators; street theatre attempts to literally hand over power to the spectators.

Ritual has a many layered or tiered structure, each level having many sectors so that it becomes an instrument for carrying out and communicating many messages at once, even of subverting at one level what it appears to be saying at another . The full meaning of the ritual emerges from the union of the text of the ritual with the performers at a given moment in a group's ongoing social process. The performative genre does not merely "reflect" or express the social system or the cultural configurations or their key relationships but has a reciprocal relationship i.e., it is either a critique (direct or veiled) of the social system that it grows out of or an evaluation of the way society handles history. This ability to critique and evaluate has been and is a need disposition of most collectivities. Street theatre carries this a bit further and uses the register of active protest in its performative process, a protest in which the actors seek to realize in the spectators a consciousness, latent until then, of the need to change the dominant power structures of the times.

Repetition, emotionality, drama and symbolism are the other principal features that most rituals share along with the whole process of order-disorder-reorder which is embedded within rituals.

II

Safdar Hashmi (1954-89) one of the founder members of JANAM, an offshoot of the then almost defunct Delhi chapter of the Indian People's Theatre Association or (IPTA) was murdered on 1 January 1989 while staging a street play called *Halla Bol* at Sahibabad on the outskirts of Delhi — a play which advocated a wage increase for industrial workers. There was a deliberate attack on the group and Safdar Hashmi fell prey to his attackers, his only fault being that he was expressing his faith in the communist movement through a play performed by a theatre company with a leftist orientation. That merely performing a street play needs to be met with such violent resistance unwittingly serves to bolster the role that such theatre can play in a developing social milieu and in the evolution of theatre itself.

What does JANAM as an agit prop theatre company wish to propagate? Apart from its belief in the Left (albeit an impartial one, not blind to the errors such ideological leanings may lead to), clearly discernible in the plays, the group claims to propagate a certain methodology of performance which is meant to change the nature of performance space. Traditionally, the dominant ideology has sought to institutionalize theatre and has also held the performance space as sacred to the performing unit and has disallowed entry of the spectator-listener into this space. It also dismisses any theatrical activity outside the mainstream as second rate and views it almost as an illegitimate, guerrilla style activity. That theatrical space has been, and can be, the catalyzing agent of revolution is something that the dominant ideology has sought to suppress. JANAM wishes to break this stranglehold and its purpose is broadly two pronged: a desacralisation of the performance space and a demystification of the actor-spectator relationship. As Safdar himself said in his *The Right to Perform*, "If we wish to confront traditional form with modern content we will first have to relieve the form of the burden of ritualism...which...appropriated it."[11] Thus the methodology of performance which this group wishes to propagate can be called, roughly speaking, "antiritualism" wherein the group wishes to break the rituals of theatre in terms of the performance space and in terms of the audience-performer relationship which mainstream (or the more "legitimate", "acceptable") theatre practices. How far is the group successful in achieving its goals? It is this that my study of both, the form and the content of *Samrath Ko Nahi Dosh Gosain*, will serve to illustrate.

III

The play begins with two actors entering the circular performance area and entertaining the spectators with a couple of somersaults and other similar antics. After a while, one actor stops and addresses the other:

Actor 1: Enough, Enough, "nough", "nough", "nough". We've shown plenty of antics and quite a few spectators have gathered. Now let's start the play.

Actor 2: Right then, here goes.

[Suddenly outside the boundaries of the performance area, there is the sound of a damru].

Actor 1: What kind of misbehaviour is this. Even this madari has to show up now! Hey you, get lost, there's going to be a play over here, right now.

[The damru continues to be played. Actors I and II strain their necks towards the sound. A third actor, wearing a police cap and wielding a stick, comes up from behind the two actors. Both of them receive a hard kick each from the policeman. Unnerved, they scamper off. Just then, cutting his way through the crowd, comes the madari]

Such a beginning to a street play is not uncommon.[12] Most of JANAM's plays begin with either the performance of antics or the sound of a percussion instrument or a brief demo style speech by the *sutradhar*. Travelling back to the *Natyasastra,* we find that most performances in the ancient Sanskrit theatre began with songs or music which was followed by an elaborate ceremony in which the performance area was sanctified and thus carefully delineated. Here, too, we can see that the ritual of initiation has begun where the members of the audience are obviously the initiates who have to be prepared for the role that is expected of them by the performers: they are a special audience who have to be aware right from the start that state control over theatrical activity (represented symbolically by the policeman's behaviour) needs to be broken into by the very activities which the state regards as innocent or passive – the audience must have a dual awareness of the traditional significance of the performing unit as well as its immediate social context. So, the point of manipulation becomes clear: now it is not the performance space that needs to be sanctified but rather, in a clear inversion, it is the audience which is being prepared for sanctification. This notion is strengthened when the text moves on to focus upon the games of the madari and his jamura:

Madari: So the play can be begun

Jamura: Can be begun

Madari: So then benefactors and patronisers,
before we begin today's play, please
clap loudly: yes, now Jamure let us
proceed with the play.

Jamura: Boss, we can start now if you wish. But
it seems that the spectators present here
have an empty stomach.

Madari: Benefactors and patronisers, my Jamura
has a bad habit. Unless and until
the public claps loudly, this bloody man
refuses to start; yes, so please clap
loudly – why brother Jamure, are you
happy now?

The madari has a "sutradhar" like role and, at this moment, I would like to pause awhile upon this common agency of the "sutradhar" employed by many street plays to assist recharacterisation of the audience.

Originally, the function of the sutradhar was to measure the land for the construction of the mandapa. In architectural literature, he is regarded as the master builder or teacher but in a text on dramaturgy like the *Natyasastra*, the sutradhar becomes the master builder of the theatrical performance. In street theatre the sutradhar, while often linking the plot together, usually provides a commentary (like the choric figures in Greek theatre). This commentary may bluntly direct the audience, as the madaris' words do – but then the madari is only LIKE a sutradhar. In other plays, the sutradhar has a special role and his commentary provokes the audience in a more insidious manner. If we look at *Hatyare*[13] we can observe the veiled incitement to the audience to protest in the sutradhar's words, for example:

> So friends, this is Aligarh – the city of locks. I guess you don't need me to introduce you to locks, 'cause nowadays almost every gentleman has had to lock his tongue.

And again,

> ...What does the police have to do? Find out who was the man killed, where, by whom, why and when? Go to the scene of crime and carry out legal proceedings, conduct or not conduct the post mortem of the dead bodies, count and identify them, tell or not tell the press? All this work is just that of the police. And Sir, to interfere in government work is legally a crime. So all you upright gentlemen are requested to become ignorant [blind yourself and forget] of what you have just seen and heard.

Obviously, the sutradhar is ridiculing government officials and is being sarcastic about the common man's submission to bureaucracy.

To return to *Samrath*, the very act of clapping at a performance which adheres to the stimulus-response code of Mounin, who argues that one way signals provoke a number of more or less automatic reflexes which cannot, in turn, communicate along the same axes, is being held up for questioning.[14] This can easily be read as a debunking of the actor-audience relationship but I think that this would be an oversimplification. Rather, it is a specific demarcation of the role that the audience has to enact – but then, this in turn delimits the role/s to be enacted by the performers as well. What must be kept in mind is that both the demarcations are being done simultaneously and it is this that brings about an apparent generation of an interactive relationship. This is a characteristic feature of ritual which can be seen as an expression of the urge for integration with the collectivity that transcends it and transfigures it. This integration does not merely reinforce notions of collectivity but also imparts a sense of individual identity to each of its members, for within the collectivity, individuals have their own status and role. By taking recourse to this fundamental feature of ritual, street theatre and here, JANAM, is only demystifying the performer-spectator relationship in so far as it is spelling out clearly the role of each: that they are interdependent but they are not the same, not one. Thus there is a recognition that theatre is a complex phenomenon composed of two units: the stage/sending/performing unit and the public/receiving/observing unit, which inter react and should not be confused as being a homogeneous mass.

That this process of sanctification is unnecessary is one of the first thoughts that may cross the mind of the reader. But I believe that while, on a proscenium stage, the curtain, the seating arrangement and the upraised stage are enough to demarcate boundaries, in street theatre it becomes important to show that nothing is inherently sacred or profane; things are sacred only in relation to, and these are mobile boundaries which shift according to the map being employed. When the madari first appears he is, semiotically speaking, loaded with a web of signifiers which establish, in the course of two circulations, that his role is that of a magician. Thus, he wears large sunglasses with frames, a bright and colourful headband with a marwari turban above it while a three metre long black sheet trails from his shoulders in the attitude of a historical figure. But within minutes the costume is dismantled and discarded. Still, we continue to regard the madari as a magician. Again,

Madari: Boy, narrate the conditions of the past future and present.

Jamura: All at once?

Madari: No, slowly or else the game will be over in a minute. Now see what I have here.

[A white 'kerchief is used by the madari to cover the damru, and lift it up]

Jamura: I've seen.

Madari: Seen what?

Jamura: A pigeon in the hand of the magician.

Madari: Alive or dead?

Jamura: Absolutely alive but scared.

The reason why the audience cooperates in the game of continuing to identify madari as magician even after he has shed his garb or in playing along with the jamura that the damru covered with a white handkerchief is a pigeon is because the text is at one and the same time creating certain variables (i.e., accidents) of ordinary life which are felt to be overwhelmingly present and powerful and then removing them precisely because the audience must be made aware of this power of the "sacra". By being used within the cut out space for performance, these signifiers must be seen not just as agents of utility but also of meaning. As Victor Turner says:

> Performative reflexivity is not mere reflex, a quick, automatic, or habitual response to some stimulus. It is highly contrived, artificial, of culture not nature, a deliberate and voluntary work of art. A 'reflex' would presuppose 'realism', a picturing of people and things as it is thought in that culture they 'really' are, without idealization or fantasization. But, of course, in art and literature even realism is a matter of artifice and what is real is ultimately a matter of cultural definition.[15]

Before we proceed further with the text, let us pause for a moment to see what is happening to the performance space in this use of ritual devices and in this knowledge of the process of ritualization. The actors are trying to show that while theatrical performances are transient by nature, they resist time by transforming the performance space into an intermediary stage where an action (being enacted) is begun – but not complete when one leaves the theatre. The performance is merely the beginning of a longer experience; it is an initiation into a large system, "It is the scorpion's bite which makes one dance. The dance does not stop when one leaves the theatre. The aesthetic value and the cultural originality of the performance are what make the sting sharp. But its precious poison comes from somewhere else".[16] Thus, the performance space is converted into a site of a demonstration.

Madari: Why am I a magician?

Jamura: For the sake of the stomach.

Madari: Why are you a jamura?

Jamura: For the sake of the stomach.

Madari: What have we eaten?

Jamura: Air.

Madari: And drunk?

Jamura: Water, from MCD's public pump.

Madari: Boy, in spite of inflation, we ate and drank.
Now do think of the rest of the public.

Jamura: I've thought.

Madari: What?

Jamura: These folks are all standing here for wheat, rice, and sugar.

Madari: Yes, that's why they're standing in a line. Will you help the people standing in this line?

Jamura: Will do.
Again,

Jamura: (Whispering) Boss, there's a policeman around. I'll tell you everything later.

Madari: So where's the sack of rations?

Jamura: Behind you.

[*The madari whips around to spot the sack. He goes and clutches it.*]

Madari: Oh dear, to hell with the passing time. The magic practiced by seven generations has not worked with a master veteran like me, yet this chit of a boy has done the same work [without the magic]…

In both these instances, what is being demonstrated is the fact that the earlier performance was looked upon as a work of art but now the performance is seen as an artistic process, in keeping with Nietzchean notions of the Apollonian and Dionysian modes of performance.[17] The Dionysian principle receives a direct impetus at the conclusion of the play when the demoralised madari wants to pack his bags and retire to Haridwar (the abode of the God-fearing) and renounce the world by taking up sanyas. At this, in an obvious bid to provoke the audience, the jamura points out:

> 'Take up sanyas?' Boss, if you take up sanyas, what will happen to these wooden owls?! They will continue to stand and watch spectacles, laugh and clap even if prices rise and even if they continue to be exploited – they will not raise even a tiny voice of protest against it. And if believers in honesty like yourself take up sanyas, then, for sure, the nation will fall apart.

So, the performative space, even as it reveals the "artistic process" becomes the site of confrontation between both, performers and spectators. It also reveals the unfinished nature of performance in a "given" space and its spilling over or extension.

Again, this very act of confrontation often takes place within a liminal space which is created by "(1) breach of regular norm-governed social relations made publicly visible by the infraction of a rule ordinarily held to be binding ...[and] (2) ...crisis, when people take sides, or rather are in the process of being induced, seduced, cajoled, nudged, or threatened to take sides by those who confront one another across the revealed breach as prime antagonists".[18]

In *Samrath Ko Nahi Dosh Gosai*, we see that for the major part of the play, the madari uses magic only to show quite literally how the body assumes a certain position or forms a particular configuration in order to become a conductor of magical power; hence the madari keeps asking the jamura to lie down, covers him completely with a cloth and, through a hypnotic process, directs the jamura to bring all the rations hoarded by the businessmen for profit-making and, later, to bring all the ministers from their ministerial homes. What happens, however, when the mantri enters the liminal space and becomes a liminal subject? With the mantri, the madari's magical powers are used differently. The mantri, on being hypnotised is not made to move magically through space but rather, inwards, into his psyche. On becoming the subject of the madaris' magic, the mantri is asked the same set of questions as the jamura was once asked such as "Why are you a mantri?" and "Who are your employers?" The mantri answers in much the same vein as the jamura, saying (and in fact, insisting) that he has become a minister for he needs to fill his stomach and that his employers are the rich businessmen and feudal landlords. But these answers are not what we expect of the mantri – we expect him to continue along the same fraudulent lines as before entering the liminal state, where he pretends devotion to the task of uplifting the "toiling masses". However, the mantri has been forced into stock taking and self scrutiny and his answers reflect his self critiquing for when the madari tries to help him to retain his "normal" self by prompting him to say that his employers are all the citizens of India, the mantri denies and resists this prompting. At this the madari allows the rare revelation of truth to continue and the mantri obliges:

Madari: Mantri, before the elections you could
be seen following people about with
folded hands. Whatever for?

Mantri: For the sake of votes, Boss! If required time comes,
one accepts even a donkey for a father.

Madari: Mantri, how did you win the elections?
Mantri: With the power of my money.
Madari: From where did the money come?
Mantri: My employers gave it to me.
Madari: What for? Mantri, tell the truth.
Mantri: To rule the country. To hike the prices, to repress the labouring farmers.

This is indeed being honest but this honesty trips when he is asked if he can make a speech to which he replies, "Of course, that is all I know. It's my family business." So the madari asks him to start, upon which the mantri (remember, he is still a liminal subject and within a liminal space) responds by standing up and saying:

> Brothers and sisters, all my sympathies
> are with you. I will take strict action
> against hoarders and collectors.

What is being demonstrated here is that the political rhetoric with which the mantri carries on his own propaganda has become routinised (effectively described by the madari as everyday, learnt by rote, battered, written by someone else, corroded with overuse) but this routinisation/ritualisation of his political rhetoric exerts such immense influence over the mantri's psyche, that it trespasses even into the liminal state of his subjectivity so that even while transcending this routinisation, he unwittingly falls prey to it and it takes over his transcendence. This is further supplemented by the immediate change in him when the madari asks him not to recite his everyday, well learnt speech but to tell the truth since the spectators were intelligent and could understand the difference between truth and falsity. At this, the mantri, turning his cap in a metaphoric gesture of playing a double role, says,

> Brothers and sisters, I don't give a damn if
> you go to hell. I wanted my seat and I've
> got that. If you think that I will go to the Lalaji's
> shop, take out all the stock and sell it among
> you all at the correct prices, then you are bloody f...ers

We observe that while pointing out to the spectators the ritual element of the mantri's political rhetoric, a rhetoric that serves as an instrument of empowerment, the text, too, has ritualized its own rhetoric of social activation. Thus, we have the familiar use of repetition in the interrogative *modus operandi* where, to quote an earlier example, even the mantri is asked the same set of questions as the jamura was and the answers, too, remain the same. This is akin to the chanting of prayers *en masse*, in response to the priest while a religious ceremony is in progress, in an effort to build up a collective spirit of religiosity and to slogans shouted by processions which effectively generate forms of hysteria. But this is a "religiosity" of a different/alternative kind and serves to highlight the "hysteria" of accumulation. When the mantri is asked the same set of questions, it is a process of integration which abolishes his privileged status as one belonging to the dominant order. Now the minister's "hunger" can be compared to the jamura's "hunger" in order to show the coercion involved in the satisfaction of the former. The same set of questions can be asked because both are now at the same level of existence and the minister is no longer protected by the institutionalized "rituals" of power. Those rituals are challenged and destroyed within another mode which thus empowers itself in order to put certain "radical" questions to this "representative" of the world of power. The text, then, is ritualizing the dramatic language for its own ends: that of social interrogation and regeneration. What has been the process of this ritualization? The text has (a) selected certain ideas as representative of the social being of the people; (b) after identifying/

locating this selection, has solidified it into a totality (therefore the madari, the jamura and the mantri, though occupying totally different positions in society, are all liable to "hungers"); (c) but the text plays upon "hunger" as "coercive ambition" and as "real need", serving to highlight the fact that the totality which it has created is one with contradiction and difference written into it, a process where power and influence are distributed in specific ways, where domination and subordination must be recognized and (d) in staging this version of a societal totality the text has begun to speak to the people but in accordance with its new social function. At this moment of its performance, the text begins to exercise its influence over the people and achieves a position of power. It has accorded itself a certain hortatory function crystallized in the rituals of empowerment by which it comes to "give itself" this moment of power. But this mode of empowerment is not the same as that by which a dominant order reproduces itself. At this moment, the text appropriates for itself the garb of a "dominant order" (in so far as it is as powerful as the dominant order). But just as we seem to move towards the logical conclusion that it is replicating a certain "fantasy" of dominance (thereby identifying itself longingly with the dominant order); that it has become yet another coercive form of dominance, the text distances itself from such a conclusion by filling the social totality it has created with an alternative set of values, where power belongs to the people.

In so far as the theatricality of this moment is made possible by ritual, the text's empowerment of itself is one which comes dangerously close to those modes/institutions/practices of power against which it is deployed. But it is precisely because these rituals form an alternative combinatory (a matrix of conventions/signifiers) that the text is able, simultaneously, to present itself as an alternative to the extra-textual in a spectacular moment of revelation. If biologically, both madari and mantri are human beings then, within the scheme of the plan, the punning on *hunger* is precisely the spectacular moment of the staging of dominance and its immediate abolition.

IV

Performers:	Audience
Demonstrators:	Potential Demonstrators
Performance Space:	Performative Space

A glance at the categories given above tells us that in spelling out the role of the performers as demonstrators and spectators as potential demonstrators (which one has observed the text to be doing), the performance space is being transformed into a performative space (since the spectators too can become performers). What is significant here is that performance space is not being done away with – there is only an extension of this space and its boundaries. So, "desacralisation" which was one of the two major aims that the group was attempting to reach, takes place only to the extent that the inherent sacredness of the performance space is being replaced by the mobility of the same.

Again, it appears that the spectators are being privileged in an attempt to demystify audience-performer relationship but, simply put, what the audience is being told is: "Look, you too can become a demonstrator – and in fact you must – if you step out of your role as the subject of the demonstration". So the very terms in which the audience is being roused into action actually strengthens the traditionally dominant role of the performing unit. There is, however, a recognition of the sacredness of the role of the spectators. It is the openness of the spectators to the ideas being presented to them in the spectacle and the vibrancy of their imagination which makes performance fruitful, that is relied upon by the performers. The performers admit to this openly but emphasise that the spectators, while no doubt wielding immense power as a collective body called the audience, should maintain this collectivity but join the ranks of the performing unit who, at that time, play a more dominant role. Another aspect to be noticed is that the performative space is a liminal space but often the power of one's role, especially one's language outside the performative space, is quite strong and can trespass into the performative space. In such a case, one needs to break into one's extra-performative role, beginning from the liminal space, and this is where the success of the performing unit's propaganda of its ideology lies.

And, finally, as has been observed earlier, the text being performed is now the new ruling opinion, so the audience does not escape from the notion of ruling opinions, but passes into a new subjection – the difference is that this "subjection" calls upon the audience to be part of a radical politics.

In this essay I have tried to problematize the notion of antiritualism and its place in defining the nature of JANAM's theatre practice. JANAM has sought to present antiritualism as an inherent principle in their theory of drama. It is the basis on which their radical cultural politics is clarified. It is at the centre of their strategies of demystification and desacralisation by which they seek to transmit certain messages regarding their political choices.

But antiritualism can also be seen as a technique which allows JANAM to carve out its own unique space. Antiritualism, thus, can be seen more as a strategy of differentiation rather than as one intrinsic to their practice. It is how JANAM seeks to project its own practice but this projection masks the fact that certain rituals, intimately linked to theatre and theatricality, are instinctively wedded to their style or mode of enactment. Indeed, to their entire theatrical experience. These rituals,

I have tried to show, exist in their practice over and beyond their avowed intentions.

This leads to a logical question. If antiritualism is the basis of JANAM's radical practice and *also* allows an effective transmission of their message, the question may be asked: Does the entry of rituals dilute the nature of the message sought to be disseminated in JANAM's kind of agit prop theatre? I suggest that the effectivity of JANAM's message is in no way marred within the terms of my reading of *Samrath*. In fact, their effectivity is dependent upon those very rituals of theatre and theatricality from which JANAM (in constructivist fashion, I have suggested) has sought to distance itself.

Notes

1 In *Seagull Theatre Quarterly*, Calcutta, Issue 16, December 1997, p.57.

2 Quoted by J.W. Lambert in "Politics and the Theatre" in *Drama: The Quarterly Theatre Review*, Spring 1977, No. 124, p.18.

3 The text I have used is *Chowk Chowk Par Gali Gali Mein*, Part 2, (Ist edn.), SAHMAT, New Delhi, 1991, pp. 23-44. The quotations from the text used in the essay have been translated by me. A brief outline of the plot of *Samrath Ko Nahi Dosh Gosain* (the title is a phrase from Goswami Tulsidas, which quite literally translates as: blame not the mighty that they are powerful) is given here. A magician (madari) performs a number of tricks upon his agent (jamura), sending the jamura finally to procure rations from the lalaji who has stored them in his godown to sell them at a higher price. This the madari does only after he himself is unable to obtain the rations through the magical powers that have so far served him so well. He is finally forced to relinquish his authority to the jamura. The jamura forcibly carries away a sack of rations from the lalaji's house where the latter is found ingratiating himself over the phone to various important people, and offering them handsome bribes in order to procure favours from them. However, the sack of rations stays only briefly with the madari and the jamura since the lalaji, with the help of the policeman whom he later bribes, retrieves the sack. The madari and jamura go in person to plead with the sethji but he turns them away, deaf to their pleas and threats. Now, the madari having decided to take ministerial help to combat food shortage and inflation again makes use of his magical powers and sends the jamura to catch hold of one of the ministers.

At first, the hapless jamura returns to report that all the ministers are away either on a holiday to some hi-fi hotel or on some innocuous visit. The relentless madari sends the jamura to the hi-fi hotel and the jamura returns bringing with him the minister (mantri). Through the madari's hypnosis, the mantri reveals his true colours to the public, shattering the mask of virtue that he dons in the beginning. The disillusioned madari wishes to renounce the world but his jamura reminds him that he must continue his work of building awareness and inciting protest

4 Victor Turner is best known for formulating such concepts as "liminality" in his book *The Anthropology of Performance*, PAJ Publications, New York, 1986, while Richard Schechner is known for his propagation of Environmental Theatre. Eli Rozik's *The Roots of Theatre: Rethinking Ritual and Other Theories of Origin*, University of Iowa Press, Iowa City, USA, 2002 is a useful book to refer to for a counterview of the relationship between ritual and theatre.

5 Eugenio, Barba . "Four Spectators" in *The Drama Review*, Vol. 34, No. 1, Spring 1990, (T125), p.96.

6 Kier, Elam, *The Semiotics of Theatre and Drama*. London and New York: Methuen, New Accents Series. 1980, p.2.

7 Quoted in Jonathan Z Smith, "Bare Facts of Ritual", *History of Religions*, Vol. 20, 1980-81.

8 *The New Encyclopedia Britannica*: Macropedia, Vol. 15, p. 866.

9 Kier Elam, ibid., pp. 62-63.

10 David I, Kertzer, 1988, *Ritual, Politics and Power*. New Haven and London: Yale University Press, 1988, p. 67.

11 From *The Right to Perform. Selected Writing of Safdar Hashmi*, SAHMAT, New Delhi, 1989, p. 50.

12 We can perceive this mood in the resistance theatres of other countries. On such example is the Madang Theatre Movement of South Korea. To quote Eugene Van Erven in his article entitled "Resistance Theatre in South Korea Above and Underground" in the journal *Drama Review*, Vol. 32, No. 3 (T119), Fall, 1988 p.158. "During my 1986 visit to South Korea, I observed two Madang performances, one in an auditorium of a Catholic college in Chonju and one in a small farmer's village an hour's bus ride further inland. All Madang performances invariably start with an ecstatic drum and dance session often with the audience actively participating. Drumming is still very much part of traditional Korean village culture. In the Chonju (indoor) performances, the drummers come in from outside, beating drums of all sizes, cymbals and gongs. In the village (outdoor) performances the next day, the drummers walked through the entire community enticing the inhabitants from their

homes to follow them to the main square where the performance was to take place. Many of the villagers joined in the drumming and dancing."

13 In December 1978,*Hatyare*, meaning *Killers*,a street play by Janam, coincided with the second phase of communal violence let loose in Aligarh. It analysed the political and economic factors which antagonized the traditional harmonious co-existence of two communities.

14 Kier Elam, ibid., pp.33-34.

15 Turner, ibid, p.24.

16 Barba, ibid., p.98.

17 Kazimierz Braun in "My Long Journey into the American Theatre" which appeared in the journal, *Drama Review*, Vol. 34, No.2 (T126), Summer 1990, p.89, states:

"...the concept of performance as a work of art is situated in what Nietzsche called the Apollonian; the concept of performance as artistic process in what he called the Dionysian. In the Apollonian mode people made art, in the Dionysian, they became art. The first great reform of theatre starting in the nineteenth century followed Apollonian principles. The second reform, originated by Artaud, returned to the Dionysian tradition. Who doesn't recall all those communal celebrations, collective works, workshops, and projects of the second reform of the 60's and the 70's? The actors were one with the public, the public was active and so many barriers were broken."

18 Turner, ibid., p.34.

Contributors

Heisnam Kanhailal is the renowned experimental theatre director of Manipur and has established the theatre group Kalakshetra Manipur in 1969. His wife and actress Sabitri has played the central role in his major productions like *Pebet* (1975), *Memoirs of Africa* (1985), *Migi Sarang (Human Cage,*1991), *Draupadi* (2000), and *Dak Ghar* (2006). Kanhailal has also researched extensively on the methodology of acting and Sabitri has played an important role in bringing this process alive to the stage. Sabitri has acted in the role of Mahadevi Akka in the short film of the same title directed by Madhusree Dutta for Majlis, Mumbai. Sabitri received the Sangeet Natak Akademi award for acting in 1991 and the Best actress award in the 3rd Cairo International Festival of Experimental Theatre in 1991.

Sabitri has been honoured with the Padma Shri Award in 2008.

Kanhailal was awarded the Sangeet Natak Akademi award for direction (1985) and the award of Natya Ratna in 1997 by Manipuri Sahitya Parishad.

Sudhanva Deshpande is an actor, director and occasional playwright with Jana Natya Manch,Delhi. He has directed along with Sanjay Maharishi, a documentary on Habib Tanvir and Naya Theatre, *Gaon ke naon theatre,mor naon Habib* (Hindi,English,Chattisgarhi,with English subtitles,75 mins.,2005). He works as editor at LeftWord Books.

Tripurari Sharma is a playwright, director and Associate Professor of Acting at the National School of Drama, New Delhi. Some of the important plays she has written are *Bahu, Aks Paheli ,Kath ki Gadi, Poshak and Azizun.* She has been directing for her group Alarippu, directed Mohan Rakesh's *Adhe Adhure* and *Kath ki Gaddi* for the National School of Drama Repertory, and worked with the famous Surbhi group in Andhra Pradesh. She has been conducting numerous theatre workshops around India to develop plays with women's groups, college students, factory workers, amateur theatre and rural performing groups. She has worked extensively with Nautanki, Tamasha and Pandvani traditional artist groups. She has written for the films *Mirch Masala* and *Hazar Chaurasi ka Ma.* She has evolved and directed *Lal Lal Hathi* with the Theatre in Education Company of National School of Drama ,1995 onwards. She is the recipient of the Sanskriti and Bharatiya Natya Sangh awards and the Safdar Hashmi award from the U.P. Sangeet Natak Akademi.

V. Padma (Mangai) teaches English at Stella Maris College, Chennai. She has been involved in Tamil theatre for more than two decades and believes in addressing various social issues relating to caste and gender-especially through theatre, street and stage.

Lata Singh teaches History in Maitreyi College, University of Delhi. A former Fellow at Nehru Memorial Trust , Teen Murti House, New Delhi, she is currently a Fellow at India Institute of Advanced Studies, Simla. She has worked on Gender and Theatre and her current focus is on Women Performers.

H.S. Shiva Prakash is author of four books of poems, two books of criticism and twelve plays in Kannada. His works have been translated into English and other Indian languages. He has been awarded four times the Karnataka Sahitya Akademi Award for best book, the Dinakar Desai award for poetry, the Sangeet Natak Akademi Award for playwrighting 1997 and the Karnataka Natak Special Award,1995. He is the Honorary Fellow of School of Letters,University of Iowa. Former Editor of "Indian Literature" (the Sahitya Akademi's Bi-monthly Journal), he is currently Associate Professor at School of Art and Aesthetics, Jawaharlal Nehru University.

Angelie Multani is Assistant Professor in the Department of Humanities and Social Sciences, Indian Institute of Technology, Delhi. Her areas of interest and research include gender studies and Indian writing in English. Some of her publications are on the performance of Moliere in Delhi and an analysis of the performance of Mahesh Dattani's *Dance like a Man*. She has edited a volume of essays on Mahesh Dattani.

GJV Prasad discusses life and literature at Jawaharlal Nehru University, where he is Associate Professor of English. His major research interests are Contemporary Theatre, Indian English Literature, Dalit Writings, Australian Literature, and Translation Theory. Prasad is also a well-known Indian English poet and novelist – his novel *A Clean Breast* was short listed for the Commonwealth Prize for best first book from the Eurasia region in 1994, and his collection of poems, *In Delhi without a Visa* (1996) is considered a path-breaking volume. His second novel, *In the Name of God*, is due to be published this year. He is a recipient of the Katha award for translation from Tamil. He has co-edited with Sara Rai a collection of stories from Indian languages, *Imaging the Other*. His academic publications include *Continuities in Indian English Poetry: nation language form* and two edited volumes of critical essays, *Vikram Seth: An Anthology of Recent Criticism*, and *The Lost Temper: Essays on Look Back in Anger.* He has edited the Penguin (now Longman) Study Edition of Samuel Beckett's *Waiting for Godot* and also of John Osborne's *Look Back in Anger*. He is the current editor of *JSL*, the Journal of the School of Language, Literature & Culture Studies, JNU, and Secretary of the Indian Association for Commonwealth Literature and Language Studies.

Jaidev Taneja is Reader in A.R.S.D. College, University of Delhi. A well-known drama critic, he has published more than 25 books and many articles on modern Hindi and Indian theatre with special emphasis on Mohan Rakesh. His articles have also been translated into various Indian languages. His most recent publications are *Adhunik Bhartiya Ranglok* and *Rangkormi Kosh (Bharatmuni Ke Adhunik Vanshaj*). The Hindi Academy ,Delhi Natya SanghAnk (Mumbai) and Sahitya Kala Parishad (Delhi Government) has also conferred awards and honours.

Dr. Archana Sharma is a poet, critic and translator. She has a Ph.D. from Delhi University on the Problem of Expression and Communication in New Hindi Poetry. She is Reader in the Department of Hindi at Jesus and Mary College (University of Delhi) New Delhi.

Dr. Vijay K Sharma is a Reader in the Department of English at RLAE College (University of Delhi) New Delhi. Recipient of four international Fellowships, he has a Ph.D. from Delhi University in the area of Contemporary American Literature. His current interests include diaspora studies, English Language Teaching (ELT), critical theory and translation studies.

Sonali Jain teaches English at Bharati College.University of Delhi. She has done her doctoral work on Vijay Tendulkar and the semiotics of cinema, with special reference to Vijay Tendulkar's *Kamla*. Her translation of Tendulkar's play *Baby* into English is to be published soon. Currently she is a Fellow at the University of East Anglia ,U.K., where she is working on the area of Creative writing and Trauma.

Maya Pandit is Professor of English at English and Foreign Languages University, Hyderabad. She is a theatre activist, actress and member of Pratyaya, an experimental theatre group in Kolhapur. She has written extensively on theatre and gender issues. Her publications include the English translation of G.P. Deshpande's Marathi play *Chanakya Vishnugupta*, Datta Bhagat',s Marathi play *Wata Pulwata*, Marathi translations of Dario Fo's plays *Accidental Death of an Anarchist* and *Awakening* and most recently the English translation of Baby Kamble's autobiography titled *The Prism We Broke*.

Swati Pal teaches English at Janki Devi Memorial College, University of Delhi. A Charles Wallace Scholar as well as the John Mc GrathTheatre Studies Scholar (2005) at Edinburgh University. Swati Pal has published essays on Beckett and Osborne. Her doctoral thesis, from JNU, looks at Agit prop in Britain from the 60s to the 90s.